PRAISE FOR *RESPONSIBLE BUSINESS DECISION MAKING*

'Responsible business decision making refers to the necessity for a workable balance between people, planet and profit. This book mentions the European Green Deal as an illustration of the European Commission's ambitious plan to invest in structural, sustainable solutions for all of society. The method of data and dialogue underlying the Responsible Business Simulator is an important instrument when formulating an innovative business case.'
Diederik Samsom, Head of Cabinet, Cabinet of Executive Vice-President of the European Commission Frans Timmermans, European Green Deal

'Facilitates decision making for systems change and sustainable practices by applying a smart framework that allows businesses to deliver a better balance between people, planet and profit.'
Lara van Druten, CEO, The Waste Transformers, and Member of the UN Advisory Board on Zero Waste

'Companies need practical instruments to keep their emissions at levels that fit with a 1.5 degree global warming scenario. *Responsible Business Decision Making* provides tools to the business community to make decisions respecting the climate, and a safe and inclusive working culture, while maintaining profits.'
As Tempelman, CEO, Eneco

'Strategic decision making in portfolio investments requires a methodology. You need data to measure both ESG and impact as well as the progress you're making. The methodology described in *Responsible Business Decision Making* is very helpful when nudging decisions in a more impactful direction and provides you with the insight on what variables to work towards for a sustainable economy. This is why this book provides distinct value.'
Guus van Puijenbroek, Director, Strategic and Family Matters, VP Capital

Second Edition

Responsible Business Decision Making

Strategic impact through data and dialogue

Annemieke Roobeek
Jacques de Swart
Myrthe van der Plas

KoganPage

First published in Great Britain and the United States in 2018 as *Responsible Business* by Kogan Page Limited
Second edition published in 2023

2nd Floor, 45 Gee Street	8 W 38th Street, Suite 902	4737/23 Ansari Road
London	New York, NY 10018	Daryaganj
EC1V 3RS	USA	New Delhi 110002
United Kingdom		India

www.koganpage.com

Kogan Page books are printed on paper from sustainable forests.

ISBNs
Hardback	978 1 3986 1230 3
Paperback	978 1 3986 1228 0
Ebook	978 1 3986 1229 7

British Library Cataloguing-in-Publication Data
A CIP record for this book is available from the British Library.

Library of Congress Control Number
2023938697

Typeset by Integra Software Services, Pondicherry
Print production managed by Jellyfish
Printed and bound by CPI Group (UK) Ltd, Croydon, CR0 4YY

CONTENTS

Readers can access the Responsible Business Simulator at

www.koganpage.com/product/responsible-business-decision-making-9781398612280

LIST OF FIGURES AND TABLES

Tables

ABOUT THE AUTHORS

Annemieke Roobeek is Professor of Strategy and Transformation Management at Nyenrode Business University and CEO of MeetingMoreMinds and GrwNxt.

Jacques de Swart is a Partner within PwC and a Professor of Applied Mathematics at Nyenrode Business University.

Myrthe van der Plas is responsible for the Data Analytics Group within PwC Consulting and is the founder of Lakisama Foundation.

PREFACE

This is the Age of Transformation. We are on our way to a greater understanding of Responsible Business in both strategy and daily practice. In this age of transformation changes, and the opportunities they offer, come along at the same time: disruptive technologies, climate change, values advocated by social movements, global tensions and new orders in geopolitics. We are in the middle of a major systems change. How can we make the right decisions to take care of People, Planet and Profit?

There is momentum for an innovative, combined quantitative and qualitative approach to strategic decision making. There is a need to move beyond the traditional spreadsheets for financially-based decision making, and to look beyond intuition and personal conviction for including non-financial aspects. The combined forces of data science and interactive strategy in the Responsible Business Simulator (tRBS) unleash the collective intelligence of the boardroom, professionals, stakeholders and the wealth of public knowledge. This combined approach provides a solid base for decisions and investments shaping the future of companies and societies.

The tipping point draws nearer for new paradigms such as climate neutral production, zero emissions, no waste and circular economy. Similarly, more people want to leave the rat race and find a healthier work–life balance. The historic Paris Agreement on climate change, adopted by 192 countries in December 2015, was a clear signal to stimulate renewable energy, cleaner technologies and massive investments in infrastructure. The rethinking of supply chains, the use and reuse of materials, modes of transport and ways of working will have a tremendous impact on reaching a better balance between people, planet and profit. Add to this the implementation of a range of disruptive technologies, ranging from ChatGPT, neuro-robotics, electrification, genomics and personalized healthcare, and the conclusion is that the world is changing at a rapid speed, and that companies and governmental institutions have to respond by making strategic decisions.

Although the tipping point is being approached through a multitude of developments, this does not mean that it is easy to implement sustainable business practices. The frontrunners, still a relatively small but rapidly growing group of companies, are leading the way, but often pay a high price for their conviction that – in the long run – they are doing the right thing for all concerned, including themselves. Many businesses and organizations are struggling with the strategic choice of structurally implementing sustainable and inclusive business practices. It is exactly in this phase, when we are moving towards the tipping point and when a turnaround in management thinking is taking place in favour of sustainable operations, that it is essential to be able to make rational decisions on the basis of facts and figures, both for financial and non-financial reasons. This is where tRBS comes into play.

Based on weighted Key Outputs, which have been identified as keys for success by management and employees in an interactive Strategic Dialogue process, tRBS can provide concrete forecasts about the impact of sustainable investments on medium-term operational results. Those forecasts are presented in digital simulations that can be fine-tuned to different conditions; hence the fact that the model is referred to as a 'simulator'.

The Responsible Business Simulator is innovative in more ways than one. It is an advanced mathematical calculation model that eliminates bias and objectifies the strategic decision-making process, because it uses weighted key outputs. In addition, it attaches value – in the form of Scenarios – to historical data about a company and to the opinions of external experts. Using these scenarios, which blend historical facts with impartial external expertise, the model is able to estimate the probability that a particular option for a strategy based on sustainability and social inclusivity will have a positive or less positive impact on the company. It simulates the reactions of decision makers and employees, presenting various probabilities in a comprehensible way. A strategic dialogue about key outputs for success is combined with weighted fact-based scenarios, and the result is calculated statistically and presented visually. The results allow the Board, management and employees to take decisions on the basis of hard facts on financial and non-financial items.

Finally, the model allows decision makers to tweak the results so that they can determine their own timeline, along which all aspects of the triple bottom line and the 3Ps of people, planet and profit can be incorporated and calculated.

In the real world, however, strategic decisions are not always rational. Other considerations always creep in. We are of the opinion that the added value of a rational model, such as tRBS, lies precisely in the fact that it can clarify highly diffuse strategic considerations. This can lead to greater insight on the part of decision makers, to better prospects for investors and shareholders, and to more transparency and accountability vis-à-vis the stakeholders – both within the company, and in society as a whole.

Our vision for balanced decision making

The combination of interactive strategic decision making and advanced data analytics gives companies, organizations and governmental agencies new insights for balanced investment decisions in the era of sustainability and an inclusive society. The strategic dialogue in an action research setting unleashes the informal and formal knowledge underlying the long-term mission of the organization and its potential to realize its goals. Data science techniques allow the comparison of large amounts of data for visualizing different scenarios. The combination of qualitative and quantitative approaches is a powerful tool for decision makers who have to meet financial and non-financial objectives in a society on the brink of a new paradigm.

The combination of these forces is what distinguishes this book from existing approaches. As authors with strategy and data analytics backgrounds we have a track record of proven results both in academia and in advising international companies and the public sector. Our purpose in writing this book was to provide a practical description of the strategic decision-making tool that we have developed and its application in highly diverse settings in companies and organizations. The book is also the gateway to an advanced software tool that allows you as the reader to play around with the data for strategic decision making.

We hope this book will inspire students at universities and business schools, as well as being a practical guide for advisors, consultants, investors and policymakers in developing a feasible sustainability strategy for companies and organizations in the private and the public sector. The book will appeal to a broad range of readers, from those who are interested in finance, economics and modelling, to those who are involved in strategy and broader sustainability and inclusivity issues. The fact that the insights and software tools can be used immediately makes it accessible to all: professionals, consultants to the financial sector, as well as to students in the classroom for reviewing the case studies. For strategists the advantage of using data science will be an eye-opener, as it is for data-driven consultancies and investors to learn from the process of strategic dialogue and the added value of iterative, interactive decision making in highly diverse teams. For all target groups the challenge is to understand the underlying complexity of factors that give evidence of the choices to be made within the internal and external contexts of the company or organization.

Strategy is no longer the exclusive domain of the boardroom, although major decisions are taken there. Both private- and public-sector organizations have seen changes in attitudes, which are advocating new ways of working, more prudent treatment of the planet, and greater consideration of people's health and wellbeing. The need for interaction with internal and external experts, as well as stakeholders and opinion leaders, has become pivotal to the successful execution of strategies. The strategy concepts in this book are underpinned by theories around multi-stakeholder management, strategic dialogue and unleashing knowledge potential by empowerment, as well as theoretical concepts underlying action research and grounded theory.

How the book is organized

The book consists of three parts. Part One describes the transformative forces and paradigm changes that are under way. In Chapter 1 we start with the rise of the concept of 'sustainability' and how we are moving from awareness to systems change in a circular economy and an inclusive society. We offer examples of frontrunners in business who are demonstrating this profound change in the economy. In subsequent chapters we go on to describe concepts that try to achieve a better balance between the interests of companies, shareholders and stakeholders. We dig deeper into the concept of 'shared value' in Chapter 2, and in Chapter 3 we argue that there is no alternative to sustainability. In this chapter we describe the potential offered by innovations stemming from sustainability and give examples of disruptive changes already taking place, alongside examples of role models demonstrating sustainability and responsibility in practice. Part Two explains the concept of 'data and dialogue' and introduces the Responsible Business Simulator (tRBS). In Chapter 4 the importance of stakeholder management and interactivity in strategic decision-making processes is elucidated. We propose that collaboration is necessary for new insights and actionable results.

Chapter 5 gives the reader a better idea of the combined forces of the strategic dialogue based on action research and the application of data science for neutralizing information and knowledge into facts and figures. In Chapter 6 we describe the methodologies used, and provide a user guide in Chapter 7.

Part Three elaborates on the application of the 'strategic dialogue' and the use of tRBS. These form the core and are illustrated in the cases presented in Chapters 8 to 14. To explain the working of the methodology and tRBS in practice we compiled a series of case studies. We applied the combined methodology of data and dialogue in various companies, from a global science-based company to a healthcare organization, and from the use of sustainable development goals in a global consultancy firm to creating a sustainable roof of a science museum – and more. We chose these highly diverse companies and organizations on purpose to investigate the usefulness of the simulation model and our combined quantitative and qualitative approach.

Each of the case studies starts with a short introduction, some facts about the company or organization, and the strategic issue at stake. They show how the strategic dialogue triggers the conversation and the search for solutions. The data process is illustrated by visualizing each of the steps in the decision-making process. Each of the cases illustrates one of the 3Ps (people, planet and profit). For example, the P of Planet is central to DSM, a globally operating company active in health, nutrition and materials, and a frontrunner in balancing people, planet and profit. For DSM the strategic issue is how to anticipate climate change by addressing their environmental and carbon footprint and finding options to reduce greenhouse gas emissions. The case study in Chapter 14, the NEMO Science Museum, discusses the decision making surrounding how to repair the roof of its landmark building in Amsterdam. Should they go for a simple repair and maintenance solution or is it possible to create a sustainable roof that gives space to an outdoor exhibition area with even more attractions for the public? In another case we shift the focus to a highly specialized metalworking company, Rimetaal, that does its utmost to score high in all of the 3Ps, but has difficulties in selling its sustainable waste collection systems to local municipalities and struggles to survive as a sustainable company. In this example we describe the surprising outcome of the process, and how the company changed its business model based on the Responsible Business Simulator.

In other cases we focus more on the P of People. In the case of IZZ, the strategic issue is one of creating a better working environment in healthcare and reducing costs of health- and stress-related absenteeism. We created the inputs for the simulation model together with the IZZ professionals. They were so eager to understand the model that they learnt how to apply it themselves, and now support decision-making processes at numerous healthcare institutions. Another example of the application of the combined methodology is the case of a global professional services firm who has applied tRBS to help them use the UN's Sustainable Development Goals (SDGs) as guidance in their organizational practices. The plight of Ukrainian refugees provides another example of how tRBS can be used to get the facts on the table while at the same time doing justice to the emotions expressed by stakeholders. The application of strategic decision making towards a sustainable economy and an inclusive society in this context has the purpose of supporting policymakers in their decision making regarding their response to the refugee crisis in a fact-based dialogue.

In most cases all 3Ps of people, planet and profit come together in different weights and balances. It is a nice illustration of clarifying the options by assessing the risk appetite for the investors. With the Responsible Business Simulator, policymakers, consultants, strategists and executives in the boardroom are able to make better decisions based on a better foundation, firmly grounded in facts, figures and the outcomes of dialogues.

In our closing chapter we invite you to explore with us the world of interdisciplinary research, collaboration and interactive strategy combined with highly advanced data science for better strategic decision making in the age of transformation and systems change.

ACKNOWLEDGEMENTS

Research is continuously developing and new theories are always being formulated to give rise to new research. Much of this happens in isolation and an interdisciplinary approach is rare rather than common. However, being affiliated to Nyenrode Business Universiteit and to advisory companies, we are used to collaborative research; interdisciplinarity is essential to answer questions that are relevant to society, the environment and organizations. We tested the resulting concept via 'action research', an interactive and iterative research process.

For the development of our strategic decision-making approach, multiple disciplines have been brought together to facilitate scientific cross-pollination, and we would like to thank everyone who has contributed to the creation of this book.

For the cases: Feike Sijbesma from DSM; Roy Wolbrink from KLIKO/Rimetaal; Agnes Kiers and Bernd Jan Sikken from de Volksbank; Michiel Buchel from NEMO; Anouk ten Arve from the IZZ Foundation; and Cees Jellema from the Provincie Utrecht for sharing his knowledge on the refugees case.

Our Nyenrode guest lecturers: Carl Koopmans (SEO), Georgette Lageman (de Volksbank) and Wouter Koerselman (Hines).

From MeetingMoreMinds: Coen Hilbrands for his insights and critical review.

From PwC: Mila Harmelink, Jasper Kunst and Christian Vijfvinkel from the Data Analytics Group for their part in improving the methodology and the Responsible Business Simulator; Thom-Ivar van Dijk, Mike Verdaasdonk and Kailey van Zomeren for their help in improving the simulation model; Wineke Haagsma, Tom Kroes, Laura van Liere, Nikki Molenaar and Paul Koster for their contribution to the SDG case; and Martine Koedijk, Oleksandra Prokopenko, Inderdeep Singh, Beau Furnee, Eva de Bakker, Ankita Shrivastava and Mylene Ingwersen for the refugees case. Our Nyenrode lecturers

Laura van Liere, Mylene Ingwersen, Manon Figee, Annabel de Goede, Leidy Kupers and Stijn Ticheloven.

Last but not least Kees Ramselaar and Chris Kuip from AIMMS for brainstorming with us on the practical implementation of the Responsible Business Simulator as a software platform; Elke Vergoossen from Boom Publishers for their support throughout the process; and of course Nick Hoar, Susan Hodgson and Isabelle Cheng from Kogan Page for their valuable input and enjoyable collaboration.

PART ONE
Relevance and context

Working towards responsibility in business and society

From awareness and evidence to systems change

Let's start by talking positively about systemic change. Change is urgently needed, but to date resistance to these changes has been hard to overcome. But now there are positive signs that resistance is weakening. There is much greater awareness of the need for bold decisions to contribute to the health, wellbeing and sustainability of our Planet, its People and company Profits (the 3Ps) in a much more balanced way. There is daily evidence of human impact on the world's climate. With the extreme weather events that have taken place all around the globe in recent years, few deny climate change any longer. The images of massive floods in Pakistan and Australia, bush fires in Southern Europe and California, shrinking icefields on the Poles and in the Alps, and the years of drought in the Horn of Africa show us the devastating impact of climate change all around the globe.

At the same time, there couldn't be a sharper contrast between the recent disappointing COP27 events in Egypt in 2022 and the optimistic mood after COP21 in 2015 in Paris, when 196 countries signed a legally binding treaty to pursue efforts to limit temperature increase to 1.5°C. The message of the highly regarded Intergovernmental Panel on Climate Change report (IPCC, 2022) was clear, and based solidly on extensive international research. The cumulative scientific evidence is unequivocal. Climate change is a threat to planetary health, human wellbeing and indeed human existence in the hardest-hit parts of the world. There is an urgency, and no time to waste. However, instead of accelerating measures to counteract the dangers, some fear further delays in reaching climate targets. There are still lobbying activities by companies seeking short-term self-interest.

The immediate challenge posed by climate change goes beyond the type of energy we are using. Fossil fuel-based energy is still dominant. The shift from fossil fuel to renewable energies, green hydro and clean technologies will certainly help to reduce the amount of greenhouse gas emissions, but it won't be enough. It will replace part of the energy demand, but the demand for energy, materials, water, food, cars, computers and data centres will continue to increase as long as the paradigm of the current economic system remains the same.

Awareness of a need for systemic change started among scientists, farmers and grassroots activists in the 1960s, when heavily polluted rivers in industrial countries were endangering food production and health. This seems a long way behind us now, with strict regulation in place in Western countries, but it does not mean the problem is solved. With the internationalization of production to developing and emerging countries, the problem has become global. In today's global community, many products are manufactured in countries in Asia, South America and parts of Africa; the mobile phone purchased in London will have been manufactured in China with intricate supply chains of rare materials, energy streams and prescribed designs that come from remote places of the world. As a consequence, the challenge to safeguard the planet as well as the health of its people with transparent governance has become even more urgent than before. At the same time, the many initiatives taken by global, regional and national organizations to bring the world into a better ecological balance show the complexity of the issues at stake.

But, notwithstanding setbacks and the powerful fossil fuel industry lobbies, change is inevitable. We have entered the age of systems change, *circular economy* and *social inclusion*, where companies, politicians, citizens, farmers, non-governmental organizations (NGOs) and the academic community have to rethink the paradigm of the economic system. *Sustainable growth* is perhaps one of the greatest challenges humankind is facing. Systemic change requires profound insight into the current economic system. The move towards a circular economy and social inclusion requires more than redesigning products and recycling. It is about shaping a safe technical, social and psychological working culture for everyone, a better work–life balance, taking into account externalities in the pricing of products and services, reducing inequality, and making the world a better place for all.

The rise of the notion of sustainability

The concept of *sustainability* has been around for more than 50 years. The notion of sustainability has been defined in the literature in an almost infinite variety of ways (Elkington, 1997) – a timeline of events is presented in Figure 1.1. When the Club of Rome, an interdisciplinary think tank, published its report titled 'The Limits to Growth' in 1972, it was the first time that the possible long-term consequences of economic actions on the climate had been presented on a global scale (Meadows et al, 1972). The report caused a great deal of concern and fuelled much debate. One of the early warnings of the need for systems change came from the late Herman E Daly (1938–2022) who worked on the topic of limits to growth even before the Club of Rome. Daly, a mathematician, laid the foundation for the ecological economy. He made a plea for a steady-state economy that respects the carrying capacity of planet Earth. Decades after his theory was derided by neoclassical economists his work gradually got more attention and he began to collaborate with Dennis Meadows of the Club of Rome, later going on to develop the 'Index of Sustainable Economic Welfare' (ISEW) with John Cobb. In recent years Daly became the inspiration for 'degrowth' economist Jason Hickel, as well as for Kate Raworth's *Doughnut Economics*, calling for a balanced growth between social, environmental and economic dimensions (Tielbeke, 2022).

The present-day activities of the Club of Rome focus less on the end of growth and more on sustainability in a broad sense. At around

Figure 1.1   Sustainability awareness and action timeline 1972–2015

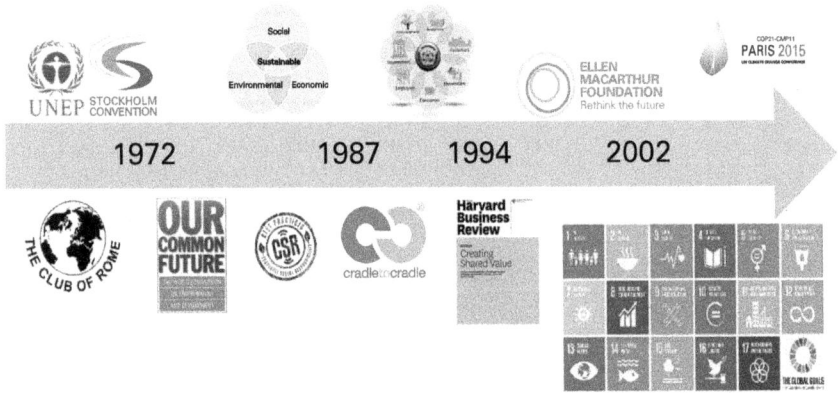

the same time as the Club of Rome's report, the term 'sustainable development' was receiving substantial attention following the United Nations Conference on the Human Environment (1972), which resulted – 15 years later – in the Brundtland Report of 1987. That report was later published in book form, under the title *Our Common Future,* by the World Commission on Environment and Development (WCED, 1987), and in which the Commission defined sustainable development as follows:

> The development that meets the needs of the present without compromising the ability of future generations to meet their own needs.

The Brundtland definition has been applied consistently during the many UN conferences held on this subject, such as the UN Earth Summit in Rio de Janeiro in 1992, the Kyoto Protocol of 1997, and the Climate Conferences in Copenhagen in 2009, Dublin in 2011, Paris in 2015, Marrakech in 2016, Bonn in 2017, Katowice in 2018, Madrid in 2019, Glasgow in 2021, COP27 in Sharm El Sheikh in 2022, and UAE in 2023. The success of the UN-organized COP meetings is mixed in terms of breakthroughs for climate change. Coming closer to consensus is a prerequisite; however, regional differences, economic opportunities and limited commitment to the goals are more common nowadays.

According to Rogers and Hudson (2011), the following four core elements can be identified from the Brundtland definition of sustainable development:

1 recognition of sustainability as a global problem, with global responsibilities

2 recognition of the limits of growth, or at least of the necessity to structure growth so as to take advantage of the options that are least destructive for the natural environment

3 recognition of social equality as an important consideration, especially in offering opportunities for economic and social progress for less-developed countries

4 giving long-term planning over future generations a new priority, and recognizing the fact that market economies tend to lean on short-term interests and are often at risk of losing sight of long-term goals

As can be seen from this explanation of the UN definition of sustainability, it is a highly complex subject and one that can be approached from a variety of directions.

With the awareness of the importance and impact of sustainability, with the *triple bottom line* (TBL) that has people, planet and profit as its pillars, the rise of *corporate social responsibility* (CSR) initiatives in companies, consultancies and NGOs started during the 1990s (Elkington, 1997). In the early 2000s the cradle to cradle (C2C) design concept became popular among companies that wanted to redesign their products and supply chains to prevent waste. All material inputs and outputs of this design concept are seen as 'nutrients' which can be reused or recycled (McDonough and Braungart, 2002). With this cradle to cradle concept a big leap forward was made towards what was coined a decade later in 2012 by the Ellen MacArthur Foundation as the *circular economy*. The Foundation advocated an accelerated transition to a circular model with numerous business and economic opportunities, within which the three pillars of the TBL become integrated (Ellen MacArthur Foundation, 2012). This integration of the people, planet and profit pillars builds on the earlier concept of *shared value creation*, developed by Porter and Kramer and adopted by many companies (Porter and Kramer, 2011).

The central premise of shared value is that there is a mutual dependence between the competitiveness of a company and the health of the communities around it. Recognition of these connections between people, planet and profit (the 3Ps) can lead to opportunities, spurring on both societal and economic progress. In a short period of time this framework has gained inroads into businesses worldwide, although criticism from economists was expressed in numerous academic articles. (We will elaborate further on this in Chapter 2 where we will dive deeper into the enhanced concept of shared value.) At a societal level, the United Nations Development Programme (UNDP) has worked on Sustainable Development Goals (SDGs). As successors of the Millennium Development Goals, these 17 SDGs cover social, ecological and economic objectives, and engage both developing and developed countries to help achieve these goals. According to the UN, businesses and companies worldwide have been and will be at the forefront of creating this change. This UNDP intergovernmental platform has made positive inroads into boardrooms' and governments' agendas. It has proven to be a workable overview that serves as an overall objective for a better world. For companies, organizations and NGOs it brings focus in defining their aspirational objectives and subsequent strategies.

We are approaching the 'tipping point' of sustainable business operations. During the past two decades more and more enterprises and organizations, including governments, have used annual reports and strategic policy papers to point out that sustainability has become a crucial factor in the way in which they design their strategy and policies, manufacture their products and deliver their services (Nidumolu et al, 2009). Many start-ups and impact-driven enterprises have sustainability at the core of their mission. These kinds of companies develop many innovative solutions that contribute to alternatives for non-sustainable mainstream products. The increasing customer demand for sustainability, the uncertainty and high cost of energy, the geopolitical shifts in power, the finite nature of raw materials, and the negative impact that present-day production methods have on the environment are all prompting more inventive and sustainable alternatives.

Sustainability reflected in the use of standards and indices

For many years international indices such as the Dow Jones Sustainability Index (DJSI, started in 1999) were paid only scant attention. Today this index is called the S&P Dow Jones Indices. A large part of a company's reputation and credibility on sustainability relies on the fact that they have a good ranking in this and similar indices. From 2020 the CSA (Corporate Sustainability Assessment) will be issued by S&P Global. It has become the basis for numerous S&P economic, social and governance (ESG) indices over the last two decades, attracting billions of US dollars in assets. One change with the years before 2021 is that, as the sustainability performance accelerates, S&P Global sees more value in rewarding groups of top-performing companies in sectors rather than focusing on individual company rankings. Companies can be ranked in Gold, Silver or Bronze class, or mentioned in the Yearbook as a member. The Gold class is for companies whose score is within 1 per cent of the top-performing company's score in their industry. There is also a category called Industry Mover. Companies in the top 15 per cent of their industry that participated in the CSA last year and the current year, who achieved an improvement in their S&P ESG score of at least 5 per cent, and who achieved the strongest improvement in their industry, are awarded an Industry Mover Sustainability Award. The frontrunners in S&P Global's *Sustainability Yearbook 2022* are listed in Table 1.1.

Stakeholders ask for more transparency into a company's ESG profile, which can be found on the S&P Global ESG Scores website. Aside from the fact that investing in sustainability provides better social and environmental conditions, companies are learning that it can also lead to cost savings in the longer term. Sustainability has become a mark of competitiveness. At the same time we must also acknowledge that 'greenwashing' with ESGs is a serious issue raised

Table 1.1 Notable frontrunners in S&P Global's *The Sustainability Yearbook 2022*

Company	Sector	Award(s)*
ABN Amro	Banking	Yearbook member
BMW	Automobiles	S&P Global Silver Class
Heineken	Beverages	Yearbook member
Shell	Oil & Gas Upstream & Integrated	Yearbook member
Randstad	Professional Services	Yearbook member
ASML	Semiconductors & Semiconductor Equipment	Yearbook member
KPN	Telecommunication Services	Global Bronze Class
Philips	Healthcare Equipment & Supplies	Global Silver Class
Yamaha Motor Co.	Automobiles	Global Silver Class
ASR	Insurance	Global Bronze Class
Samsung	Conglomerates Industrial	Yearbook member
Ahold Delhaize	Food & Staples Retailing	Global Silver Class
Signify	Electrical Components & Equipment	Global Gold Class
Siemens	Industrial Conglomerates	Global Gold Class
DSM	Not included	Not included
ING	Not included	Not included
Unilever	Personal products	Global Gold Class
Air France/KLM	Airlines	Yearbook member

*These companies are a selection of the many different S&P awards discussed above

by critics. According to Investico and Follow the Money (Change Inc, 2022) almost half of the most sustainable (dark green, article 9 under SFDR – Sustainable Finance Disclosure Regulation) category investment funds is (still) being invested in shares and bonds of companies in the fossil fuel industry or airlines. Both Actiam Blackrock and BNP Paribas launched supposed 'green' funds which still invested in fossil fuel companies. The dark green label should not be misused as a marketing tool, but as a promise to the investors.

The triple bottom line standard uses a somewhat wider definition of sustainability, and aims to measure the financial, social and environmental performance of a company over time, rather than merely the traditional measure of corporate profit. TBL is based on three pillars: people, planet and profit (PPP or 3Ps). These pillars were formulated by John Elkington in his book *Cannibals with Forks: The triple bottom line of 21st-century business* (1997). Even then they were not entirely new: the concept of people, planet and profit had already been broached in the United Nations Brundtland report of 1987 (WCED, 1987).

What makes the triple bottom line – whether expressed as TBL or as PPP – such an interesting framework is the fact that in 2007 it became the UN standard for the full-cost accounting of the public sector. It is used to calculate eco-footprint and goes beyond the scope of the S&P Global indices in the sense that economic operating results are not considered solely in terms of sustainability, but are appraised in conjunction with social aspects.

It ought to be noted that one difficulty posed by the TBL is the fact that it is extremely difficult to capture environmental and social standards in one single value. In order to 'weigh' the 3Ps against each other, one must account for profit in the same terms as people and planet. The Responsible Business Simulator (tRBS), which will be introduced in Chapter 5, provides a solution to this problem.

Corporate social responsibility (CSR) is used as an umbrella term derived from the TBL to describe entrepreneurial behaviour. In the case of the TBL, it is explicitly clear that companies must not only account for their performance to shareholders but also to other stakeholders (Wheeler et al, 2003). The concept of profit has to be 'weighted' against the other two pillars. A stakeholder is anyone who is or becomes directly or indirectly involved in or is affected by the activities of a company or organization. The TBL puts a great deal of emphasis on the reciprocity between a company, the community within which it operates, the natural resources it uses and the people who work for it (Rogers and Hudson, 2011). A company that operates according to the principles of the TBL/3Ps will not use toxic substances, cause environmental pollution, trade in arms or weapons, or use child labour.

Increasing awareness of the important role played by stakeholders has led to positive results for companies who act upon it. For example, Nike and Tesco received severely negative responses from their customers around 2010 and were forced to reconsider some of their practices in countries where social and environmental standards were not regulated. Now they are more transparent about their supply chains being aware of the importance of stakeholders increasing appreciation of fair trade and good labour practice. A positive example of a company that has increased awareness among its stakeholders of its environmental impact is PUMA, the sportswear company based in Germany. PUMA was the first to develop an environmental profit and loss account in 2010, which revealed that the impact of the company's activities on the environment was equivalent to almost 72 per cent of its profit. It turned out that PUMA's supply chain was responsible for 94 per cent of this environmental impact. This information helped PUMA to focus innovation on their supply chain and on designing products with less environmental impact (Puma, 2011).

In the financial services industry standards are improving. In particular, the trend has been set by the leading pension funds that have massive amounts to invest. The so-called ESG considerations include environmental, social and governance aspects that can or should be taken into account in assessing investments in countries, companies or projects, and include the following:

- *Environmental* considerations are, for example, sustainable resources, clean technology, climate change and low carbon.
- *Social* considerations include controversial weapons, repressive regimes, adult entertainment, landmines, gambling, tobacco, diversity and alcohol.
- Considerations under *governance* are, for example, board independence, majority ownership, financial planning, financial reporting and executive pay.

In the meantime the increase in ESG assets has gone up to such an extent that 'greenwashing' becomes a serious issue.

The UN Global Impact Assessment (2015) on the transformation of business speaks of 'a modern corporate sustainability movement'.

The assessment concludes that the UN Global Compact, as the world's largest corporate sustainability initiative, together with new initiatives from the business community on sustainability as described above, have had a significant impact on the development of sustainability over the past 15 years. Business has become more strategic, systematic, integrated, transparent and collaborative regarding sustainability.

In the last 15 years, space has been created for alternative ways of running a business, based on concepts of social enterprises, B Corps and shared value creation, described by Porter and Kramer (2011), and which will be addressed extensively in Chapter 2 (Austin and Reficco, 2009; Eggers and Macmillan, 2013; Mair et al, 2012; Short et al, 2009). The enterprise or organization is not an isolated entity, and its purpose should not only be to create value for shareholders. It must continually assess the impact of its actions on the various parties directly and indirectly involved: the stakeholders. Shell used to call this a 'licence to operate', and businesses these days are increasingly finding that they need some sort of social certificate of good conduct to be able to continue their activities. Nowadays companies who want to do good, also want to do better. The focus is not only on a licence to operate, but also on social and environmental impact, transparency and good governance.

This new attitude increases the complexity of strategic and investment decisions. When you add external factors such as limited resources, energy transition, future demographics, hyper-transparency, the growing wealth gap and an exponential increase in technology into the mix, it becomes clear that data science is not a luxury to unravel the different variables in a decision-making process. Recently, interesting European initiatives have been announced, all focused on speeding up the implementation of policies and company strategies to reduce net greenhouse emissions, and measures to increase the resilience of the EU-wide energy system. The European Green Deal (2019) is a five-year plan to adopt a set of climate proposals. These include reducing net greenhouse emissions by at least 55 per cent by 2030. During COP27 in 2022 the EU increased the target to at least 57 per cent. Another target is no net emissions of greenhouse gases by 2050 and economic growth decoupled from resource use. From a social perspective it is worthwhile to mention that in the European Green Deal no person and no place should be left behind. In June 2021, the EU introduced the European Climate Law with a legally binding target of net zero by 2050. An EU taxonomy for sustainability in finance came into being in 2020, developed in close consultation with the EU financial institutions. In May 2022, the REPowerEU plan was launched to rapidly reduce dependence on Russian fossil fuels and fast-forward the green energy transition.

It will be clear that there are now many more factors and actors to be taken into account than there were in the past. But what value should you attach to them in relation to the strategic goals you are trying to achieve? How can you translate those values into concrete and manageable actions? How can you visualize the various options? And which decision best suits your enterprise or organization? The strategic decision-making process and the Responsible Business Simulator help to reduce that complexity to manageable proportions for decision makers and advisors in the world of business. Making use of the results of data and dialogue is a powerful way of getting a better oversight on decision making.

The circular economy as integrating approach

Our current economy can largely be described as a linear one. From resource extraction to production process to consumerism, it is a one-way ticket. This take–make–dispose approach results in a highly inefficient and, more importantly, unsustainable use of our resources. Not only does this lead to an increasing scarcity of resources, it also brings with it waste and pollution, which imposes enormous costs on the public sector. Here we discuss the phenomenon of a *circular economy*, the inevitable perspective for an economy with limited resources.

A circular economy, as defined by the Ellen MacArthur Foundation (2012), is an economy that is restorative and regenerative by intention and design, and which aims to keep products, components and materials at their highest utility and value at all times. So a circular economy is very careful with resources, trying its best to 'circulate' them throughout the economy indefinitely without wasting any of them.

There are six trends visible that move an economy towards becoming a circular one. Although this list is not exhaustive, we see these as the main drivers for a circular future:

1 *Increasing demand for resources and energy*. With an increasing global population, coupled with a sharply increasing middle class, the demand for resources and energy surges.

2 *Innovative technologies*. Using new technologies (e.g. Internet of Things, Big Data, etc) enables producers to increase the value in their production chain, to analyse the material life cycle and employ new design and production methods.

3 *Urbanization*. The increase in urbanization makes it easier and more cost-effective to track, gather, reclaim and share parts or whole products and materials.

4 *Government pressure*. Governments and legislators are becoming more aware of sustainability issues and are creating legislation to contribute to these issues (e.g. Paris COP21).

5 *More aware consumers*. Consumers are becoming more critical of their own consumption behaviour, being more conscious of their impact. There is societal momentum directed towards sustainability.

6 *Consumers get used to access over ownership*. People are getting used to having access to the performance of a product instead of simply owning one (e.g. car sharing via Uber or house sharing via Airbnb); this leads to an increased efficiency in the use of products.

Within a circular economy one can distinguish two 'sub-circles', based on the 'compostability' of waste: a biological circle and a technological one (Figure 1.2). A linear economy essentially leads to treating both types of 'waste' the same, meaning they are being dumped in landfills and incinerated, resulting in large amounts of toxins being released into the environment. The first step towards a circular economy is making the essential distinction between biological and technical materials.

Figure 1.2   The circular economy

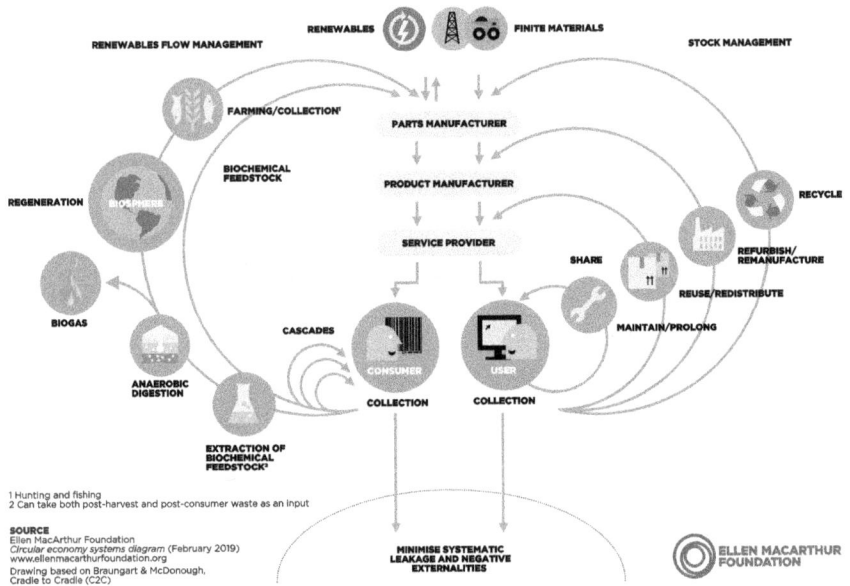

SOURCE Ellen MacArthur Foundation, 2019

The difference lies in the return of biological nutrients to the food chain, which is not possible with technical materials. The focus within the technical realm is consequently on the reuse, remanufacturing or recycling of these waste materials. Keeping soil at its highest possible value is a crucial part of sustaining this biological circle. Through this new circle process, the quality of all materials is optimized, which results in the pressure being taken off the manufacturing end of the model, as well as the waste disposal end. As both ends of the model are being 'pushed down', the first steps towards a circular economy are taken. Last, but definitely not least, the energy necessary to fuel this cycle should be renewable by nature, to decrease resource dependence and increase system resilience (Ellen MacArthur Foundation, 2015).

Although the public in general values recycling highly, from a circular perspective it is the last resort when aiming to 'close the loop'. Recycling often reduces the quality of materials ('downcycling') which limits their usability. While regaining raw material from used products in this way we lose valuable information related to these used products, such as product idea, design and technical specifications. The different sub-circles, as shown in Figure 1.2, are focused on maximizing the use and reuse of the materials and resources in the products, distinguishing them on the basis of their inherent characteristics.

Products that need the least change in order for them to be reused are represented in the innermost circle. Typically, these products require maintenance and should be prevented from entering the outer cycles of remanufacturing and recycling, in order to optimize potential savings on the shares of material, labour, energy, capital, and the associated externalities (such as greenhouse gas emissions, water and toxicity). The next circle, as one moves towards the outside, focuses on reuse and redistribution. If, due to the specific characteristics of the product this is not possible, remanufacturing, refurbishing and, last, recycling are the options, in that order. Needless to say, the more products that stay within the inner circle, the less the negative impact on the environment and the more positive impact on profit through potential saving (such as material, labour, etc). Consequently, the leakage to landfill and incineration is minimized (Ellen MacArthur Foundation, 2015).

Critics propagating the unsustainable character of a linear economy usually focus on how deeply consumerism is embedded in our Western society. Instead of including every aspect of the take–make–dispose approach, these critics limit their solution thinking to one side of the coin. Consumerism might be the engine that keeps the manufacturers manufacturing, the producers producing and waste disposal at full throttle; nevertheless, changing the population's attitudes to consumerism has proven to be nearly impossible. By taking the economy as a whole within the loop of circular economy, other solutions come to mind. Stahel (1982) developed a new economic model that helps to facilitate the changes necessary for a circular economy. As he re-evaluates how we look at ownership, he introduces 'performance-based contracting'. In this model, ownership as we know it today makes way for a fee that the user pays for the performance of a product. Consumers do not pay for ownership of the product, but instead pay for the performance the product delivers. The producers keep ownership, which means, ideally, that the product is returned to the producer after the consumer has enjoyed its performance. Convincing consumers to recycle their products is taken out of the equation by returning the control over the product to the producers once the performance has been fulfilled. A recent voice in the public debate is Kate Raworth, author of *Doughnut Economics*. She writes that the traditional system of economics is broken and that radical reframing of economics for a new generation is necessary, given the challenges at stake (Raworth, 2017).

Circular economy examples in business practices

Society is coming to regard the concept of circularity as increasingly important. We see this reflected both in economic studies, and by circular thinking and acting in industry: materials passports in building and construction; the recycling of electronics, where the shortage of rare earth materials forces companies to reuse materials, and the circular use of materials inside electronic car batteries will become essential.

In September 2014, the European Commission adopted a zero-waste programme, establishing a legal framework for an EU-wide circular economy. Not only did the Commission predict that this new framework will boost recycling and prevent the waste of valuable materials, but that it would also create new jobs, economic growth, new business models, and reduce greenhouse gas emissions. By 2030, EU citizens can expect at least 7 per cent of their municipal waste to be recycled and at least 80 per cent of all packaging materials. On top of that, it is estimated that the circular economy can save European businesses €600 billion (European Commission, 2014). With the Green Deal in 2020 more ambitious goals have been set.

On McKinsey's website the company states in a White Paper (Gatzer et al, 2022) that it estimates that portfolio transformation, green business building, green premiums, and green operations focused on circularity can help European consumer goods companies shift to circular value pools of more than €500 billion of annual revenues by 2030. The primary driver will be a shift in consumer demand, with younger generations in particular expressing their values in their purchasing choices. McKinsey research shows that sustainability is 'highly important' for about 40 per cent of European consumers, amid rising demand for recycled, refurbished and reused products.

We give some examples here, drawn from the list of S&P Award winners, of leading companies who practise circular economy principles. Most of the information is from the companies' own websites, from articles in trusted press, and the Ellen MacArthur Foundation, who prepared some company case studies.

Patagonia

Patagonia is an example of a brand that sets environmental values and circularity as key priorities, and has done so for decades. All Patagonia products are specifically designed to have long economic life cycles. Through 'Worn Wear' repair hubs, the company encourages its customers to repair items instead of buying new ones. In September 2022, the company went a step further to spread its missions and values; the owning Chouinard's family made 'the planet' their only shareholder by donating 98 per cent of the company's stock to the Holdfast Collective, which is a non-profit organization aiming to fight the environmental crisis, protect nature and biodiversity, and support thriving communities as quickly as possible. The remaining 2 per cent of the shares and all decision-making authority was donated to a trust, which will oversee the company's mission and values (*The Guardian*, 2022).

Royal Philips

Royal Philips has been a top-ranking company in the DSJI and S&P rankings for many years. The healthcare technology company has made major strides to integrate the circular economic principles into their core business systems. As of 2020, all of their sites are fully powered by renewable energy sources, and all emissions from production, travel and logistics are CO_2 compensated. The company is already carbon neutral in its operations and aims to further reduce its CO_2 emissions to adhere to international global warming mitigation targets. The company has set a number of ambitious economic objectives, such as increasing its circular economy revenue to 25 per cent of sales and ensuring that 100 per cent of products meet the company's EcoDesign principles (of which circularity is a key pillar) (Ellen Macarthur Foundation, 2021a).

Heineken

Royal Heineken has been on a mission to enhance its circularity since 2010, when it presented its 'Brewing a Better World' ambition to reduce CO_2 emissions and increase the use of renewable energy in production (Heineken, 2016). Since 2020, all Heineken beer for the Dutch market is produced using 100 per cent green energy. In 2021, the company set new goals to become fully circular by 2030. Before this year, Heineken aims to decarbonize its production, eliminate waste disposal to landfills in production, accelerate the use of returnable and recyclable packaging and significantly reduce water use in production (Heineken, 2020).

IKEA

Circularity is one of three focus areas in IKEA's sustainability strategy. The company aims to become a climate-positive, circular business by 2030 by giving products and materials a longer life. Today, 55.8 per cent of the materials sourced by IKEA are renewable, like wood and cotton, and 17.3 per cent are recycled, and the company is making efforts to increase these numbers. IKEA has started auditing its products based on circular product design principles; products are designed for easy assembly, disassembly and reassembly. Additionally, the company has started a number of initiatives to go beyond the simple sale of furniture. The company is experimenting with renting options for their furniture, sale of refurbished products, and aims to prolong the lifetime of products by providing customers with spare parts (Ellen MacArthur Foundation, 2021b).

Unilever

Unilever is an example of a global company incorporating circular principles in their corporate strategy. Under Paul Polman, one of the former CEOs who supported the SDGs from the start, a new awareness about the planet and Unilever's contribution was developed. Through the Unilever Compass strategy, launched in 2020, the company is committed to the transition to regenerative agriculture practices and to use 100 per cent reusable, recyclable or compostable plastic packaging by 2025. Additionally, the company's Clean Future strategy sets out Unilever's ambition to use 100 per cent renewable or recycled carbon in the development, production and processing of all their cleaning products before 2030. An example of reusable packaging at Unilever is the *Cif* eco-refill. This refill containing super-concentrated cleaning product can be attached to used *Power & Shine* bottles filled with water. The refill is made using 75 per cent less plastic than new bottles, is 100 per cent recyclable and saves 97 per cent water over new cleaning products. According to Unilever, this innovation will remove 1.5 million plastic bottles from UK supermarkets alone (Ellen MacArthur Foundation, 2021c).

As we transition to a circular economy, disruption will be experienced in many economic systems, affecting every sector imaginable. We expect change in the following five sectors to be most influential, and disruptive, in the near future:

- *Logistics*: waste flows from one company will form the resources for another. Logistics companies will have to connect companies from different material chains in increasingly complex networks. Trucks will probably never drive completely empty.

- *Retail and marketing*: circular products and services will need accompanying revenue models. To regain resources and efficiently process them producers will probably remain owners of their products or use buyback schemes.

- *Finance*: a change from ownership to usage has many finance-related consequences for producers and consumers alike. Risk needs to be addressed and financial instruments, like mortgages, need to be overhauled. Banks can also become important players in connecting different chains.

- *Product design*: products will have to be designed for circularity; they should be reusable and modular, meaning they are easy to take apart. These parts then need to be easy to replace or repair, and the product as a whole needs to be easily refurbished.

- *Material design*: materials should be made from resources that are already reused without loss in value and that can be reused again. Moreover, circular materials and parts should either consist of only one material or be easily separable into single materials.

The Responsible Business Simulator and the circular economy

Benefits of making strategic decisions based on data and dialogue

1 Unleashes the combined power of explorative and strategic dialogue with the art of advanced modelling.

2 Operationalizes circular economy-related issues.

3 Facilitates boardroom discussion with facts, figures and visuals that are created on the spot.

4 Captures every element brought up in strategic dialogues.

5 Integrates the financial and non-financial objectives of strategic decisions and clarifies potential trade-offs.

6 Stimulates out-of-the-box thinking.

7 Creates robust, sustainable decisions.

8 Provides many visual displays to explain complex interdependencies.

9 Creates shared value for multiple stakeholders.

10 Creates transparency in business dynamics.

11 Documents all assumptions, steps and sources underlying a strategic decision.

12 Allows users to incorporate new insight into existing models without programming.

13 Extends the two-dimensional world of spreadsheets into a highly multi-dimensional world.

14 Provides access to all types of data sources.

15 Discloses, combines and projects all available data on the strategic decision at hand.

16 Supports any strategic decision.

17 Detects the vital few factors that influence the outcomes of decisions the most.

The transition to a circular economy inevitably implies a paradigm shift. The Responsible Business Simulator (tRBS) can be used as a tool to accelerate that shift. Businesses working towards ameliorating social goals, such as shifting towards a circular economy, need incentives. Sustainability for the environment and people has, however, traditionally been regarded as merely representing a corporate philosophy; a charitable corporate strategy that is often seen as just a burden and a necessity for marketing. As opposed to this, increase in profit typically functions as the largest incentive for any business, sometimes indeed at any cost when it comes to the environment and people. Not surprisingly, the most important barriers to implementation of circular economy practices are high upfront investment costs and risks for businesses (Preston, 2012). The Responsible Business Simulator, however, combines these two seemingly contradicting doctrines – environmental/social and economic benefits – operating within the framework of shared values (people, planet and profit). In this respect, tRBS makes the complexity of the value chains in a circular economy more transparent. Sustainability in the long term is more beneficial to a company's profit than short-term destructive use of resources and disregard for the social dimension.

The importance of shared values for the company's long-term continuity is clearly demonstrated and confirmed through this strategic decision-making process and the use of tRBS, in which profit is an integral component. The Responsible Business Simulator actively takes stakeholders' interests into account in attaining strategic goals. The stakeholders' interests can be found in the 3Ps, which in turn find their expression as performance indicators in the model. This brings us one step closer to attaining the goals of a circular economy by getting the biggest players in the field, businesses, on board the train to circularity: no negative effects on human life, people, or the ecosystem, planet.

References

Austin, J and Reficco, E (2009) Corporate social entrepreneurship: a new vision for CSR, in *The Accountable Corporation*, eds M Epstein and K Hanson, Praeger Publishing, New York, 237–47

Change Inc (2022) How is it possible that half of the 'greenest' investments funds invest in fossil? (Hoe kan het dat de helft van de 'groenste' beleggingsfondsen toch in fossiel investeert?) 25 November

Eggers, WD and Macmillan, P (2013) *The Solution Revolution: How business, government, and social enterprises are teaming up to solve society's toughest problems*, Harvard Business Review Press, Boston, MA

Elkington, J (1997) *Cannibals With Forks: Triple bottom line of 21st-century business*, Capstone Publishers, Mankato, MN

Ellen MacArthur Foundation (2012) Towards the Circular Economy 1: Economic and business rationale for an accelerated transition, www.ellenmacarthurfoundation.org/assets/downloads/publications/Ellen-MacArthur-Foundation-Towards-the-Circular-Economy-vol.1.pdf (archived at https://perma.cc/5UB3-L439)

Ellen MacArthur Foundation (2015) Ellen MacArthur Foundation, www.ellenmacarthurfoundation.org (archived at https://perma.cc/4QX8-BUDN)

Ellen MacArthur Foundation (2019) Circular economy diagram, https://ellenmacarthurfoundation.org/circular-economy-diagram (archived at https://perma.cc/L63N-T9VS)

Ellen MacArthur Foundation (2021a) The circular economy in action at Philips, ellenmacarthurfoundation.org/philips (archived at https://perma.cc/D88X-DDT5)

Ellen MacArthur Foundation (2021b) The circular economy in action at Ikea, ellenmacarthurfoundation.org/ikea (archived at https://perma.cc/C57D-FMZ7)

Ellen MacArthur Foundation (2021c) The circular economy in action at Unilever, ellenmacarthurfoundation.org/unilever (archived at https://perma.cc/Y6AE-THR4)

European Commission (2014) Communication from the Commission to the European Parliament, the Council, the European Economic and Social Committee and the Committee of the Regions Towards a Circular Economy: A zero waste programme for Europe, eur-lex.europa. eu/legal-content/EN/ALL/?uri=CELEX:52014DC0398R(01) (archived at https://perma.cc/8YWF-BFXD)

Gatzer, S, Helmcke, S and Roos, D (2022) Playing offense on circularity, McKinsey, www.mckinsey.com/industries/consumer-packaged-goods/ our-insights/playing-offense-on-circularity-can-net-european-consumer-goods-companies-500-billion-euros (archived at https://perma.cc/ L3YF-FZ6T)

The Guardian (2022) 14 September, http://www.theguardian.com/us-news/2022/sep/14/patagonias-billionaire-owner-gives-away-company-to-fight-climate-crisis-yvon-chouinard (archived at https://perma. cc/5FGB-LQSN); hq.misio.io/patagonia-case-study-how-to-drive-profit-with-purpose (archived at https://perma.cc/E6W6-3UA5)

Heineken (2016) Sustainability Report 2015: Brewing a better world, Heineken, Amsterdam www.theheinekencompany.com/newsroom/ heineken-launches-2030-brew-a-better-world-ambitions/ (archived at https://perma.cc/XA3K-SEE8)

Heineken (2020) Heineken beer has been brewed using 100% green energy, Press Release, 31 August, www.theheinekencompany.com/ newsroom/heineken-beer-has-been-brewed-using-100-green-energy (archived at https://perma.cc/AGK7-X3LD)

IPCC (2022) www.ipcc.ch/working-group/wg3/ (archived at https://perma. cc/MR5H-QJV2)

McDonough, W and Braungart, M (2002) *Cradle to Cradle: Remaking the way we make things,* North Point Press, New York, NY

Mair, J, Battalina, JL and Cardenas, J (2012) Organizing for society: a typology of social entrepreneuring models, *Journal of Business Ethics,* **11**, 353–73

Meadows, DH et al (1972) *The Limits to Growth*, Universe Books, New York, NY

Nidumolu, R, Prahalad, CK and Rangaswami, MR (2009), Why sustainability is now the key driver of innovation, *Harvard Business Review*, **87** (9), 56–64

Porter, ME and Kramer, MR (2011) Creating shared value: how to reinvent capitalism – and unleash a wave of innovation and growth, *Harvard Business Review*, **89** (1/2), 62–77

Preston, F (2012) *A Global Redesign? Shaping the circular economy*, Chatham House, London, 1–20

Puma (2011) Environmental profit and loss account, about.puma.com/en/sustainability/environment/environmental-profit-and-loss-account (archived at https://perma.cc/VZ6B-5F3A)

Raworth, K (2017*) Doughnut Economics: Seven ways to think like a 21st-century economist*, Random House Business Books, London

Rogers, K and Hudson, B (2011) The triple bottom line: the synergies of transformative perceptions and practices for sustainability, *OD Practitioner*, **43**, 3–9

S&P Global (2022) *S&P Global Sustainability Yearbook 2022*, www.spglobal.com/esg/csa/yearbook/2022/downloads/spglobal_sustainability_yearbook_2022.pdf (archived at https://perma.cc/6P6G-HJS5)

Short, JC, Moss, TW and Lumpkin, GT (2009) Research in social entrepreneurship: past contributions and future opportunities, *Strategic Entrepreneurship Journal*, **3**, 161–94

Stahel, W (1982) *The Product-Life Factor*, Product Life Institute, Geneve

Tielbeke, J (2022) Herman E Daly, 21 July 1938 – 28 October 2022, *De Groene Amsterdammer*, www.groene.nl/artikel/herman-e-daly-21-juli-1938-28-oktober-2022 (archived at https://perma.cc/3K5Y-N9SR)

UN Global Compact (2015) *Impact: Transforming business, changing the world*, www.unglobalcompact.org/library/1331 (archived at https://perma.cc/654C-2WSG)

WCED (1987) *Report of the World Commission on Environment and Development: Our common future*, www.un-documents.net/our-common-future.pdf (archived at https://perma.cc/95GB-8TWY)

Wheeler, D, Colbert, B and Freeman, RE (2003) Focusing on value: Reconciling corporate social responsibility, sustainability and a stakeholder approach in a network world, *Journal of General Management*, **28**, 1–26

Creating shared value as a framework for shaping strategy

02

It is interesting to see how concepts and frameworks have been developed in recent decades in order to achieve a better balance between the interests of enterprises and shareholders on the one hand and the interests of society and stakeholders on the other. Over the years, various articles from Michael Porter and Mark Kramer have provided fuel for the debate from the perspective of business administration (2002, 2006, 2011). In this chapter, we will first discuss the concept of 'shared value' as introduced by Porter and Kramer (2002). They developed the concept in practice with first-mover companies like Nestlé. After that, we will outline Porter and Kramer's arguments as to why there does not necessarily have to be tension between economic and social goals and the role the Responsible Business Simulator (tRBS) can play to integrate social and economic goals in the decision-making process. The concept of 'creating shared value' (CSV) is not free from academic debate. We will discuss critical contributions by De los Reyes et al about the importance of ethics in what they call the CSV+ framework (2017, 2019). To overcome the problem that profitability and social advantage appear to be at odds in business, more focus on sustaining the moral legitimacy of business decisions is needed, as well as a closer look at the ethics and behaviour of management. In short, going beyond compliance and making the real miles to go for a balanced People, Planet and Profit strategy.

The concept of shared value

In 2002 Porter and Kramer wrote that companies could use their phil-anthropic efforts to improve their competitiveness within the business environment that shapes their productivity. The intellectual develop-ment path illustrated by these authors is a good reflection of thinking within the field of sustainability in business in the past decades. The leaders in the field are becoming quite adept; they are attracting disci-ples and a real movement is emerging. The shared value concept was demonstrated very clearly at the Paris 2015 COP, at which eco-conscious frontrunners such as Unilever and DSM were actively call-ing for an acceleration in global efforts to reduce CO_2 emissions and keep global warming under 1.5°C, as well as promoting the UN SDGs development goals. The core of these frontrunners' development programmes is shifting towards integrating societal objectives into corporate strategy, previously the exclusive domain of purely com-mercial economic objectives. Porter and Kramer (2002) describe the development of the concept of philanthropy or charity from what was merely a peripheral consideration to one that shapes corporate social responsibility (CSR), but they do also express some criticisms.

In their later article (2006), Porter and Kramer move on to corpo-rate social integration (CSI) as a way to explain that CSR must not become a discrete activity for a small group within a company, but must be directly and firmly connected to the enterprise's commercial economic objectives. From CSI they go on to speak of how important it is for businesses to create social value. Some radicalization is dis-cernible in their later articles (2011), in which they advocate a re-definition of capitalism with shared value as the underlying principle. It is their conviction that commercial enterprises can offer an answer to today's major social questions by being innovative and sustaina-ble, and showing respect for people, the planet and the social envi-ronment. It is the ultimate amalgamation of societal interests and a reinvented form of entrepreneurship that arises from the common values, the shared value, being pursued.

Even though the concept of creating shared value has received a lot of attention among management scholars and within the business community, there have also been some critics. Crane et al (2014) published an assessment on the topic outlining both the strengths and weaknesses of shared value creation. The strength of their approach, according to these authors, mainly lies in the fact that Porter and Kramer elevate social goals of enterprises to a strategic level as well as including the role of the government in the social initiatives of companies. The main weakness these authors put forward is that Porter and Kramer focus too much on corporate self-interest in the sense that enterprises only engage in socially responsible behaviour if it serves the economic objective of the company. The authors state that Porter and Kramer neglect the possibility that companies can have a social purpose, and that they also neglect the possible tension between economic and social goals. However, Crane et al do acknowledge that the concept of shared value does add value to the debate on the role of business in society, and it may well contribute to the rise of business practices that are beneficial to society.

From a slightly different perspective De los Reyes et al (2017) criticize Porter and Kramer, but eventually they plead for a more enhanced concept of shared value, which they call CSV+, which stands for creating social value plus ethics and moral legitimacy. The authors stress the importance of looking beyond the firm and taking the perspective of the business environment and supply chains to have a broader impact on unregulated pollution and labour conditions during steps in the production and delivery processes. The second basis of their scepticism towards Porter and Kramer's approach is the narrow focus on compliance by business and their management. De los Reyes et al (2017) consider this as naïve, or, as Crane et al (2014) state, as essentially a form of greenwashing. The authors emphasize that simply telling managers that they are assumed to be complying with ethical norms does not help them do so. Their answer is that a true strategy to protect the business's reputation is to act legitimately.

In our approach with tRBS, we can provide managers with convincing facts and figures. In that sense, we can overcome the problems in Porter and Kramer's approach of shared value that have been subject to criticism. In their article on a systemic review and integrative perspective on creating shared value, Menghwar and Daood

(2021) acknowledge that CSV is a meaningful, incremental addition to the literature, but it is not a revolutionary concept. CSV provides a strategic approach that integrates social problems with corporate strategy. They stress the importance of the firm's decision processes when it comes to adopting a CSV strategy.

The outcome depends on opportunity costs and transaction costs. In their opinion there are many ways to create shared value rather than a single universal way. Daood warns of the lack of radical innovativeness in CSV, and this is also heard in the writings of Beschorner and Hajduk (2017), Crane (2014) and Dembek et al (2016). Notwithstanding the criticisms, there is always a kind of unspoken jealousy displayed by economists who see Porter and Kramer's framework being adopted and adapted by the business community. Perhaps one of Porter and Kramer's main achievements has been knowing how to engage with the pivotal frontrunners in their endeavours to move business in the direction of doing good for people and the planet, while making profits. Their ideas have had a major impact on businesses, giving them the confidence to become more radical to push harder for creating shared value. Looking at the movement they have created among business leaders and organizations around the world, the evidence clearly supports them.

In this book, we take 'shared value' as a framework for the shaping of corporate strategy and the decision making that underlies that strategy. Pinpointing what exactly the shared value in a company is, and the importance of that shared value for the company's long-term continuity, can be simplified and underlined with facts and figures. The Responsible Business Simulator makes the company's shared value transparent.

Balancing societal and economic objectives

When a company is socially active within its own competitive context, the effort it puts into achieving a particular charitable objective will have a social dimension, but economic benefit can often be derived at the same time. Porter and Kramer (2002) suggest that in the longer term, far from causing conflicts, this leads to an amalgamation of societal and economic objectives. They suggest, quite correctly, that at the point where social and economic benefits converge, the focus on corporate strategy is of great significance. After all, if you can 'do good' and achieve the commercial objectives of your company at the same time, you can draw multiple objectives into the scope of the same strategy.

This argument by Porter and Kramer is supported by meta-analytic findings (over 35 years of empirical data) in studies by Orlitzky et al (2003) and Margolis et al (2007). These findings suggest that corporate social performance (CSP) is likely to pay off, thus being positively correlated with corporate financial performance (CFP). Above all, it becomes clear that market forces do not penalize companies that have high CSP levels. Rather, the market rewards businesses for building sustainability into their corporate strategy. In addition, social audits, which often result in receiving public endorsements from federal or international agencies, can have a positive effect on CFP (Porter and Kramer, 2006).

At the same time we must listen carefully to critical comments. De los Reyes et al (2017) give the example of increasing labour safety standards in the global apparel industry that may hurt profitability and make the business case less likely as profits for global brands will be lower. In a more recent article De los Reyes and Scholz (2019) are sceptical about the potential of CSV to generate transformative innovation for corporate sustainability. Optimizing legacy business by offsetting or mitigating impact that is ecologically destructive perhaps reduces any harm, but does not lead to breakthrough solutions. The authors state that there are multiple reasons why CSV will not get rid of destructive businesses altogether. In their opinion more focus should be placed on providing a framework to managers with adequate normative guidelines in regulatory voids (De los Reyes et al, 2017).

Looking at the effectiveness of CSV from a different angle, Jones and Wright (2016) take a closer look at the fashion industry and ask the question: Does creating shared value pay? Their accounting and financial views shed new light on CSV. Their findings, based on a sample of ASX 300 companies taken over a five-year period (2008–2012) show a strong statistical association between the CSV proxies and a range of financial performance indicators. According to the authors these companies also tend to be larger and have higher growth opportunities. However, statistical tests of causality indicate that superior financial performance leads to greater CSV activity, rather than CSV activity driving financial outcomes. The findings suggest that successful companies may well be adopting CSV-type practices as an outcome of management fashion rather than because of their tangible contribution to the financial performance of the firm. Successful companies see CSV activities as a way of further harnessing their performance in building new capabilities, efficiencies, products and markets as it should be doing (Jones and Wright, 2016).

We can similarly position Fernández-Gámez et al (2020) on the positive impact of creating shared value on hotels' online reputation and financial performance. Their research shows that the relationship between CSV and operational results (OR) in the hotel industry is relevant for reconceiving products and redefining productivity in the value chain. CSV has proved to be related to company value (Choi et al, 2018). Specifically, the tourism industry shows results in promoting 'green engage'. Intercontinental Hotels Group (IHG) has stimulated CSV for green impact, and at the same time it also contributed to higher efficiency of resources and reduced costs in hundreds of hotels in the hotel chain (Hsiao and Chuang, 2016). Better economic results and reinforced and improved relationships with clients may be seen as a positive impact of CSV (Spitzeck and Chapman, 2012). Porter and Kramer's concept (2011) is further substantiated by Jin (2018), who says that the CSV strategy has important implications for companies' competitiveness, for their behaviour towards customers and for the company's value and performance. Research carried out by Awale and Rowlinson (2014) on CSV effects on company competitiveness has shown that CSV increased company competitiveness through the improvement of its business and social conditions. This is in line with the original ideas of Porter and Kramer (2011).

Moreover, it has been found that bad environmental performance has a negative effect on the market value of publicly traded companies. A study by Konar and Cohen (2001) has shown that the emission of toxic chemicals generally has a negative effect on the intangible asset value of companies, and that reducing these emissions increases market value. A more recent investigation into the effect of corporate sustainability compared 180 US companies, grouped as either High Sustainability or Low Sustainability companies (Eccles et al, 2014). The high sustainability companies were characterized as being early adopters of sustainability policies. Evidence showed that these companies outperformed the others, especially over the long term, both in accounting and stock market performance.

Another, more internal way in which social and economic benefits converge is illustrated by the following example: at first sight, investing in better-qualified personnel means increasing wage costs. But those same personnel can provide the basis from which to develop more sophisticated products or services and thus create more added value for the company. If we take this example a stage further, and the company invests actively and deploys its employees in activities to raise the level of education in disadvantaged areas, that investment not only has value in terms of the reputation of the company but also ensures that more people are encouraged to continue to learn and therefore to have a better chance of finding work and generating income. This in turn creates new consumers and – at the same time – reinforces the self-sufficiency of the local community. 'When corporations support the right causes in the right ways – when they get the *where* and the *how* right – they set in motion a virtuous circle' (Porter and Kramer, 2002).

In their article titled 'Strategy and Society' (2006), Porter and Kramer take this positive image of philanthropy a step further. By 2006, corporate social responsibility (CSR) was well established. Porter and Kramer argue that CSR should not exclusively be seen as an expense, but that it can also be the source of new opportunities, innovation and competitive advantage. They were quick to see that sustainability fits so well into the P for planet in the triple bottom line of people, planet and profit. However, integrating sustainability into an organization demands a sense of stewardship from that organization. To give substance to the concept of sustainability is to show respect for the natural environment and it is the moral duty of enterprises to do so in such a way that future generations will be able to fulfil their own needs (Porter and Kramer, 2006). People, planet and profit have to be seen as equal partners in this process of integration.

It is extremely short-sighted that often people and planet are only used in the service of profit, or only used to bring about profit. The critical note that the authors sound in their 2006 article is that enterprises frequently use CSR to obtain a 'licence to operate' and to uphold stakeholder satisfaction in the short term. In this context, Porter and Kramer specifically mention the energy and chemical industries, both of which are pragmatically engaged with CSR but nonetheless have not allowed it to penetrate to the core of their strategy. The authors argue that in the case of companies such as Ben & Jerry's, Patagonia and The Body Shop, cited as prime examples of long-term commitment, social responsibility and CSR did find their way into the core of corporate strategy. They can be said to have achieved true integration between the 3Ps of people, planet and profit.

In terms of our positioning of strategic decision making and the Responsible Business Simulator, it is interesting to note that Porter and Kramer (2006) state that:

> The essential test that should guide CSR is not whether a cause is worthy, but whether it presents an opportunity to create shared value – that is a meaningful benefit for society that is also valuable to the business.

But a further step is necessary to integrate corporate objectives and societal needs. This entails creating different relationships both within and outside the organization, creating transparency in operational management about objectives and how they are achieved, being explicit about values and, finally, accounting candidly in reports. According to the authors, CSR should no longer be perceived as a separate discipline; a progression needs to be made from CSR to corporate social integration (CSI). Corporate social integration is far more than a simple name change. In their view, social responsibility should be seen as creating shared value. And that calls for more than simple damage control or the organization of public relations campaigns with a short-lived result (Porter and Kramer, 2006).

A good example of non-integrated CSR is illustrated by the following example. The International Organization for Standardization (ISO), as one of the world's largest developers of voluntary international standards, has published guidelines for incorporating CSR into business practices. These guidelines, ISO 26000, were launched in 2010 and are aimed at clarifying what CSR is, as well as helping businesses and organizations translate these principles into effective actions. CSR is defined according to seven generic principles: accountability, transparency, ethical behaviour, respect for stakeholder interest, respect for the rule of law, respect for international standards of conduct, and respect for human rights. These principles are then to be implemented within different CSR subject areas such as the environment and human rights. The ISO 26000 guidelines for implementing CSR principles in core subject areas are expressed in a complex body of definitions and rules that reflect the nature of CSR as a separate discipline (ISO, 2010).

Opting for sustainable business practices is a strategic choice

Where sustainability was seen for a long time as 'doing good' or at least observing a minimum set of rules (compliance), it is now seen as a strategic choice that goes to the heart of business practices. And that applies just as much to the private as to the public sector. A government that opts for sustainability, circularity and social inclusion will take decisions about the design of public spaces, drinking water quality, mobility, or the purchasing process for the apparatus of government quite differently than one for which sustainability has a low priority.

The double political standards seen in some countries – saying one thing but doing the opposite – has nevertheless not deterred some states (such as Germany, the Scandinavian countries, Italy and Austria) and some multinational enterprises (those that want a high ranking on the *S&P Global Sustainability Yearbook*) from purposefully taking up the baton. They do so not only because it is better for the climate, but because they realize that sustainability is a strategic choice for the long term. Persistence is called for if the necessary institutional changes are to be implemented in either a country or an enterprise. Countries can create the necessary conditions by means of regulation, legislation, an appropriate tax regime and institutional adaptation. In doing so, they also create a stimulating investment climate for businesses. Businesses can look upon opting for sustainability as a necessary investment to enhance their competitiveness. They choose to distinguish themselves through sustainable, innovative products, production chains and stakeholder management.

As a strategic choice, sustainability calls for a rational analysis that goes far deeper than responsible business practices or CSR. It also goes further than eco-efficiency (Dyllicki and Hockerts, 2002). It hinges on a strategic choice that is fundamental to the management and direction of the enterprise: its investments, internal working processes and employees' competences, interactions with its environment, its offices and factories, raw materials input and the chosen combination of energy sources, its processing methods (throughput), and its output.

It goes without saying that such a complicated assemblage of steps will be fraught with uncertainty. So much can go wrong, and well-intended efforts might not amount to much. If a successful strategy for sustainability in the management of an enterprise is to be achieved, the operational implementation of that strategy will need to be given due consideration in the decision-making process from the earliest stages. More often than not, that will be seen as an extra layer of complexity, but if sustainable practices are to be put in place it will be desirable to ensure the involvement of the entire organization and its stakeholders.

Towards creating a shared value strategy

In 2011, Porter and Kramer published an article about creating shared value which was very well received by companies that already had some experience with CSR (Porter and Kramer, 2011). In this article, the authors take the line set out in previous publications one step further still. They speak about 'rethinking capitalism'; Michael Porter makes it clear that he advocates a radical change. The tenor of the article is that the concept of shared value has the potential to release a new wave of global growth – a growth that is characterized by innovation and that can be beneficial to both business and society as a whole. Earlier in this chapter we mentioned authors who have published critical commentary on the rather general, often bold claims made by Porter and Kramer, without paying too much attention to theoretical substance behind them. However, one should not underestimate Porter and Kramer's impact on the world of business and change, simply because their work is very accessible and easy to understand.

Such a drastic change as proposed by Porter and Kramer (2011) will require businesses to make some fundamental strategic decisions. A switch from short-term to long-term vision, for example, from relocating production facilities because of lower wages to investing in high-tech production processes which are closer to the customer, from waste mountains to recycling and reprocessing waste and 'leftover' material. Another factor is their observation that although businesses pay lip service to CSR it doesn't seem to be getting them anywhere because the impact remains inconsequential. The authors realize that creating social value unlocks enormous potential to develop new products and satisfy societal needs and challenges. According to the authors, businesses that can identify societal needs and respond to them with innovative products and services will enjoy competitive advantage over businesses that are unwilling to stray beyond the well-known boundaries of capitalism. They recommend a different business model, based on the needs of the enterprise and society, that can create value for both the enterprise and society by using the resources of the enterprise to address society's challenges.

In their article on strategic decisions regarding shared value Mühlbacher and Böbel (2019) describe the conditions for successful shared-value strategy implementation. They stress five conditions in a theoretical framework:

- shared value-oriented entrepreneurial vision
- strategic alignment
- shared value-oriented innovation (SVI)
- networking capabilities
- impact monitoring

The framework is an important step in supporting management efforts to reorient their companies from zero-sum strategies to win–win shared-value strategies. In Mühlbacher and Böbel's view, managers need to align their strategic focus with solutions to problems relevant to the business domain of the company in an environmentally conscious manner, while balancing the interests of all stakeholders. Transparent monitoring systems are important to enable management to see progress (or not). It gives a sense of belonging to the greater goal of sustainability. It also shines light on the opportunities to invest in innovations that will benefit customers, stakeholders and the company and will have an impact on the problem at hand.

It is also interesting that their five conditions require the development of networking capabilities. This is not only valuable internally within companies, but even more valuable with external companies, organizations and stakeholders, and emphasizes the importance of leadership, behaviour and new networking skills to collaborate and co-create solutions. In doing so, Mühlbacher and Böbel contribute to a more holistic enabling model to implement strategic value creation in companies, networks and ecosystems (Mühlbacher and Böbel, 2019).

This is a nice bridge towards Kramer and Pfitzer's earlier article on 'The ecosystem of shared value' in the *Harvard Business Review* (Kramer and Pfitzer, 2016). Based on their earlier research and observations they see barriers for implementation of shared value due to the fact that companies do not operate in isolation, but operate in ecosystems. Government policies and cultural norms present further limitations. Therefore they plead for 'collective impact' efforts that involve all players in the ecosystems. Collective impact is based on the idea that social problems arise from and persist because of a complex combination of actions and omissions by players in all sectors (Sánchez-Hernández et al, 2017). This can only be solved by coordinated efforts of those players. Think about issues such as education, pollution, childhood obesity, job creation, etc. In ecosystems, different perspectives from expert to experiential can be brought together, as well as the data needed to come to decisions for innovative solutions. The first step in collective impact initiatives is a shared understanding of the problem. To implement this collective solving of the problems, five elements are needed: a common agenda, a shared measurement system, mutually reinforcing activities, constant communication, and dedicated 'backbone' support from one or more independent organizations.

'Value' is defined in the following chapters as benefit in relation to costs, not just as benefit in isolation. What matters is that businesses not only seek to make a profit, but also seek to create strategic and collective shared value. According to Porter and Kramer (2011), this is the ultimate legitimization of an enterprise. In Kramer's contribution (2016) it is not only relevant for business, but also for organizations, the public sector and for governments. Therefore the ecosystem approach with more parties involved is an inspiring perspective.

Rolling out shared value through the Responsible Business Simulator

The route that Porter and Kramer have taken from philanthropy, via CSR to CSI, and from there to shared value, networks and collective impact in ecosystems, is fairly consistent. In the course of their research, they have observed that increasing numbers of enterprises want to 'do good', but more often than not that wish is translated into short-term opportunistic intentions, ways of keeping stakeholders happy, avoiding reputational damage, supporting good causes at random, etc. From that perspective, social responsibility (CSR) will continue to be side-lined, while social and environmental challenges continue to increase and call for precisely the corporate approach the authors and the critics describe. Bringing the two sides together is what leads to shared value with impact.

Since 2015 the concept of B Corporations (B Corps) has taken off in Europe. B Corps started in 2006 in the United States and its global headquarter is in New York. B Lab is the non-profit network transforming the global economy to benefit all people, communities and the planet, and its members are the so-called B Corps. B Corps are for-profit organizations that meet rigorous standards of environmental and social performance, as well as the corresponding accountability and transparency. These companies are certified by B Lab. Moreover, there are currently many social enterprise start-ups, and social impact financing is on the rise. This movement shows that an increasing number of eco-conscious entrepreneurs and companies want to do more than the average business does, and certainly more than mere compliance demands.

In their argument for shared value, Porter and Kramer give a number of examples of businesses who are indeed thinking along these lines, but they give no indication of what the potential value could be in terms of actual outcomes for people, planet and profit. They do contend that these considerations should have a place in any major decision taken in or by a business. To achieve this, they say that concrete and tailored metrics are needed for each business unit in each of the three areas (Porter and Kramer, 2011). Although their critics basically agree with the strategic intent of shared value, and although there are many studies providing positive evidence of shared-value initiatives in various industries and individual companies, there is not a model that substantiates the strategic decision-making process towards shared value with facts and figures. In Part Three of this book the cases will show how that can be done with the underlying methodology of the data and dialogue of the Responsible Business Simulator.

The concept of strategic decision making in combination with tRBS builds further on this premise and shows that strategic objectives can be achieved with due observance of the 3Ps of people, planet and profits, that then find expression in the principal key outputs of the decision-making process.

References

Awale, R and Rowlinson, S (2014) A conceptual framework for achieving firm competitiveness in construction: A creating shared value (CSV) concept, in *Proceedings Thirtieth Annual ARCOM Conference*, Association of Researchers in Construction Management, 1–3 September 2014, 1285–94, eds A B Raiden and E Aboagye-Nimo, Portsmouth, UK

Beschorner, T and Hajduk, T (2017) Creating shared value: A fundamental critique, in: J Wieland (2017) *Creating Shared Value: Concepts, Experience, Criticism*, 10.1007/979-3-319-48802-8 (archived at https://perma.cc/5KZY-FM2T)

B Lab (nd) What are B Corps? B Corporation, www.bcorporation.net/what-are-b-corps (archived at https://perma.cc/RQZ8-GQ6D)

Choi, S-J, Ko, JK and Jung, S (2018) A Conglomerate's effort for co-prospering with its subcontractors and firm value: Evidence from Korea, *Sustainability*, **10** (7), 2512, doi.org/10.3390/su10072512 (archived at https://perma.cc/9DDT-CC4U)

Crane, A, Palazzo, G, Spence, LJ and Matten, D (2014) Contesting the value of 'creating shared value', *California Management Review*, **56** (2), 130–53

De los Reyes, G, Scholz, M and Smith, NC (2017) Beyond the 'win-win': creating shared value requires ethical frameworks, *California Management Review*, **59** (2), 142–167, doi.org/10.1177/0008125617695286 (archived at https://perma.cc/EMK2-VGEY)

De los Reyes, G and Scholz, M (2019) The limits of the business case for sustainability: don't count on 'creating shared value' to extinguish corporate destruction, *Journal of Cleaner Production*, 221, 785–94, doi.org/10.1016/j.jclepro.2019.02.187 (archived at https://perma.cc/83JY-WEQ3)

Dembek, K, Singh, P and Bhakoo, V (2016) Literature review of shared value: A theoretical concept or a management buzzword?, *Journal of Business Ethics*, **137**, 231–67

Dyllicki, T and Hockerts, K (2002) Beyond the business case for corporate sustainability, *Business Strategy and the Environment*, **11**, 130–41

Eccles, RG, Ioannou, I and Serafeim, G (2014) The impact of corporate sustainability on organizational processes and performance, *Management Science*, **60** (11), 2835–857

Fernández-Gámez, MA, Gutiérrez-Ruiz, AM, Becerra-Vicario, R and Ruiz-Palomo, D (2020) The impact of creating shared value on hotels online reputation, *Corporate Social Responsibility and Environmental Management*, **27** (5), 2201–211, doi.org/10.1002/csr.1958 (archived at https://perma.cc/K6N3-ZF84)

Hsiao, T-Y and Chuang, CM (2016) Creating shared value through implementing green practices for star hotels, *Asia Pacific Journal of Tourism Research*, **21** (6), 678–96, doi.org/10.1080/10941665.2015.1068194 (archived at https://perma.cc/2M4P-NXNL)

ISO (2010) ISO 26000: 2010 guidance on social responsibility, International Organization for Standardization, www.iso.org/obp/ui/#iso:std:42546:en (archived at https://perma.cc/H5XY-A8E3)

Jin, CH (2018) The effects of creating shared value (CSV) on the consumer self–brand connection: Perspective of sustainable development, *Corporate Social Responsibility and Environmental Management*, **25** (6), 1246–257, doi.org/10.1002/csr.1635 (archived at https://perma.cc/2CGF-B7JS)

Jones, S and Wright, C (2016) Fashion or future: does creating shared value pay? *Accounting & Finance*, **58** (4), 1111–139, doi.org/10.1111/acfi.12243 (archived at https://perma.cc/SZX5-KML4)

Konar, S and Cohen, MA (2001) Does the market value environmental performance?, *Review of Economics and Statistics*, **83** (2), 281–89

Kramer, MR and Pfitzer, MW (2016) The ecosystem of shared value, *Harvard Business Review*, October

Margolis, JD, Elfenbein, HA and Walsh, JP (2007) Does it pay to be good? A meta-analysis and redirection of research on the relationship between corporate social and financial performance, Working Paper

Menghwar, PS and Daood, A (2021) Creating shared value: a systematic review, synthesis and integrative perspective, *International Journal of Management Reviews*, **23** (4), 466, doi.org/10.1111/ijmr.12252 (archived at https://perma.cc/P7FN-MWNW)

Mühlbacher and Böbel, I (2019) From zero-sum to win-win: organizational conditions for successful shared value strategy implementation, *European Management Journal*, **37** (3), 313–24, doi.org/10.1016/j.emj.2018.10.007 (archived at https://perma.cc/FE47-3GTC)

Orlitzky, M, Schmidt, FL and Rynes, SL (2003) Corporate social and financial performance: a meta-analysis, *Organization Studies*, **24** (3), 403–41

Porter, ME and Kramer, MR (2002) The competitive advantage of corporate philanthropy, *Harvard Business Review*, **80**, 56–69

Porter, ME and Kramer, MR (2006) Strategy and society: the link between competitive advantage and corporate social responsibility, *Harvard Business Review*, **84**, 78–92

Porter, ME and Kramer, MR (2011) Creating shared value: how to reinvent capitalism – and unleash a wave of innovation and growth, *Harvard Business Review*, **89** (1/2), 62–77

Sánchez-Hernández, MI, Bañegil-Palacios, TM and Sanguino-Galván, R (2017) Competitive success in responsible regional ecosystems: An empirical approach in Spain focused on the firms' relationship with stakeholders, *Sustainability*, 9 (3), 449, doi.org/10.3390/su9030449 (archived at https://perma.cc/SZD2-QYGM)

Spitzeck, H and Chapman, S (2012) Creating shared value as a differentiation strategy: The example of BASF in Brazil, *Corporate Governance: The International Journal of Business in Society*, **12** (4), 499–513, doi.org/10.1108/14720701211267838 (archived at https://perma.cc/2NFH-NPAZ)

Innovation and sustainability as catalysts for responsible growth

03

For the majority of businesses and governments, sustainability and innovation have become pivotal to their efforts to jump to a new era. Fossil fuel will still be a dominant source of energy, but the acceleration of the transition towards renewable energy has led to a new landscape. Geopolitical dependencies are an important reason to stimulate more initiatives that give more autonomy. The Green Deal of the European Commission in 2020 and the further refinements and actions in the years after are a clear illustration of this. The same can be said of the US Inflation Reduction Act, signed by the White House in August 2022. This Act should be seen as part of a broader attempt by the United States to become less dependent on China for semiconductors and to become more active on climate change. With the Act trillions of US dollars will become available for innovation, sustainability, energy transition, infrastructure and social welfare, particularly for children (Tankersley, 2022).

Sustainable operations can be the leverage to achieve cost savings and an incentive to find new sources of income and stimulate innovation. This was the main message set out by the late management guru Prahalad and his co-authors Nidumolu and Rangaswami in their 2009 article titled 'Why sustainability is now the key driver of innovation'. In this article, the authors argue that sustainability should be the touchstone for innovation. They contend that any business that sees sustainability as an objective will have a competitive edge. It does, however, demand adaptation of business models, products, technology and processes, and such far-reaching interventions can take many years to implement. The authors suggest a step-by-step approach to take on the challenge of sustainable operational management, to acquire the necessary new competences and to identify innovative opportunities.

In this chapter, the step-by-step approach introduced by Nidumolu, Prahalad and Rangaswami is further elaborated upon. Moreover, we will discuss the importance of innovation in moving towards responsible growth. The approach we developed for the Responsible Business Simulator (tRBS) seamlessly follows the suggestions made by Prahalad and his co-authors. In this time of transformational change the relevance of taking decisions based on data and dialogue are becoming even more important. Long-lasting impact can be secured by decisions and the (tax) money that becomes available, but only if these decisions are well founded, accepted and executable.

Innovation for sustainability is the way to go

According to Nidumolu et al (2009) there is no alternative to sustainability. Businesses may well complain about the extra costs and compartmentalize sustainability along with CSR, but just like Porter and Kramer (2002, 2006, 2011), Nidumolu et al contend that by doing this they are missing opportunities and their competitive power will decline.

Social and financial objectives do not have to cancel each other out, but they can go hand in glove. Research among 30 major corporations showed that '... sustainability is a motherload of organizational and technological innovations that yield both bottom-line and top-line results' (Nidumolu et al, 2009). By using fewer raw materials, applying recycling and energy-saving measures, using sustainable energy and making logistic processes more efficient, costs can be reduced and the quality of products can increase (Nidumolu et al, 2009). Sustainability is a catalyst for innovation, and that could mean new possibilities for further growth for many businesses (Ellen MacArthur Foundation, 2015, 2019).

This is a powerful argument to persuade us to take a closer look at overall operational management and the existing business models. The authors recommend looking for those links in the business chain where internal adjustments can be made, and similarly where opportunities can be found for sustainability interventions in the external network.

Interestingly enough, this causes external developments such as legislation, standards and regulation in the domain of sustainability to be seen as positive factors. Strategically, it is smarter to be a forward thinker, to adapt operational management and change production processes, rather than simply complain and delay the inevitable. The first-mover advantages become greater as soon as change is linked to innovation with a positive social impact. Sustainability is the driver for far-reaching renewal and rethinking of business models. The enterprise, the employees, the customers, the suppliers and even society can profit from these innovative impulses (Nidumolu et al, 2009).

Sustainability as an incentive for rethinking the economic paradigm

We are almost a quarter of the way through this century and at the moment of writing we are in the midst of a whirlwind of transitions, from energy sourcing to healthcare reform, and from flexibilization of working conditions after Covid-19 to changes in the geopolitical spectrum.

The start of the Millennium was characterized by the burst of the internet bubble in 2003. In 2008 we experienced the bankruptcy of Lehmann Brothers and its serious effects on the finance industry, followed by the euro crisis. With so many 'too big to fail' financial institutions in trouble there was an immediate effect on the global economy. The result was a deep crisis that lasted five years until 2013. Unprecedented monetary actions from the Federal Reserve and the European Central Bank led to cheap money, low inflation and lower interest rates. Lending became the answer for financing innovation and policy adjustments at the level of companies and nations. Then, after extraordinary years of growth, Covid-19 brought the global economy to a standstill in the first quarter of 2020. The lack of an available vaccine was devastating for hundreds of thousands of people worldwide in 2020–2021. Unequalled, far-reaching measures, such as lockdowns lasting months, impacted social and economic life as never before. The world stood still with no flights or trains, and curfews across the globe. Economic support packages were huge and the role of the state became extremely important. After more than 30 years of neo-liberalism, politicians, even sometimes the convinced free marketeers, demanded immense financial support from the state for companies and their employees across entire industries. Covid-19 has been the unexpected black swan, a catalyst that had immense impact on all important actors in both the economy and our social life. Working from home became the new normal. The long-lasting impact of Covid-19 on the global economy will be revealed in the years to come. But in the meantime, another change on the international chessboard has occurred, with the military invasion by Russia of Ukraine in 2022.

Nowadays, the economic tide looks brighter and the economy has shown a remarkable resilience. Many technology-based companies explore and exploit new business models: many more buying to lease and 'as a Service' models are now offered. The challenge is finding a new ecological balance between technological change and new working environments. We are living in an exciting era, a time of transition from a global mass-production model to a flexible decentralized quality model based on the principles of the circular economy and social inclusion. Good examples of the 'old' quantitative model can be found in the traditional energy producers (coal, gas, oil, nuclear power), and the mass production of foodstuffs also falls into this category, with the concentrated production of deep-frozen ready meals as a prime example. However, regional, sustainable food producers from local farmers to socially responsible food processors are recognized as the new normal and no longer as the outcasts. Certainly the producers of renewable energy (from solar, wind, water and biomass sources) have a place in the 'new' qualitative model with new paradigms, transparency of origin and a stronger consumer perspective.

Over the past century, an extensive infrastructure with accompanying logistics systems has been set up for the mass-production model, but an entirely different infrastructure is needed for the new model. For example, the development, construction and implementation of a new smart grid for decentralized sustainable power generation and distribution to end users would in fact provide an excellent impetus for the economy.

This argument for sustainable growth in a reviving economy after the financial and economic crisis of 2008–2013 finds its origins in the climate issue. It is not without reason that the authors repeat a quote from Josef Ackermann, until 2013 the CEO of Deutsche Bank: 'Make no mistake: a new world order is emerging.' The race for leadership has already begun. For the winners, the rewards are clear: 'Innovation and investment in clean energy will stimulate green growth; it will create jobs; it will bring greater energy independence and national security' (Jaeger and Jaeger, 2011).

Furthermore, the 2015 United Nations climate change conference in Paris was largely successful and the largest three polluters, the United States, China and India, committed to join the agreement. In April 2016 it was ratified, which was a unique moment in history. Shortly after US President Biden started his presidency in 2020, he re-ratified the Paris agreement to underline the importance of investment in climate change measures. His predecessor, former President Trump (2016–2019), withdrew the United States from the 2015 Paris Agreement as a political act, denying the importance of climate change for the planet. In the meantime, other countries were stepping up and doubling their efforts in the light of global climate concerns and arguing for competitiveness, job creation and business risk management (Zlotnicka, 2017).

The impact of sustainability on neoclassical business models

The one thing that makes sustainability fundamentally different from other challenges faced by businesses is that changes need to be made at each and every level of the organization. Moreover, sustainable business practices call for a reassessment of the values underlying the entire business. Sustainability calls for sharing actual experiences, beyond the borders of organizations, economic sectors and even countries. After all, sustainability issues are unfettered by borders and demand a communal, holistic approach. For that reason it is prudent to switch from a purely competitive model to a model in which collaboration and networking can take place. In the literature, this is often referred to as a 'co-opetitive model' (i.e. simultaneously competing and collaborating in the market), whereby enterprises and organizations join together to tackle the pressing issues surrounding sustainability (Brandenburger and Nalebuff, 1996). Organizations in which sustainability has permeated through all layers develop new business models, create an open work culture and develop initiatives based on sustainability. Instead of seeing sustainability as simply an 'add-on', it is perceived to be an integral part of the business. Profit becomes a result and the facilitator of environmentally friendly and socially sustainable activities. Ideally, sustainability should be a goal from both an ethical and an economic perspective (Bansal and Roth, 2000). In other words: it is the 'right' thing to do and the 'smart' thing to do.

The dominant business models are based on neoclassical theories: maximization of profit for the shareholders is taken as the principle on which an enterprise is founded (Brenner and Cohrane, 1991; Stormer, 2003). In this perspective, social and ecological goals are seen as minor considerations, or perhaps not considered at all. This classic paradigm is therefore less suitable as a backdrop to the achievement of social and ecological goals. We therefore need to seek out new business models and management paradigms to help us look beyond 'the organization as an economic entity' (Dunphy et al, 2003; Shrivastava, 1995). The neoclassical model cannot simply be supplemented with social and ecological objectives. The entire model must be transformed into a model in which sustainability plays an essential role in both determining the mission or driving force of the organization and decision making (Wicks, 1996; Raworth, 2017). In the neoclassical model, sustainable objectives are only pursued if they are in the interests – usually the short-term interests – of the organization, if required by legislation (compliance), under pressure from shareholders, or to achieve greater corporate legitimacy (Bansal and Roth, 2000). In the neoclassical model, organizations must constantly be competitive in order to acquire the best 'resources' (in terms of both human capital and raw materials). The production cycle of a business is often based on a linear 'take–make–waste' approach, without any consideration being given to – let alone responsibility being taken for – the element of 'waste' (McDonough and Braungart, 2002).

The discussion of governance and business models goes further than a readjustment of the classical models. The book *Governance and Business Models for Sustainable Capitalism* (Midttun, 2022) touches upon many of the central themes of today's debate on business and society. It draws attention to a recurrent tension between efficiency, innovation and productivity on the one hand, and fairness, equity and sustainability on the other. It argues that in spite of the popular corporate sustainable responsibility (CSR) agenda, business is still too transient and too limited in its motivation to carry the regulatory burden. The author makes a plea for the adoption of a much wider concept of 'partnered governance', where advanced states and pioneering companies work together to raise the social and environmental bar.

This fits well with the business ecosystem framework as developed by James Moore in the early 1990s (Moore, 1993, 1996, 2006, 2013). Although the concept of business ecosystems did not fit in the neoliberal high days, his ideas were picked up by large consultancy firms after the financial–economic crisis in 2008–2013 (Deloitte, 2015; IBM 2014). Collaboration between public and private organizations is central in business ecosystems thinking, as is the collaboration among competitors for speeding up innovation for challenges that are too big to solve for one party on its own. Ecosystems capture new value and are an important way to discover new business models when collaborating with very different parties where not everything is monetized and the focus is on the long term in a shared ecosystem with mutual benefits. It is the collaboration and networking in the ecosystem environment that leads to new insights, innovations and solutions for climate change. Ecosystems are a promising way to organize innovation for sustainability. In *Organizing for Sustainability: A guide to developing new business models,* Jonker and Faber show how to develop business models that have a positive impact on people, society, and the social and ecological environment (2021). Given what we now know, it is clear that neoclassical models are out of date and other priorities need to be set that comply to the balance of People, the Planet and Profit.

Consequences of sustainability and innovation for a circular and inclusive economy

We hear from various disciplines in the academic world about the systemic changes that are occurring as a result of the progression towards a circular economy. The philosophies and frameworks within which production processes and operational management have been organized until very recently are no longer working effectively; you could in fact say that they are proving to be a hindrance to the revival that is just around the corner.

Each era has its challenges, but at the moment it seems we are faced with an unusual concurrence of factors. Just consider the possibilities offered by data science, ICT and the internet for services and products that we could not even have imagined just a decade ago. Figure 3.1 presents possible future scenarios by Frank Diana, a futurist at Tata Computer Services, who demonstrated the importance of forging links between the innovative technologies to create the building blocks for potential future scenarios.

He calls this 'combinatorics' where convergence between building blocks of future development are simulated (Diana, 2015; 2021). The stream of new applications is only possible because of the mobile internet infrastructure. That same infrastructure has brought drastic changes to education with online learning. During Covid-19 hundreds of millions of people experienced the advantage of working or learning from distance, but with the possibility to interact with others in virtual offices or classrooms. Changes in education have a far-reaching impact on the economy, on social structures, and on the way we live and interact. Where revenue models were previously built around the products that were delivered, they are now increasingly oriented to the services that keep the economy afloat, towards 'performance-based contracting' and business models based on Service as a Product (SaaP): service production and delivery models in which a productized service is sold via sellers or vendors on websites or platforms.

Another disruption can be found in the drastic changes that are occurring in the way we work. In the past 15 years, there has been a shift from a homogeneous working population towards a population of highly differentiated expert professionals, who are just as likely to use their expertise as a self-employed person as they are to work for a major company. Where it used to be almost inconceivable that someone would work from multiple locations, these days millions of people can work from their homes or a meeting place and still connect and collaborate with others. Covid-19 with the lockdowns were a game changer in this respect. The main technology behind this connectivity is the ever-growing 'Internet of Things' (IoT). These days everything from thermostats to cars, from buildings to refrigerators, is collecting and exchanging data through a network. This trend has had sweeping consequences for logistics and transportation, for offices and real estate. The name of the game is data science and creating algorithms for predicting the most likely outcome.

Along the same lines, the Organisation for Economic Co-operation and Development (OECD) reached the conclusion, based on their data, that there is a correlation between shorter working hours and greater productivity. Working fewer hours, meaning employees get more time off to focus on their life outside work, apparently leads to a more committed and stable workforce. In the Swedish city of Gothenburg, the municipality started an experiment by cutting an

Figure 3.1 Innovative technological scenarios

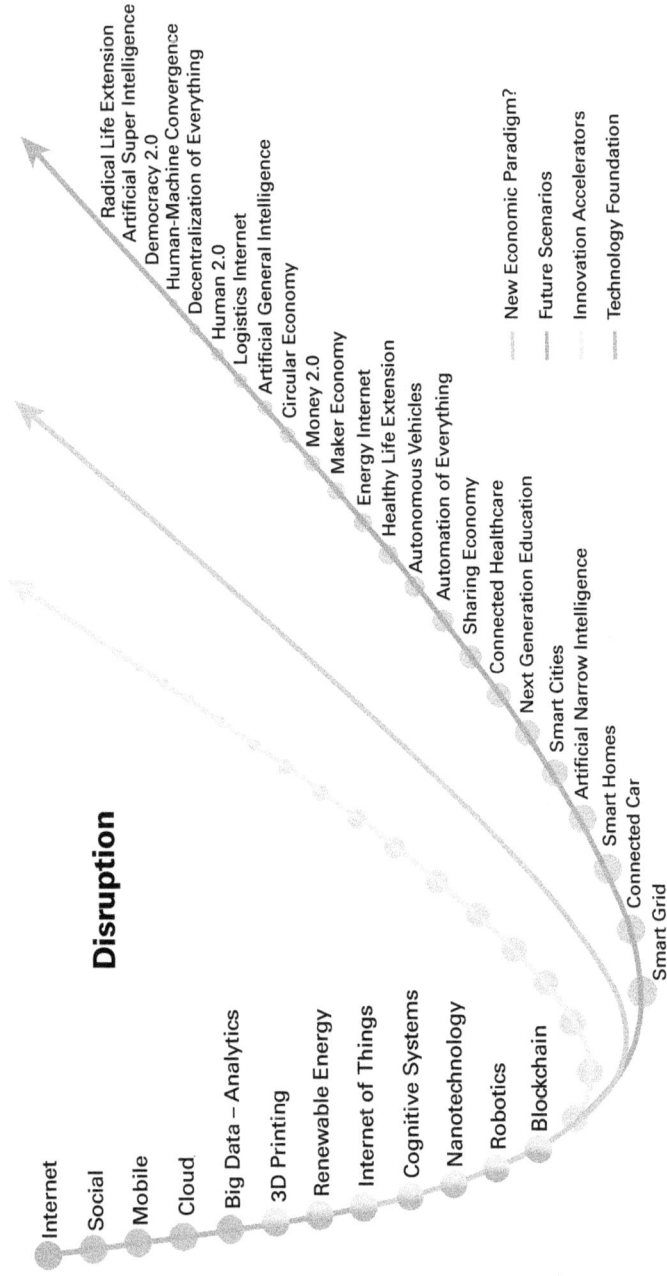

Internet
Social
Mobile
Cloud
Big Data – Analytics
3D Printing
Renewable Energy
Internet of Things
Cognitive Systems
Nanotechnology
Robotics
Blockchain

Disruption

Smart Grid
Connected Car
Smart Homes
Artificial Narrow Intelligence
Smart Cities
Next Generation Education
Connected Healthcare
Sharing Economy
Automation of Everything
Autonomous Vehicles
Healthy Life Extension
Energy Internet
Maker Economy
Money 2.0
Circular Economy
Artificial General Intelligence
Logistics Internet
Human 2.0
Decentralization of Everything
Human-Machine Convergence
Democracy 2.0
Artificial Super Intelligence
Radical Life Extension

New Economic Paradigm?
Future Scenarios
Innovation Accelerators
Technology Foundation

SOURCE Frank Diana, TCS, 2015; 2021 updates

hour off the daily working hours of a group of employees and then comparing the results to a control group working regular hours. Wages in both groups were kept the same, and the results showed a correlation between fewer working hours and greater productivity. It is therefore likely that employers will be able to save money when cutting working hours and employees will feel mentally and physically better (OECD, 2015). With high levels of stress from work and consequently high levels of absenteeism, working costs are becoming higher for employees. Looking for new business models that take into account the savings brought about by less stress and more satisfaction while keeping productivity levels up is exactly what we did with tRBS in the IZZ case (see Chapter 11).

There is an even clearer systemic character to the combination of climate change and the transition to sustainable energy. The transition from a power system based on fossil fuels to a system in which sustainable energy sources hold sway is bringing about changes in the techno-economic system of society. Energy forms the bedrock of the system. Every company, every home, every gymnasium or workplace will be affected. The business models that apply to nearly every product or service will be affected. It is precisely these systemic challenges that call for innovative business activities and an adjustment of the present government regulatory framework, tax systems and the mindset of all concerned.

The key challenge in transitioning from fossil fuel-dependent vehicles to electric vehicles, a disruptive innovation, has been the cost and capacity of their battery packs (Nykvist and Nilsson, 2015). Seeing electric vehicles as an inevitable step in the evolution of cars, Elon Musk decided on a long-term business strategy that would bring about mass production of electric vehicles. Tesla first entered the high-end, low-volume car market to create a revenue stream to invest in electric charging infrastructure, cheaper and higher-capacity battery packs, and to develop a medium-end car. The success of the high-end Tesla electric car has been a challenge to the German luxury car market, but will not be so for much longer, as the temporary tax schemes available to electric car manufacturers, and from which Tesla benefitted, have now been withdrawn. However, competition is stepping up, not only from the German automotive industry, but also from Chinese players. There is also a strong demand from consumers and car lease companies. These trends will disrupt the current economic systems in place and demand innovative business models, and as we will explain in the following chapters, tRBS is a useful tool in quantifying all financial and non-financial benefits of the investment in new business models.

Industrial and service sectors transition differently towards a sustainable situation. The global food market started a slow transition towards organic foods decades ago, but has been picking up pace in recent years, especially in North America and Europe. In contrast to some years ago, we now find organic food and beverages in almost every supermarket. This market has grown by more than 15 per cent each year and it is projected that this growth will continue for some years. Worth $84 billion in 2014, the organic food and beverages market in 2022 was $208.18 billion with a revenue forecast in 2030 of $564.22 billion. This is a growth rate (CAGR) of 13 per cent from 2022 to 2030 (Grand View Research, 2022), a huge growth rate that indicates the tipping point for sustainable food production and hence large opportunities for businesses. FrieslandCampina, the world's largest dairy cooperative, is one of the companies capitalizing on this transition to sustainability. Their motto is the very fitting 'Nourishing by Nature'. FrieslandCampina has introduced a new separate price system for organic milk due to increasing demand, incentivizing farmers to switch to organic farming (FrieslandCampina, 2016). At the same time it is difficult to change the way mass-production farmers operate, evidenced by the many farmers' protests in the Netherlands and Belgium in recent years. The European Union is an important force for change giving guidance to more sustainable farming by setting strict standards for CO_2 and methane emissions and not allowing exceptions to the rules any more.

The end result of these systemic shifts, prompted as much by sustainability as by technological opportunities, is that it will become ever more relevant for businesses and organizations to take a long and critical look at their present business models. The approach that we call responsible business decision making to achieve strategic impact based on data and dialogue can take all this into account: from the changing circumstances and environment, disruptive innovations, the expectations of employees, customers and stakeholders, to all the other demands that sustainable growth imposes on a business.

References

Bansal, P and Roth, K (2000) Why companies go green: a model of ecological responsiveness, *Academy of Management Journal*, **43**, 717–36

Brandenburger, A and Nalebuff, B (1996) *Co-opetition*, Doubleday, New York, NY

Brenner, S and Cohrane, P (1991) The stakeholder theory of the firm: implications for business and society theory and research, *IABS Proceedings*, 449–67

Deloitte (2014) *Business-Ecosystems Come of Age*, Deloitte University Press, 5

Diana, F (2015a) An interview with Gerd Leonhard, thefuturesagency. com/2015/02/20/an-interview-with-gerd-leonhard/ (archived at https://perma.cc/CJ8M-8BER)

Diana, F (2015b) Expanding disruptive scenarios, frankdiana.net/2015/06/26/ expanding-disruptive-scenarios/ (archived at https://perma.cc/LDC3-QGZK)

Diana, F (2021) Combinatorial, frankdiana.net/tag/combinatorial/ (archived at https://perma.cc/HS6T-YEFU)

Dunphy, DC, Griffiths, A and Benn, S (2003) *Organizational Change for Corporate Sustainability: A guide for leaders and change agents of the future*, Routledge, London

Ellen MacArthur Foundation (2015) *Towards a Circular Economy: Business rationale for an accelerated transition*, www.ellenmacarthurfoundation. org/assets/downloads/TCE_Ellen-MacArthur-Foundation_9-Dec-2015.pdf (archived at https://perma.cc/9U5A-5L79)

Ellen MacArthur Foundation (2019) Circular economy diagram, https:// ellenmacarthurfoundation.org/circular-economy-diagram (archived at https://perma.cc/N8T6-UPL9)

FrieslandCampina (2016) *Annual Report 2015*, www.frieslandcampina. com/app/uploads/sites/2/2016/03/FrieslandCampina-annual-report-2015-English-A4.pdf (archived at https://perma.cc/T6DW-XQ8B)

Grand View Research (2022) Organic food and beverage market report 2022–2030, www.grandviewresearch.com/industry-analysis/organic-foods-beverages-market (archived at https://perma.cc/P54M-U2UW)

IBM (2014) *The New Age of Ecosystems. Redefining partnering in an ecosystem environment*, New York

Jaeger, CC and Jaeger, J (2011) Three views of two degrees, in *Regional Environmental Change*, **11**, 15–26

Jonker, J and Faber, N (eds) (2021) *Organizing for Sustainability: A guide developing new business models*, Palgrave Macmillan

McDonough, W and Braungart, M (2002) *Cradle to Cradle: Remaking the way we make things*, North Point Press, New York, NY

Midttun, A (2022) *Governance and Business Models for Sustainable Capitalism*, Routledge

Moore, J (1993) Predators and Prey: A new ecology of competition, *Harvard Business Review*, **71** (3, May–June), 75–86

Moore, J (1996) *The Death of Competition: Leadership and strategy in the age of business ecosystems*, HarperBusiness, New York

Moore, J (2006) Business ecosystems and the view from the firm, *The Antitrust Bulletin*, **51**, 1 (spring), 31

Moore, J (2013) *Shared Purpose: A thousand business ecosystems, a connected community, and the future*, CreateSpace

Nidumolu, R, Prahalad, CK and Rangaswami, MR (2009) Why sustainability is now the key driver of innovation, *Harvard Business Review*, **87** (9), 56–64

Nykvist, B and Nilsson, M (2015) Rapidly falling costs of battery packs for electric vehicles, *Nature Climate Change*, **5** (4), 329–32

OECD (2015) *OECD Employment Outlook*, www.oecd-ilibrary.org/employment/oecd-employment-outlook-2015_empl_outlook-2015-en (archived at https://perma.cc/7Z5H-PA3X)

Porter, ME and Kramer, MR (2002) The competitive advantage of corporate philanthropy, *Harvard Business Review*, **80**, 56–69

Porter, ME and Kramer, MR (2006) Strategy and society: the link between competitive advantage and corporate social responsibility, *Harvard Business Review*, **84**, 78–92

Porter, ME and Kramer, MR (2011) Creating shared value: how to reinvent capitalism – and unleash a wave of innovation and growth, *Harvard Business Review*, **89** (1/2), 62–77

Raworth, K (2017) *Doughnut Economics. Seven ways to think like a 21st-century economist*, Random House Business Books, London

Shrivastava, P (1995) Ecocentric management for a risk society, *Academy of Management Review*, **20**, 118–37

Stormer, F (2003) Making the shift: moving from 'Ethics Pays' to an inter-systems model of business, *Journal of Business Ethics*, **44**, 279–89

Tankersley, J (2022) Biden signs climate, health bill into law as other economic goals remain, *New York Times*, 16 August

The Tesla Team (2016) The week that electric vehicles went mainstream, www.teslamotors.com/nl_NL/blog/the-week-electric-vehicles-went-mainstream (archived at https://perma.cc/D7YP-TTTB)

Wicks, A C (1996) Overcoming the separation thesis: the need for a reconsideration of business and society research, *Business & Society*, **35**, 89–118

Zlotnicka, E (2017) The path ahead after US leaves Paris Agreement. What is the real impact of President Trump's move to pull the US out of the global accords to combat climate change?, Morgan Stanley, www.morganstanley.com/ideas/us-path-after-paris-agreement (archived at https://perma.cc/S85W-UKKC)

PART TWO
Concept and methodology

Dialogue and stakeholder engagement in decision making

04

An effective decision-making process must be based on a combination of robust evidence from hard data, multiple dialogues with internal and external stakeholders who can offer insights into informal aspects of the organization, and transparent communications and responsibilities in its execution. In the strategic decision-making process, using the Responsible Business Simulator (tRBS), data science and advanced econometric calculation techniques are combined with interactive dialogue sessions with employees, management and external stakeholders. It is the interactive and iterative *use of evidence from data* and *interpretation via dialogue* that creates the value of tRBS for the decision-making process.

This qualitative and quantitative combination is unique because – during the progression towards a strategic decision – it brings transparency to the identification and linkage of the hard, financial objectives and the non-financial objectives. This interaction takes place in dialogues during the action learning sessions that are held within the businesses and organizations, and during sessions held with external stakeholders. By bringing together true cross-sections of employees, management and stakeholders, thereby guaranteeing a diversity of knowledge, experience and latest insights, the process becomes an active exercise. It is no longer a 'black box', as can be the case when advisors are allowed to conjure statistics from Excel files like rabbits out of a hat. In this chapter we discuss the role of the dialogue with stakeholders and the applicability of action learning to the strategic decision-making process with the use of the Responsible Business Simulator.

Integrating stakeholder engagement into the decision-making process

In an analysis of stakeholder engagement research over a 15-year period with a literature review of over 90 articles in leading academic journals focusing on stakeholder engagement in business and society, management and strategy, and environmental management and environmental policy literatures, Kujala and his co-authors come to a definition of stakeholder engagement. Based on their research they stated that 'stakeholder engagement' refers to the aims, activities and impacts of stakeholder relations in a moral, strategic and/or pragmatic manner (Kujala et al, 2022). The aims are linked to the participants' interest and to purpose, reasons and incentives. In their review they see that many authors see legitimacy, trust and fairness as important moral aims of stakeholder engagement. For the same reason, corporate social responsibility (CSR), responsibility, environmental and sustainability concerns, and enhancing inclusive stakeholder engagement are all seen as important moral aims. Other authors analysed in their review stress pragmatic aims such as strengthening stakeholder relationships, collaboration, and dialogue, co-generation of knowledge, problem solving and reaching consensus, and bringing change that benefits societies. In the same way, reducing and resolving conflicts of interest also relates to informing, consulting and making joint decisions with stakeholders (Kujala et al, 2022). A common denominator in the articles reviewed by Kujala and his co-authors is that stakeholder engagement has a strategic impact on efficiency due to reduced transaction costs and firm performance (ROE), effective use of resources, competitive advantage, reducing uncertainty, achieving control, and maintaining corporate autonomy and flexibility in operations. Pragmatic impact is seen in shared norms, values and objectives. In short, stakeholder engagement can contribute to many positive 'nudges' in decision-making processes. The dialogue process in stakeholder engagement is key to building the foundation of trust in decision making.

Dialogues with stakeholders for understanding, co-creation and acceptance

To manage the transition towards sustainability and social inclusion, we need new business governance models that do justice to the complexity of that transition and the involvement of stakeholders. This includes making allowances for a long-term timeline, assessing uncertainties, and ensuring that the opinions of stakeholders are taken into account (Loorbach et al, 2010). To put innovation and more sustainable business practices into operation, an enterprise needs to reinvent itself; organizations must learn to see themselves as actors in a much larger societal system and think about their own interactions with that system. Organizations no longer exist in isolation, but have become open, dynamic systems that operate in constant interaction with their environment. The advancement of business ecosystems with interlinking networks of networks is an indication of this. Good practices regarding business ecosystems can be found in the report *Business Ecosystems Come of Age* (Deloitte, 2015).

It is in this environment that the term 'stakeholder' plays a pivotal role. We also saw this element in Porter and Kramer's concept of shared value (Porter and Kramer, 2011; Kramer and Pfitzer, 2016). The aim of organizations that apply tRBS is not only to realize a profit and create a good working environment for their employees, but also to improve the sense of stakeholders' wellbeing. These can be widely diverse parties, from local residents to NGOs, suppliers or customers, and in a circular economy all actors related to the same material chains. Sustainable companies adjust their perspective from one that focuses exclusively on shareholders to one that also includes other stakeholders. The stakeholder concept was traditionally limited to people or groups with a particular political or economic impact; people or groups that were in a position to help – or hinder – organizations.

Businesses, however, operate in a particular natural environment; some are even dependent on that environment. That is manifestly the case for businesses in the agricultural and energy sectors, but it actually applies to any business. Businesses have long ceased to be isolated entities, static systems that have no need to take account of various other external parties or of their possible dependence on such parties. Stakeholders should not be perceived as 'the others' or simply 'external' to the organization, but as partners and even co-creators whose future and interests are closely interwoven with those of the organization. In this way, the concept of 'stakeholder' acquires not only a politico-economic meaning, but also an element of moral legitimacy whereby the 'parties' – the people and the environment on which you, as a business, can exercise some influence – are also perceived as stakeholders in that business (Carroll, 1993).

The importance of interactivity in decision-making processes

Decision making with data and dialogue is not a linear process, but an interactive and iterative process. In commerce, sustainability is often expressed as the *triple bottom line* (TBL), whose central themes are social, ecological and economic objectives, in other words People, Planet and Profit objectives. This TBL model, coined by John Elkington in 1994, emphasizes the relationships between the three elements and all three objectives are, ideally, pursued equally, in an effort to create a 'triple-win' situation. Nonetheless, tension can arise between these three objectives. The aim is therefore not to treat the three objectives as individual goals, but as a single unified goal.

However, decision making on sustainability issues is often complex, especially when this initial tension is evident. According to Rogers and Hudson (2011), decision making on sustainability issues should therefore take place at a higher level of systemic abstraction. In other words, decisions need to be taken in a far broader societal context. This is obviously not 'business as usual', since managers must be thinking beyond the confines of their own organization. It could even be argued that experts who are not part of the upper echelon of an organization, but who see themselves as part of a far greater social totality, are in a better position to embrace this broader approach than the members of the upper echelon themselves. It is therefore important to involve employees in this shift towards sustainability. After all, employees of an organization are also members of society. The encouragement and empowerment of employees helps to create a sustainable mindset within the organization. It is not simply a matter of change. What is called for is a far-reaching transformation or revitalization, as it is termed by Pascale et al (1997):

> Providing a permanent impetus for individual creativity and responsibility, an enduring transformation of the internal and external relationships of the organization, and a lasting behavioural change within the organization.

Conversely, it is also the case that employees of an organization where socially responsible business practices are the norm are generally more satisfied in their work and also feel that they are treated more fairly. This is because sustainability satisfies their desire for honesty and justice (Aguilera et al, 2007; Tziner et al, 2011). It also exerts a positive influence on the way employees perceive their organization, making them prouder to work for that organization (Galbreath, 2010), which in turn has a positive influence on the commitment of the employees (Peterson, 2004). Getting employees involved in sustainable business practices will therefore not only help to actually achieve the sustainability objectives, but will help create a workforce that is passionate about and committed to the business. This is precisely the reason that we use a round-table format and conversations when applying strategic decision making and tRBS, so that employees and management alike are involved in working towards a sustainable strategy that does justice to the triple bottom line. Also, customers and external stakeholders can be involved. In this way developing new business models is a co-creating process where value is created in a mutual stakeholder context resulting in value portfolio, the term used by Freudenreich and co-authors in their article on business model research and value creation for sustainability (Freudenreich et al, 2020).

Interactive adjustment and determination of key outputs

Once a corporate team gets started on strategic decision making with the use of tRBS, the first priority is to establish the main hard (financial) and not-so-hard (non-financial) key outputs. In this action learning setting, knowledge is exchanged over the course of several sessions, and at the same time incremental decision making takes place about the principal key outputs that serve to achieve the enterprise's strategic objective. The choices for particular financial and non-financial objectives can be adjusted during the sessions once the outcomes of the computational process show what effect that choice of key outputs and the value that team members ascribe to them will have on a possible strategy. The fact that this computational model shows the outcomes in a graphic form is an important factor for the team sessions, because even the less mathematically minded can immediately see what could be the impact of applying certain values and weightings to the financial and non-financial objectives.

The interesting thing is that the process is completely transparent, and adjustments can immediately be made visible. This clears the way for a decision-making process towards finding a sustainable business model that is free of subjective values ('we believe in sustainability' or 'we believe in social inclusion'), while the action learning sessions nonetheless provide an opportunity for the expression of subjective opinions. The combination of tweaking the input in a team session and learning in an informal setting what the impact of possible choices might be makes this a sophisticated, yet low-threshold method. One important advantage is that strategic choices can be made, on the basis of the objective outcomes of the computational model, that go hand in hand with the phase in which the enterprise finds itself in terms of the triple bottom line (people, planet, profit). By incorporating the time dimension into the simulation model, any enterprise – whether it is just starting to become sustainable or has already progressed some way along the route – can make the strategic choices that best suit its current situation. It can pinpoint where investments in the coming years are going to pay off, and how the enterprise or organization could evolve.

Complex issues require an interdisciplinary approach

It follows from the above that sustainable business practices take place within a highly complex framework. We can call this the 'management of complexity'. Sustainable management covers a wide spectrum of aspects, and can be approached from a variety of different angles. In the dialogue there is room for different lenses on the same subject. The subject as seen from the accountancy and finance angle will differ from the subject as seen from the business administration or human resources angle. Looking from an ethical perspective, different facets will be considered than from the perspective of operational research, risk management, strategy or climate science. Each discipline looks at the matter through its own spectacles, and adds its own specific knowledge. In this context, Pojasek (2007) mentions the creation of an 'interdisciplinary body of knowledge' that will ultimately lead to a framework for business sustainability. In this respect the interactive and iterative process is part of the action learning and the exchange of insights and informal knowledge. Getting this firsthand increases the mutual understanding, even if one does not have the same opinion. The facilitator of the dialogue can ask more searching questions as to the why and why not, which brings the conversation to the next level. In combination with data, facts, figures and evidence from proven studies, prejudices can be eliminated, giving a much clearer perspective.

Businesses do not operate in isolation but in a social context, one in which technology, economy, culture, biological and technological material chains and institutions play a leading role. In recent years inclusion, diversity and gender balance have received more attention. To be able to understand the transition to sustainability, we need to take a systemic approach in which the roles played by and the interrelationships between government, commerce and society are explained (Loorbach et al, 2010; Rotmans et al, 2000). Eamonn Kelly reintroduced the concept of business ecosystems in a highly accessible study with practical insights on shaping business environments for innovation with highly diverse public and private actors (Kelly, 2015).

Limiting sustainability to the level of the enterprise gives an imperfect view of the complexity and the persistent institutional problems that hinder the transition towards sustainability. According to Loorbach et al (2010):

> The complexity and persistent nature of sustainability issues pose new challenges on business, which requires new conceptual models for researching in relation between firms and the natural environment.

In the same article, Loorbach et al argue – on the basis of articles by Porter and Kramer (2006), Korhonen and Seager (2008) and Seager (2008) – that it is necessary to include knowledge about sustainability in strategic decision making. If we add the principles of the triple bottom line, do justice to Porter and Kramer's principle of shared value, and envision the transition to a circular economy and inclusion, it will quickly become clear that we need to approach sustainable business practices in a much wider social context with stakeholder engagement and from an interdisciplinary perspective (Elkington, 1998, 2006; Ellen MacArthur Foundation, 2012; Kujala et al, 2022; Freudenreich et al, 2020).

Collaboration for new insights and actionable results

The desire to do more than draw conclusions from the perspective of individual disciplines is reflected in a 'collaborative research' approach taken in our research into sustainability and social inclusion with tRBS as a tool for strategic decision making. At the heart of this research approach is the fact that we concentrate on specific strategic issues, bridging and blending knowledge from academic disciplines in the simulation model. This yields new insights, based on well-founded academic theories, knowledge and practical experience.

This unique combination of academic and experiential, practical knowledge has been put to good use in exploring, explaining, applying and testing tRBS in real-world business environments. The members of the team reviewed the intermediate outcomes in iterative sessions. During the course of the research, we held various review and discussion sessions in an academic setting with the businesses and stakeholders involved in the action research projects. In this way, we did our best to replicate the complexity surrounding sustainable business practices. At the same time, we also realized the necessity of ensuring that our research had practical applicability for businesses and organizations. A significant reciprocal benefit was gained from the combination of on-site action research, modelling using sophisticated calculation programs, and the reflection sessions with the academic staff.

We also presented the results of our research on tRBS to students in Bachelor's, Master's and MBA programmes and to participants in executive programmes at various business schools, universities and at conferences with business professionals. We still do so to learn and enrich the foundations of the Responsible Business approach. We have examined whether modelling using tRBS can be made more comprehensible, and whether it is something that can be picked up fairly quickly. Thanks to the interdisciplinary approach and the iterative research method used –the testing, reflection and modification – the modelling has been given extra depth. The Responsible Business Simulator has made complexity manageable. It can now be put to practical use in the decision-making processes within businesses and organizations. In the next chapters a series of case studies will be described giving a real-life context to the application of the Responsible Business Simulator.

References

Aguilera, RV, Rupp, DE, Williams, CA and Ganapathi, J (2007) Putting the S back in corporate social responsibility: a multilevel theory of social change in organizations, *Academy of Management Review*, **32**, 836–63

Carroll, AB (1993) *Business and Society: Ethics and stakeholder management*, South-Western Publishing, Cincinnati, OH

Deloitte (2015) Business ecosystems come of age, www2.deloitte.com/content/dam/insights/us/articles/platform-strategy-new-level-business-trends/DUP_1048-Business-ecosystems-come-of-age_MASTER_FINAL.pdf (archived at https://perma.cc/3UV8-2V9D)

Elkington, J (1998) *Cannibals with Forks: Triple bottom line of 21st-century business*, Capstone Publishers, Mankato, MN

Elkington, J (2006) Governance for sustainability, *Corporate Governance: An International Review*, **14** (6), 522–29

Ellen MacArthur Foundation (2012) *Towards the Circular Economy 1: Economic and business rationale for an accelerated transition,* www.ellenmacarthurfoundation.org/assets/downloads/publications/ Ellen-MacArthur-Foundation-Towards-the-Circular-Economy-vol.1.pdf (archived at https://perma.cc/AN7H-UB8C)

Freudenreich, B, Lüdeke-Freund, F and Schaltegger, S (2020) A stakeholder theory perspective on business models: Value creation for sustainability, *Journal of Business Ethics*, **166**, 3–18, doi.org/10.1007/s10551-019-04112-z (archived at https://perma.cc/A38D-Y6C6)

Galbreath, J (2010) How does corporate social responsibility benefit firms? Evidence from Australia, *European Business Review*, **22**, 411–31

Kelly, E (2015) *Introduction: Business ecosystems come of age*, Deloitte University Press, Westlake, TX

Korhonen, J and Seager, TP (2008) Beyond eco-efficiency: a resilience perspective, *Business Strategy & the Environment*, **17** (7), 411–19

Kramer, M and Pfitzer, MW (2016) The ecosystem of shared value, *Harvard Business Review*, October, 81–90

Kujala, J, Sachs, S, Leinonen, H, Heikkinen, A and Laude, D (2022) Stakeholder engagement: past, present, and future, *Business & Society*, **61** (5), 1136–196, doi.org/10.1177/0007650321106659 5 (archived at https://perma.cc/5PVH-WMFD)

Loorbach, D, van Bakel, JC, Whiteman, G and Rotmans, J (2010) Business strategies for transitions towards sustainable systems, *Business Strategy and the Environment*, **19**, 133–46

Pascale, R, Millemann, M and Gioja, L (1997) Changing the way we change: how leaders at Sears, Shell, and the US Army transformed attitudes and behavior – and made the changes stick, *Harvard Business Review*, **75**, 126–39

Peterson, DK (2004) The relationship between perceptions of corporate citizenship and organizational commitment, *Business and Society*, **43**, 296–319

Pojasek, RB (2007) Quality toolbox: a framework for business sustainability, *Environmental Quality Management*, **15**, 81–88

Porter, ME and Kramer, MR (2006) Strategy and society: the link between competitive advantage and corporate social responsibility, *Harvard Business Review*, **84**, 78–92

Porter, ME and Kramer, MR (2011) Creating shared value: how to reinvent capitalism – and unleash a wave of innovation and growth, *Harvard Business Review*, **89** (1/2), 62–77

Rogers, K and Hudson, B (2011) The triple bottom line: the synergies of transformative perceptions and practices for sustainability, *OD Practitioner*, **43**, 3–9

Rotmans, J, Kemp, R, Geels, FW and Asselt, M (2000) *Transities en Transitiemanagement: De casus van de emissie-arme energievoorziening*, International Centre for Integrative Studies (ICIS), Maastricht

Seager, TP (2008) The sustainability spectrum and the sciences of sustainability, *Business Strategy & the Environment*, **17** (7), 444–53

Tziner, A, Oren, L, Bar, Y and Kadosh, G (2011) Corporate social responsibility, organizational justice and job satisfaction: how do they interrelate, if at all? *Review of Psychology of Work and Organizations*, **27**, 67–72

The Responsible 05
Business
Simulator

The heart of the strategic decision-making process

Making strategic decisions to benefit People, the Planet and Profits is an interactive process with stakeholders that addresses both financial and non-financial aspects. The interactive process comprises a seven-step process that leads to a clear strategic choice based on data and dialogue (Roobeek and de Swart, 2013). The process is empowered by unique, open-source modelling software named the Responsible Business Simulator (tRBS). With the help of this software, broadly based decisions are taken around balancing the people, planet and profit (PPP or 3Ps) objectives of an organization by investigating multi-dependencies between these objectives. Which aspects are weighed up, why, and with what impact?

The seven-step decision-making process can be broken down into three phases:

- The first phase is about unleashing collective intelligence to specify the strategic challenge that requires a decision. The setting of this phase is an explorative dialogue with stakeholders and experts from multiple disciplines.

- The second phase is the research phase in which additional data is collected via desk research and – optionally – field research, and the simulation model is constructed. Although the participation of various experts is preferable, to disclose and combine existing knowledge, the setting of this phase focuses less on dialogue.

- The third phase is about analysing output from the simulation model such that the decision-making process results in a well-balanced strategic choice. The setting of this phase is strategic dialogue in the boardroom of the organization.

The Responsible Business Simulator has three objectives:

1 to facilitate the decision-making process by capturing all its elements in a structured way

2 to allow for an easy implementation of the simulation model specified in the research step

3 to help analyse the output from the simulation model in a graphical and interactive way

We named this the 'Responsible Business Simulator' because it calculates the future financial and non-financial effects of potential decisions on the basis of a simulation model in a business context. Putting tRBS at the heart of the decision-making process gives decision makers in organizations a tool that they can use, with the aid of strategic dialogue, to make clear and well-founded choices. This makes the transition from a vague 'gut feeling' to clear strategic decision making a far simpler step than we often imagine.

Making strategic decisions to benefit people, the planet and profits uses an approach that is advanced, yet at the same time transparent. Advanced, because the approach facilitates advanced econometric modelling. Econometric formulae are not, however, everyday fare for the average employee, manager or even director. It is therefore not necessary that they fully understand the underlying calculations, let alone be able to carry them out: we have modelling specialists for that. These specialists do not have to program the model themselves. By using the open-source programming language Python (van Rossum and Drake, 2009; CWI, 2013) and the tRBS package in Python (de Swart and van der Plas, 2023), they can restrict themselves to just supplying the type of relationship and the parameters in that relationship. On the other hand, what must be made transparent for the participants of round-table sessions in dialogue form are the non-trivial assumptions underlying the simulation model and the mutually interdependent importance of performance in the domains of people, planet and profit.

We have applied and fine-tuned the methodology in a variety of organizations during multiple sessions. This form of action research formed the basis of this seven-step decision-making process in which Q&Q (quantitative and qualitative) aspects are combined, thereby giving realistic estimates of the values around the themes of people, planet and profit. This finally leads to strategic choices based on shared value.

We also tested the developed methodology in both the Bachelor's and Master's degree programmes in business administration at Nyenrode Business Universiteit. We observed that it is possible to teach how modelling works through the medium of workshops as interactive round-table sessions in which the participants are guided through the decision-making process.

In this chapter we elaborate on the seven-step decision-making process depicted in Figure 5.1. For simplicity we have presented a sequential stepwise approach here. However, in practice several feed-back loops and iterative actions take place during the decision-making process.

Chapter 7 describes the supporting software, the Responsible Business Simulator, more extensively. In Part Three of the book we illustrate the use of the developed methodology in practical situations using a number of case studies. We therefore give here only a brief general description of each of the seven steps. Further explanation can be found in the case studies, which will give the reader a much clearer impression of the methodology in action.

Step 1: describing the strategic challenge that requires a decision

The first step in the decision-making process is to describe the *strategic challenge* that requires a decision. In this step questions such as 'What is the decision about?', 'Who is the decision maker?', and 'Which stakeholders should be accounted for?' are discussed. In addition, a

Figure 5.1 The decision-making process: three phases and seven steps

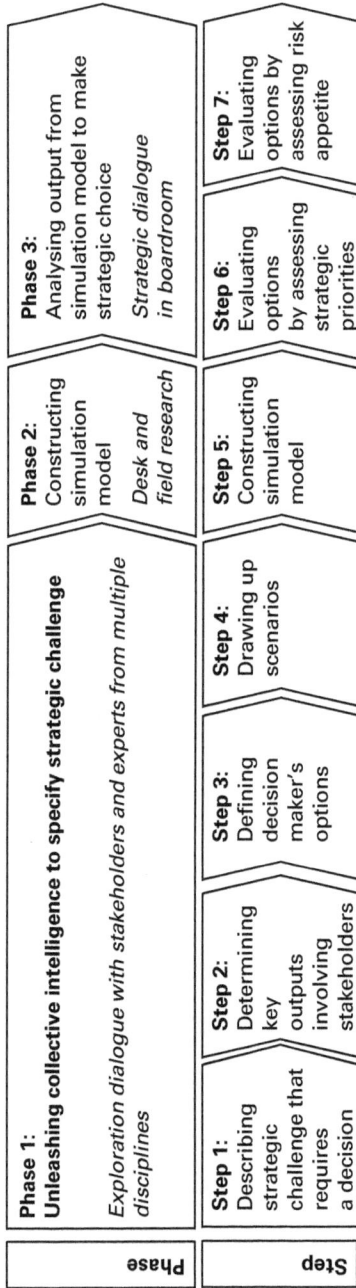

Phase	Phase 1: Unleashing collective intelligence to specify strategic challenge	Phase 2: Constructing simulation model	Phase 3: Analysing output from simulation model to make strategic choice
	Exploration dialogue with stakeholders and experts from multiple disciplines	*Desk and field research*	*Strategic dialogue in boardroom*

| Step | Step 1: Describing strategic challenge that requires a decision | Step 2: Determining key outputs involving stakeholders | Step 3: Defining decision maker's options | Step 4: Drawing up scenarios | Step 5: Constructing simulation model | Step 6: Evaluating options by assessing strategic priorities | Step 7: Evaluating options by assessing risk appetite |

high-level qualitative assessment is performed regarding the impact of potential decisions on the decision maker and the stakeholders. The essence of the methodology is that this impact is considered beyond profit only. Finally, the stakeholders and other experts who need to be involved in the first phase are listed.

Although this step may seem a no-brainer, it is a crucial step. This methodology is about facilitating specific decision making rather than generic impact measurement. Questions such as 'What is our societal impact and what can we do to improve it?' are less suitable to be answered via this approach. Examples of relevant strategic challenges that may result from this step are: 'How to sustain employability', impacting the financial result and employee wellbeing; or 'How to source energy', impacting the financial and environmental bottom line. Examples of stakeholders that may be listed in this step include regulators, clients, opinion leaders, shareholders, employees and local residents.

Step 2: defining key outputs involving stakeholders

After the strategic challenge of the decision has been described, it is now crucial to involve the stakeholders listed in Step 1. Together with the decision maker, the stakeholders determine the outputs upon which the decision maker will base their decision, the so-called *key outputs*. Key outputs can be thought of as the basis for the decision criteria. Note that a key output does not have to be a decision criterion or business requirement yet, since such a criterion typically needs a target value for the key output as well. For example, if payback period is a key output, then 'payback period should not be longer than 1.5 years' may be a decision criterion.

Step 2 of the decision-making process normally takes place by first formulating a longlist of outputs which will then be reduced to a shortlist of key outputs, again in an interactive setting. A group of participants working under guidance can quickly learn how to pinpoint outputs and then place them in order of priority. Progressing from a longlist to a shortlist of key outputs is also a way to focus attention: in which areas the organization needs to achieve success or concrete results; which areas should be given priority; who are the key stakeholders whose interests should be taken into account. Hence, when defining key outputs, it is of crucial importance to take into account the views and standpoints of all stakeholders as formulated in Step 1. Chapter 7 will clarify that there are more types of outputs than key outputs. However, key outputs matter to the boardroom. These are often referred to as *key performance indicators* or KPIs. Existing key output definitions on which the organization already reports are the best sources, for two reasons. First, since the key output definition is not a result of this step, discussions on the quality of the definitions can be avoided or at least not be held on the back of this step. Second, since the organization already reports according to the existing key output definition, a measurement system and a baseline are already available. Sources for existing key output definitions include an annual sustainability and/or social report, a so-called integrated report, which includes both financial and non-financial information, the GRI framework (Global Reporting, nd), the European Sustainability Reporting Standards (EFRAG, nd), to which many corporates have to adhere by 2023 according to the Corporate Sustainability Reporting Directive (CSRD) (EU Commission, 2021). In the context of CSRD it is interesting to observe that this Directive not only focuses on reporting various non-financial key outputs, but also on disclosing how an organization embeds these outputs into its decision-making process (ESRS 2, article 46(c)). The seven steps described in this chapter automatically fulfil this reporting requirement.

Often, key outputs together cover the 3Ps. There might be cases where not all of the 3Ps are relevant, but key outputs together should preferably address at least two of them in order to exploit the potential of the Responsible Business Simulator concept. However, even if all key outputs belong to just one P, but have been defined such that they are hard to compare because they have different units (for example, internal rate of return next to payback period and net present value), this strategic decision-making methodology may be useful to study the multi-dependencies between these key outputs and find the right balance. Examples of key outputs addressing people and planet include change in employee commitment and change in percentage of energy consumption from sustainable resources. In practice, most of the time it is enough to work with the themes people, planet and profit, but users of tRBS can specify the themes themselves. For example, Chapter 8 illustrates how SDGs are used to specify themes.

Step 3: determining decision maker's options

In order to define the options facing a decision maker, we first introduce the concept of *internal variable inputs*. Internal variable inputs are in the hands of the decision maker. Within the field of operations research (OR), a discipline within econometrics that focuses on the application of analytical methods to support operational decision making, these are known as endogenous or in-control inputs (Pintér, nd). Although we focus on strategic decision making rather than operational decision making, it is still interesting to exploit the computational practices used in OR, since these are far more developed than those in strategic decision making. The values of these internal inputs are adjusted during the decision-making process. Each internal variable input can be thought of as a single aspect on which a sub-decision needs to be made. First we need to determine the internal variable inputs by answering the question, 'What actions can the decision maker possibly take?' A decision maker's option can then be formulated by assigning a single value to all internal variable inputs. This assumes that every option within the scope of the decision can be completely described by one value per internal variable input. Since there is typically more than one internal variable input, a decision maker's option can be thought of as a set of potential sub-decisions, where each potential sub-decision is represented by choosing a single value for the corresponding internal variable input. For example, when a municipality decides on a new waste collection system, it may not only need to select a supplier, but also decide whether the maintenance will be outsourced or not.

It is important, in this step, that any participant who wants to submit a proposal for an alternative option is given the opportunity to do so, so that this alternative can be added to the collection of options to be evaluated. This can often be done during the workshop, by selecting a new combination of values for the internal variable inputs and saving them as a new option. As soon as there are more than three options to be evaluated, it is recommended that the options are given names that illustrate the nature of the option clearly, so that it is not necessary to inspect the values of each of the internal variables.

In many cases, it helps to include a 'nil option'. This nil option boils down to not making a decision, and leaving everything as it was. Formulating a nil option provides a good check on the formulation of the key outputs. Just as in a normal business case assessment, the outputs may illustrate the incremental effect of the decision. Quite often this means evaluating all outputs in the nil option at zero, but that is not always the case. Take, for example, the decision of whether or not to insulate the leaking roof of a science centre (Chapter 14). The nil option would mean doing nothing to the roof. Consider now the key output reflecting the energy saving to be achieved by insulating the roof. This output should, in principle, reflect the energy saving in comparison to maintaining the present situation. If the roof is still leaking, however, the option of doing nothing may cause the leaking to become even worse, thereby leading to an even higher energy consumption than the actual energy consumption. Normally, insulating the roof would automatically remedy the leakage. In that case, the output for energy saving can be given a negative value for the nil option, as is the case in Chapter 14.

Step 4: drawing up scenarios

In order to define scenarios, we first introduce the concept of *external variable inputs*. External variable inputs are the inputs that are not in the hands of the decision maker and hence also known as exogenous variables or out-of-control inputs. The values of these external inputs are adjusted during the decision-making process. Each external variable input can be thought of as a single aspect of external uncertainty affecting the outcome of the decision in scope. A scenario is defined by assigning a single value to all external variable inputs. It assumes that every possible future outcome of all external uncertainty with respect to the scope of the decision can be completely described by a single value per external variable input. Since there is typically more than one external variable input, a scenario can be thought of as a coherent combination of future developments, where every single aspect of external uncertainty is represented by choosing a single value for the corresponding external variable input. For example, both the future interest rate and the future price of solar panels may have to be set when designing a scenario in the context of an energy sourcing decision.

Just as formulating the decision maker's options consists of multiple rounds of filling in data for the internal variable input, so the drawing up of scenarios consists of filling in data for the external input several times. Since the external input cannot, by definition, be influenced by the decision makers, the challenge of the latter task is many times greater than that of the former step. During the workshop some basic scenarios will be formulated by the participants, and these – together with the key outputs and internal variable inputs – will be further investigated, updated and completed outside of the workshop. The data to fill in the scenarios is collected from a combination of existing research, historical data, expert opinions and simulation. The objective of the exercise is not per se to fill out the scenarios as realistically as possible; it is more important to gain access to the sources that can be made available within a reasonable amount of effort, and to make the remaining uncertainty more transparent.

It is desirable to draw up at least three scenarios at this stage: a base-case or neutral scenario (in which all external output is given a 'most plausible' value), along with pessimistic and optimistic scenarios to represent the rather negative and positive reactions of the environment to the decision. Once again, all participants in the workshop must feel that they are free to add or adapt scenarios. This might include adding specific stress scenarios so as to test extreme settings of external input, or adding alternative base-case scenarios if there is a difference of opinion among the experts as to what the most probable values actually are.

As tRBS is uncommonly patient, and the addition of a scenario is a simple task, there is no limit to the number of scenarios that can be considered. Therefore, it is important to ensure that the names of the scenarios reflect the intention clearly, at first sight, without the need to inspect the individual values of the external input.

Typically, not all values needed to define scenarios can be produced on the fly in this step. Desk and even field research may be needed to complete scenario definitions. Historical data may be involved, and/or other experts may be consulted. Since these activities are too time-consuming to perform in the explorative dialogue setting in the first phase of the decision-making process, these are postponed until the next phase: the construction of the simulation model.

Step 5: constructing the simulation model

The primary objective of Step 5 is to specify the *simulation model* in the form of a set of formulae that compute key outputs based on the decision maker's options and scenarios. Constructing this simulation model typically involves more than just writing down as many formulae as there are key outputs. First, the model may become more transparent by breaking down formulae in a number of steps, thereby generating a set of intermediates. For example, instead of calculating the total cost of ownership (TCO) of a new asset, it may be wise to break down TCO into capital expenditure, capital charges and operational costs, calculate these components separately and then aggregate them. Second, more inputs than just the internal variable input and external variable input defined in Steps 3 and 4 are often needed to model the relationship between these inputs and key outputs. Since there is less focus on understanding the dependency of key outputs on the changes in these additional inputs, we call these *fixed inputs*. For example, in order to calculate maintenance costs, the cost per hour of a maintenance operator has to be known. Third, besides key outputs it may be useful to compute additional outputs to create additional insights and/or simple validation possibilities. For example, besides the decrease in energy usage, the new level of energy usage might be communicated as well.

The secondary objective of Step 5 is to complete all input data needed to feed the simulation model. As explained in the previous section, Steps 3 and 4 take place in a boardroom setting and focus on defining the decision maker's options and scenarios respectively. These only require setting the values of the internal and external variable inputs. However, data needs to be collected for all additionally defined fixed input as well. This is typically done using desk research and – if no useful secondary data is readily available – using primary data collection, historical data, expert opinions and/or Monte Carlo simulation. From the point of view of efficiency it is, of course, preferable to use existing research that is directly applicable to the situation being modelled. A great deal of relevant quantitative data is often already available from previous research, somewhere. Nonetheless, non-statisticians often find it difficult to access such results and relate them to the results of other existing research. It can also be considered difficult to superimpose the results of this research onto the situation in hand. Our experience has been that tRBS provides an excellent aid to accessing, disclosing and combining existing research, and translating that combination of research to the business context of the organization at hand. The use of historical data that has a direct relevance to the decision-making process sits in well-deserved second place after using insights from research. In practice, however, such relevant historical data is rarely available. First, data of this nature cannot always be made readily accessible. Second, we need data that describes the future, not the past, and extrapolating historical data realistically into the future is no trivial task. Third, sustainable decision making often has an innovative character and this more or less precludes the possibility that historical data will be applicable. However, it can still help to collect historical data of vaguely similar situations. In all cases it is recommended that historical data, as a source, is combined with expert opinions. This can be achieved by giving experts the opportunity to adjust the historical data (up or down) to make it more representative for the future. In credit risk modelling, this method became known as 'judgemental overlay'. Conversely, experts can also arrive at more reliable estimates if these are based on historical data rather than on guesstimates. At the same time, experts might forfeit their impartiality if they allow themselves to be unduly influenced by historical data that has only a limited relevance. This effect – known as 'anchoring' – is one of the pitfalls of decision-making processes (Hammond et al, 2006). The final source of data for the external input is simulation. This source can be considered a last resort in the event that there is absolutely no relevant previous research, no historical data is available, and/or the experts are reluctant to make any rigorous estimates.

We use the Monte Carlo simulation method for this purpose. This technique entails estimating a probability distribution for each external input so that each possible future end result corresponds with a draw from each of the distributions. Historical data and expert opinions can, of course, help to determine the type of probability distribution and its parameters. Subsequently, we ask the software to compute, say, 50,000 draws of future end results for each highly uncertain input. Ultimately, therefore, we have 50,000 observations for each output and these are then aggregated into the most plausible value. A 95 or 5 percentile of those 50,000 observations can also be calculated as output. By 'promoting' the parameters of the probability distribution to the status of external inputs, and allowing them to vary per scenario, it is possible to obtain the desired level of variation in the environment being studied. The process of investigating, updating and completing scenarios is often rather time-consuming, because the members of the modelling team need to speak to co-workers and to external experts to obtain the data. It is therefore sensible to do this in the intervals between modelling sessions; besides, it is an instructive intervention to request reports and information from others within the organization, and from suppliers and customers as well. Not infrequently, informal knowledge is thus brought to light that can be used to refine the definition of key outputs and the decision maker's options.

Reaching these two objectives is supported by two sub-steps in tRBS: specifying the formulae encompassing the simulation model, and collecting data. More details on these sub-steps will be given in Chapter 7.

After the simulation model has been constructed, all the information gathered in the foregoing steps of the decision-making process has been processed within the model, and the simulation model has been validated, tRBS calculates the key output scores, and we can proceed to the selection of the best strategic choice. For that, two steps remain: assessing the strategic priorities (Step 6) and the risk appetite of the decision maker (Step 7).

Step 6: evaluating options by assessing strategic priorities

Strategic priorities are discussed by assigning weights to key outputs. This discussion is the start of Phase 3 and takes the form of a strategic dialogue in the boardroom. The Responsible Business Simulator also allows for assigning weights to themes instead of key outputs. Since every key output is linked to one or more themes, weights per theme can be transformed to weights per key output and vice versa. It depends on the situation at hand whether it is preferable to work with weights per theme or per key output. Irrespective of this choice, weights depend on the mission and vision of the organization that is making the decision. This mission and/or vision should in fact reflect how the equilibrium of its performance in terms of the 3Ps is perceived. An organization that is primarily profit-driven, but wants to show its customers that it also has an eye for people and planet, will assign more weight to (key outputs attached to) profit than will a charitable institution that sees financial performance as little more than a peripheral condition. Changing the weights assigned to the key output enables the decision maker to get a feeling for the relationships between inputs and key outputs and also shows the decision maker to what extent his or her mission and/or vision are aligned with the decision they are about to take.

An organization that wants to be sustainable will need to score on all the 3Ps, or at least two of them, but there can be large discrepancies between different organizations in the proportionality of the scores on the individual Ps. A construction company that devotes its efforts to enhancing the sustainable employability of its staff will assign a greater weight to people-related outputs than a tomato grower whose objective is to operate an energy-efficient greenhouse. The tomato grower will value planet-related aspects more highly. It is a no-brainer that the maturity of an enterprise – in terms of sustainability – influences the proportionality of the importance assigned to the different Ps. An organization that is just beginning to make its production chain sustainable will be different from an enterprise that has been high in the rankings of sustainable businesses for many years. Using this strategic decision-making process, it is possible for employees and management to work together to find a balance that is appropriate to the situation, context and possibilities of the organization.

Even more important than the current sustainability status is the fact that there is a vision and a desire at the top of the organization to have the corporate strategy and operational management practices calibrated objectively against values determined by employees and management alike. By visualizing the proportionality between people, planet and profit in various constellations, everyone can gain insight into the consequences of potential choices. The Responsible Business Simulator brings shared value creation to life in a strategic dialogue with all relevant stakeholders. As discussed in Step 2, key outputs may well have been linked to these stakeholders. Often, stakeholders link directly into the themes reflecting the different aspects of the impact of a decision. As such, weights assigned to key outputs are also weights assigned to stakeholders. The more weight one assigns to a stakeholder, the more one tends to 'listen' to that stakeholder when making decisions.

A dialogue to establish strategic priorities thus leads to the assignment of weights to each key output or theme. The simulation model uses these weights to aggregate the three-dimensional set of scores per key output per decision maker's option per scenario into a two-dimensional set of scores per decision maker's option per scenario. Before key outputs can be aggregated, tRBS transforms the different units that key outputs typically have into one, unitless, scale by means of *appreciation functions*. In this context, appreciation means the value induced per key output. This valuation concept will be further explained in Chapter 7, but should for now be considered as the instrument to ensure that key outputs can be compared even though they have different base units (e.g. euros or kWh). Now that the key outputs are comparable, tRBS calculates the weighted sum of the appreciation per key output for each combination of options and scenarios. Figure 5.2 shows how placing 50 per cent weight on the key output relating to planet and dividing the remaining 50 per cent evenly between the people- and profit-related key outputs produces an overall score per decision maker's option for three possible contextual scenarios: pessimistic, neutral and optimistic. The attractiveness per option depends on the scenario: option A is to be preferred in the optimistic and pessimistic scenarios, whereas B is the prevailing option in the neutral scenario.

Interestingly, as we will see in the case studies, the outcomes are often unexpected. Experience has shown that in many cases an initial focus on sustainable objectives in terms of people and planet often leads to better profit results in the longer term. The assumption is often that sustainability is expensive, but better educated personnel can be more effective in their work and need less management, as a result of which savings can be made. Sustainably produced goods often last longer and need less maintenance or repair. We have also seen that the overall costs can actually be reduced significantly by adding a time factor to the equation.

Figure 5.2 Input of strategic priorities leads to scores per option per scenario

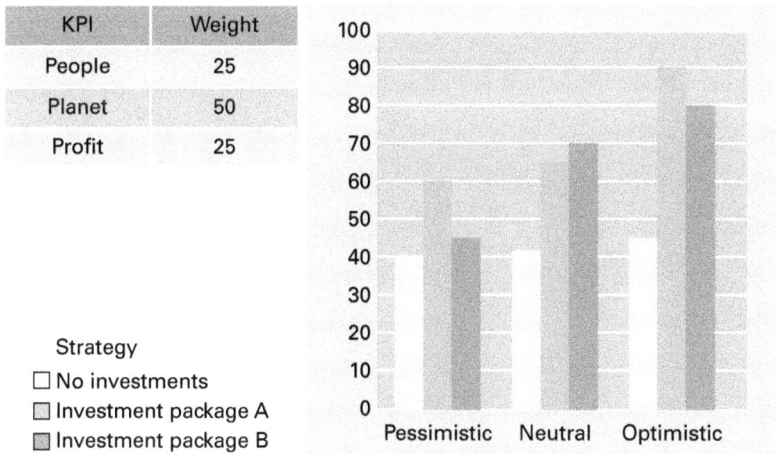

Step 7: evaluating options by assessing risk appetite

Risk appetite is discussed by assigning weightings to scenarios. The weights depend on the risk appetite of the organization, which might be risk-loving, risk-averse or risk-neutral. The risk appetite should in fact reflect how the organization perceives the equilibrium of its performance in terms of risk aversion. An organization that is risk-averse will assign more weight to a pessimistic scenario than one that is risk-neutral. Once the weightings of the scenarios have been set, tRBS has sufficient information to be able to express the desirability of each strategic option in numerical terms. This is done by taking the weighted sum of the scores per scenario for each strategy. The option with the highest score corresponds with the decision that the organization should take, taking into account all the assumptions made throughout the seven-step decision-making process.

In Figure 5.3 we see how a relatively low risk appetite is translated into weights that result in one overall score per option.

On the basis of the chosen strategic priorities and the risk appetite, as translated into weights for key outputs and scenarios, the enterprise would therefore choose option A. This analysis makes it clear what the assumptions are to finally choose one of the available options. By

Figure 5.3   Processing risk appetite leads to one score per option

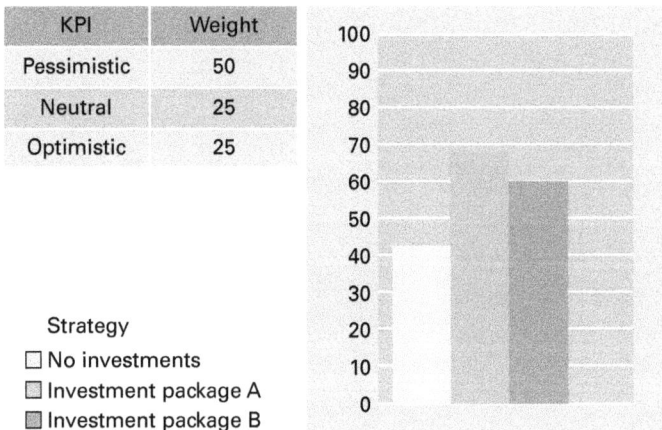

KPI	Weight
Pessimistic	50
Neutral	25
Optimistic	25

Strategy
☐ No investments
☐ Investment package A
☐ Investment package B

establishing these assumptions in a dialogue setting together with all relevant stakeholders and experts from all relevant disciplines, a 'black box' experience can be avoided. Instead, there is a hands-on process of weighing up the options that is a perfect fit for the specific situation in which the organization finds itself.

References

CWI (2013) National ICT 2013 Award for Python and SIG, www.cwi.nl/en/news/python-and-sig-win-national-ict-award-2013/ (archived at https://perma.cc/35UU-VS3N)

de Swart and van der Plas (2023) tRBS source code. Available at www.koganpage.com/product/responsible-business-decision-making-9781398612280 (archived at https://perma.cc/Q942-JG3)

EFRAG (nd) ESRS Exposure Drafts, www.efrag.org/lab3#subtitle6 (archived at https://perma.cc/4YUA-P3U4)

European Commission (2021) Communication from the Commission to the European Parliament, the Council, the European Economic and Social Committee and the Committee of Regions: EU Taxonomy, Corporate Sustainability Reporting, Sustainability Preferences and Fiduciary, 21 April

Global Reporting (nd) GRI Standards, www.globalreporting.org/standards (archived at https://perma.cc/UU3F-PZNK)

Hammond, J S, Keeney, R L and Raiffa, H (2006) The hidden traps in decision making, *Harvard Business Review*, 84 (1)

Pintér, J (nd) Operations Research, *Mathworld*, www.mathworld.wolfram.com/OperationsResearch.html (archived at https://perma.cc/8TFT-VMUK)

Roobeek, A and de Swart, J (eds) (2013) *Sustainable Business Modeling*, Academic Service, The Hague

Van Rossum, G and Drake, F L (2009) *Python 3 Reference Manual*, CreateSpace, Scotts Valley, CA

Strategic decision making based on data and dialogue

06

Strategic decision making using the Responsible Business Simulator (tRBS) is a communal activity, one in which employees and management both play an active role in providing input. This can also be extended to external stakeholders. The facilitator or advisor stimulates the strategic dialogue and renders that input transparent in the computational model. During the sessions, all participants are on an equal footing. Entering into a dialogue with each other about the direction a business or organization should take, or about the interests that particular stakeholders have in realizing a specific strategy, is an important part of the strategic decision-making process. Everyone is able to speak openly to one another during the sessions, and in between sessions, reports, figures, comparative studies, data and other information is collected. These documents, for instance consulting or engineering reports, which are often already available within the business, are frequently found to contain important hints for constructive dialogue. The process brings a large volume of existing information and data to the surface, avoiding the usual tendency to reinvent the wheel. For example, an engineering consulting firm might already have produced a report with hard facts about what is needed for the repair of a roof (see the NEMO case study in Chapter 14). Such details can then be included in the computational model.

Even more important is the identification of unsubstantiated assumptions, which can sometimes prove vital to altering the way the strategy is looked at. In the NEMO case, what proved to be an important hint was found in a casual comment in the report about the roof at the Science Museum. The engineers suggested that a sustainable roof could well have a positive effect on visitor numbers; our research team then had these effects calculated in the Responsible Business Simulator. For the engineers, this was barely relevant information; they had after all been called in to look at the technical side of the options for the roof repairs. But tRBS encompasses all the factors that provide information about People, Planet and Profit. From the holistic perspective, this comment about visitor numbers was an important factor that brought together various strategic objectives, namely a sustainable roof that could become an additional exhibition space, making the roof even more attractive to visitors and the city alike, and that would generate more revenue in terms of admission tickets sold and an even better reputation in the city of Amsterdam. This example also demonstrates why tRBS is not the introvert activity of a stand-alone calculator sitting at a computer, but an *interactive activity* between employees and management so as to bring extra dimensions into the equation and to appraise them in terms of their value for a sustainable, widely supported strategy instead of just taking a decision on a single aspect and losing sight of all the rest.

Action research as suitable method

The method that we used in the development of tRBS and its application in real-world corporate environments can best be described using the action research method. *Action research* can be defined as a process that is suitable for situations in which you simultaneously wish to realize change ('action') and acquire academic insight ('research') (Dick, 2002). Since our research had a strong practical and pragmatic component, we contend that it is impossible to achieve a thorough understanding of tRBS without having practical experience of its application on the one hand, and a fundamental knowledge of current practice within the participating organizations on the other. For a more extensive overview of the action research method and related theories than we present here, see the *Handbook of Action Research* by Reason and Bradbury (2001).

Dick (2002) explains that action research can be 'cyclical' or 'spiral', whereby action and critical reflection continually alternate. You begin by studying either the present practices or the policy currently pursued in the organizations. This is an exploratory phase, which is carried out from an unbiased perspective. A setting is subsequently created in which key persons within the organization can arrive at new insights that help to improve the current organizational processes. Action research can be described as progressing through cycles of intervention, reflection and investigation. With the unprecedented development of information systems and IT, the use of action research proved to be highly relevant. In particular, the practitioner/researcher interactions, as well as the group dynamics among practitioners themselves, lead to much more personal investment in the research than is found with traditional research methods.

Action research is a form of research that takes place outside experimental laboratories in the real world and is common practice at universities, corporate consultancies and knowledge-intensive companies in domains such as pharmaceuticals and IT. Action research is carried out in a real-life environment with the people from businesses or organizations. The research is carried out under normal conditions as far as possible, so that the true impact of interventions can be determined. The researchers are conscious of the interventions that they are implementing, and they communicate about them. This introduces a form of subjectivity, something that is considered to be impure science within traditional scientific circles.

However, not every issue is suitable for dissection in the unnatural environment of a technical laboratory, simply because the input needed to arrive at the heart of the matter cannot be poured out of a test tube but has to be delivered in collaboration with the real actors involved. Baskerville (1999) states that the key assumptions of the action researcher are that (1) the social settings cannot be reduced for study, and (2) action brings understanding. These assumptions are clearly valid for corporate strategic decision making. Although scientists are sometimes reticent about action research, the phenomenon has existed for a long time and it is applied in practice on a large scale in the social sciences and in the world of corporate consultancy. Lewin (1946) already defined action research as 'a spiral of steps that proceeds from planning to action to observation and finally to reflection'.

In their review article on action research in business and management, Shani and Coghlan (2021) state that action research operates in the realm of strategies, practical tasks, and structured hierarchical organizational systems in diverse industries and across multiple business functions and disciplines. The key difference between standard academic research and action research is that the impact of the latter is the generation of immediate actionable knowledge that is co-developed with the actors involved. The validation is part of the action, which improves the chances that the outcome of the action research will be executed. It leads to common knowledge on common ground. For innovative environments, this is important, because it then leads to speeding up innovation and implementation. Shani and Coghlan quote Mohrman and Winby (2018) who state that the renewed global interest in sustainability and sustainable value provides an opportunity for action research to engage and have impact.

Society also has a great need for research that is connected to a concrete action element, especially in the transition to a circular economy, as timely action is required. The unknowns in this transition are widespread and plentiful, such that most strategy decisions made will involve some of these unknown factors. 'Learning by doing' fits this scenario. The action research method suits research into sustainability and social inclusion while the economy is in such an unprecedented transition because knowledge acquired can be directly utilized in the next iteration of the research cycle.

Action research to unleash collective intelligence

In the Responsible Business Simulator approach we unleash the 'collective intelligence' of a group of highly diverse experts for strategic decision making. As shown by Woolley et al (2010) it is this collective intelligence that explains the performance of a group, not the individual intelligence of group members. Moreover, Woolley et al found evidence that group intelligence does not correlate strongly with the average intelligence of group members, but that it is correlated with the 'average social sensitivity of group members and the equality distribution of conversational turn-taking', which affirms the importance of using a round-table format (Woolley et al, 2010). Specifically, collective intelligence has been found to be crucial in settings that incorporate research (Buecheler et al, 2010) and the use of computer applications to support human interaction and decision making (Gregg, 2010). This evidence illustrates that tRBS and its interactive setting are very effective in dealing with complex issues.

Action research forms a counterbalance to the so-called 'extractive research', whereby researchers extract knowledge from a group of subjects while no changes are brought about in the situation of the subjects investigated (Tromp, 2006). Action research's iterative method of working allows participants to learn informally and ensures that new insights fall into place as the research progresses.

This is a highly desirable situation when developing well-supported strategy and processes of change because it only strengthens the outcome. From a steady state perspective, however, it is disturbing that living actors live up to their epithet and continually switch tracks during the process on the basis of those new insights, instead of continuing on the original track. This is a fundamentally different perspective from that taken in a physics laboratory; it is impossible to return to the starting situation of the initial experiment, because the actors have already undergone change. In the context of the social environment, however, this is self-evident, and appropriate to this research method (Roobeek, 1996).

Action research can be distinguished from conventional research in two ways. First, there is close collaboration with key persons within the organization. In other words, the organizations are not merely the subject of the research: they actively participate. According to Boonstra (2012), the underlying principle here is that insight, reflection and perspective lead to actions, and that sustainable change can only be achieved through participation. Knowledge is acquired because people reflect on their actions. The second distinguishing characteristic is that 'action' is the aim of the research. The goal is to achieve a positive change, not simply to describe present state findings. One comment that describes the core of action research really well is: 'Practice follows theory, theory follows practice' (Boonstra, 2012).

Action research places itself outside the realm of the paradigm that is otherwise dominating science at the moment, namely that of logical empiricism. That movement centres around a model in which the researcher as an 'objective and value-free' observer tries to understand the object of their research as well as possible. Action research, on the other hand, is set up as a communal learning process involving researcher and investigated subjects in which all parties jointly decide which objectives and values are to be achieved by the research. Participative research is based on the principle that there is a close relationship between the development of theory and the search for practical solutions. This does not, however, mean that action research is not objective. Wilmsen (2006) indicates that the most successful projects are those characterized by reciprocity: relationships that are characterized by open communications, trust and exchange between the researchers and the investigated subjects. This situation maximizes the use of the group's collective intelligence, as mentioned earlier in this chapter. According to Tromp (2006), this form of research actually has the potential to enhance objectivity, because there are extra control opportunities. An open attitude and controllability increase reciprocal confidence, and this in turn increases openness. In this way, reciprocity enhances the effectiveness of knowledge; Tromp suggests that this can be seen as an alternative way of interpreting conventional reliability and validity criteria.

Action research entails trying to 'reframe' the problems that have been identified so that they can be viewed in a different light. It is based on a systematic dialogue rooted in factual data which fits perfectly with the way we have designed our research. Existing knowledge is used, combined and tested by means of an econometric simulation model. Before such complex simulation models were possible it was already recognized by Baskerville and Wood-Harper (1996) that the action research method is ideally suited to the study of information systems and technology in its human context. Our research is specifically aimed at this. The goal is improving theory and technology, the Responsible Business Simulator, in order to support the interactive processes that integrate sustainability into all layers of the organization.

Although everyone feels that the transition towards a circular economy and social inclusion is important, organizations do not know how to use the insights gained from their current performance against these topics. When applying data and dialogue as we do in tRBS, organizations can place sustainability and social inclusion strategically as aims within their decision-making processes. This fits well with the findings of Schaltegger et al (2019) in their article on 'the business case for sustainability'. They state that some see sustainability and the business case as contradictions and thus emphasize the existence of trade-offs, while others highlight how business cases can be created by managing ecological, social and economic aspects. For these authors, the business case is not a given phenomenon, but has to be co-created in the exchange between and with contributions from various stakeholders. Our research adds to the gap Schaltegger and his co-authors notice, namely that we put the 3P values in the centre of the decision making with the active contribution of stakeholders. The aim of our action research is explicitly to move sustainability from the side-lines into the heart of the organization. To this end we have collaborated actively with businesses and organizations; in applying the model in the real world we have ourselves learnt a great deal and been able to introduce improvements. In addition, we invited various parties to join us at the university so that we could all reflect critically on our findings. The results served as input for the further refinement of the model, and also helped to enhance our understanding of the obstacles that are inherent in business strategies. Collaborative research proved its worth through the process of cyclical reflection and through providing tips for the further research process. Making maximum use of each participant's expertise – the mathematician, the financial expert, the organizational expert, the strategist – we were able to develop a simulation model that enhances insight into which interventions carried out at what juncture would have the greatest impact on sustainability and profit objectives alike. The ultimate aim was to create sustainable interventions based on hard data rather than on intuition and assumptions. The results of the action research proved that this is a feasible method, and strengthened the content of the process of strategic decision making with the use of the Responsible Business Simulator.

Data science in strategic decision making

Interest in data science has increased enormously over the past decade. According to the *Economist* (2010):

> A new kind of professional has emerged, the data scientist, who combines the skills of software programmer, statistician and storyteller/artist to extract the nuggets of gold hidden under mountains of data.

Davenport and Patil called data scientist 'The sexiest job of the 21st century' in the title of their article in the *Harvard Business Review* (2012). Interestingly, 10 years later the same authors asked themselves, 'Is data scientist still the sexiest job of the 21st century?' (Davenport and Patil, 2022). They say that the job is more in demand than ever with employers and recruiters due to the increased demand for AI model developers. They also say that the job of data scientist has changed, not only because its scope is redefined and (deep learning) technologies and open-source technology have developed, but also because the importance of non-technical expertise, such as ethics and change management, has grown. The turning point for data science ethics, according to Davenport and Patil, was probably the 2016 US presidential election, in which data scientists in social media attempted to influence voters and polarized the debate. In current discourse, but also in university programmes, attention is paid to the bias in algorithms and the use of AI (Davenport and Patil, 2022).

In this and the following paragraphs we look at some of the obstacles that arise when applying data science in practice and focus on how tRBS offers a practical way of creating business impact by applying data science in strategic decision making.

The challenge of applying data science in practice lies not so much in having enough statistical modellers, or data managers, or professional strategists who have the ability to present their views with impact in the boardroom, but rather in the combination of these three capabilities. This combination is what truly creates business and social impact.

In our business practice, we have seen many examples of organizations who could combine only two out of these three when making decisions. Just IT and analytics together typically lead to advanced models on real data that cannot, however, be used in an optimal way in boardrooms. For decisions with impact, a collective interpretation is necessary from the data experts and statistical modellers (internal or external), in combination with the (interactively operating) strategists and the participants in the company.

Avoiding the pitfalls of spreadsheet modelling

We still see companies making big decisions based on spreadsheet models. These models typically implement a discounted future cash flow analysis, leading to a net present value (NPV) and internal rate of return (IRR) that pass the hurdle rate set by the company. Although in principle it is possible to create a transparent spreadsheet model doing much more than such a cash flow analysis, there are a number of fundamental limitations to this approach:

- *Risk of goal reasoning.* A spreadsheet reporting an NPV or IRR not meeting the hurdle rate will probably not make its way to the boardroom. This automatically creates some pressure to set so-called fudge factors (uncertain inputs to the model having high impact on NPV and/or IRR) to values that favour the decision preferred by the author of the spreadsheet. This confirmative, deductive reasoning is actually deeply embedded in many forms of practical analytics. One of the promises of Big Data is to be more open for explorative, inductive insights as well as confirmative insights. In other words, data should not only be used to find answers to predefined questions, but also to pose new ones. In statistics there is a similar trend. Frequentist statisticians are still mainstream in academic education and scientific journals. As soon as the p-value, which represents the risk that there is no relationship in reality, is smaller than 5 per cent, students and researchers typically conclude that they have found enough proof to conclude that there is a relationship. This is a deductive reasoning, since only the relationships that pop up in the brain of these students and researchers are being tested. So there is no room for discovering relationships that were not thought of before. Also, it gives the opportunity to commit fraud by generating artificial data that is in line with the relationship on which the researcher plans to publish an article. One may argue that the ways to detect such fraud have been improved (e.g. Horton et al (2020) use Benford's law to detect fabricated data sets). However, one does not even need to generate artificial data to prove a non-existent relationship. If in reality no relationship exists and the researcher divides the data into 20 buckets, one bucket will reveal the relationship by coincidence. The fraudulent researcher just has to make sure to delete the other 19 buckets. The inductive counterpart of frequentist statistics is Bayesian statistics and allows for updating prior knowledge with data, potentially resulting in new insights. Machine learning models typically apply such inductive reasoning as well. Figure 6.1 displays the conceptual difference between the two approaches. In sum, spreadsheets are primarily focusing on confirmative, deductive, frequentist analysis and are of limited use when implementing exploratory, inductive, Bayesian analysis.

- *Proneness to errors.* Spreadsheet models can easily introduce errors. Many examples of this can be found in the horror stories section on the website of the European Spreadsheet Risks Interest Group. This group estimates that at least 90 per cent of spreadsheets contain errors (European Spreadsheet Risks Interest Group, 2022).

- *Non-transparency.* The complexity of spreadsheets is often measured by counting the number of distinct formulae; spreadsheets supporting big decisions often contain thousands of these. On the one hand this should not be a problem, as there are many ways to structure these spreadsheets adequately. Microsoft's Excel has functionality to trace precedents and dependents and there are also many good add-ons available to create more transparency around spreadsheets, such as OAK (Operis Analysis Kit, nd) and Spreadsheet Professional (Audit Excel, nd). On the other hand, however, these mitigating measures are not always used and even if they are, it may still be hard for non-experts to get a grasp of what is really going on in these large spreadsheets. We encounter many spreadsheets that are unattractive for those who want to challenge or learn from the model.

- *Focus on traditional business functions.* Spreadsheets are typically used by business professionals. However, for responsible business decision making there is a *mer à boire* of key insights from other disciplines, such as environmental impact and human behaviour, that are not automatically disclosed via spreadsheets. This also explains why a lot of spreadsheets still tend to focus on financial effects.

- *Inefficiency.* In our experience, many organizations spend lots of time on creating spreadsheets for decision making. Although spreadsheets allow for automatic interfacing with databases, this functionality is typically used more for reporting purposes than for decision making. Also, for many decisions, a new spreadsheet is built from scratch, although many elements are the same in all these spreadsheets, such as a discounted future cash flow analysis.

- *Two-dimensionality.* Spreadsheets try to project a complex world onto the two-dimensional world of rows and columns. Ways of increasing the number of dimensions to more than two by using multiple sheets or blocks typically increase the error count.

- *Inflexibility.* The addition of an extra product, time period, region or cost category to a dimension within a data structure which already contains more than two dimensions is often cumbersome.

- *Suboptimal access to more advanced statistical techniques.* Although there are many good add-ins available such as @Risk (Palisade Corporation, nd) for decision trees and Monte Carlo simulations, many powerful algorithms, such as solvers for mixed integer problems, are still not easily accessible. As an example, the Goal Seek function in Microsoft Excel is one-dimensional and may have difficulty in solving non-linear problems.

- *Lack of handling large data sets.* Although the number of rows and columns is not particularly small (up to 1,048,576 and 16,384 respectively in Microsoft Excel 2023), opportunities offered by Big

Figure 6.1   Many spreadsheets for decision making still follow confirmative reasoning

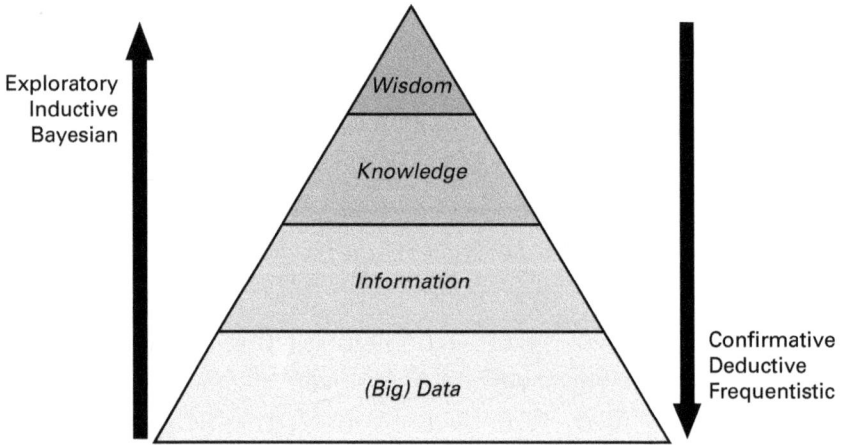

Exploratory
Inductive
Bayesian

Wisdom

Knowledge

Information

(Big) Data

Confirmative
Deductive
Frequentistic

SOURCE Tuthil, 1990

Data may require more. Also, spreadsheets are not primarily designed to handle sparse data sets. If a two-dimensional data set has 20 million rows and 20,000 columns, but only contains 1 million non-zeros, then it will not be straightforward to work with this data in Microsoft Excel.

Strategic decision making via the Responsible Business Simulator

We developed tRBS to overcome the obstacles encountered by spreadsheet models for strategic decision making. Just as a spreadsheet model is built within a spreadsheet software environment – typically Microsoft's Excel – the Responsible Business Simulator is available in two non-spreadsheet environments: Python and AIMMS.

AIMMS (2023) is a mathematical modelling software environment. The main advantages of AIMMS over a spreadsheet environment are that AIMMS has been designed to create graphical user interfaces around multi-dimensional models and offers access to advanced mathematical techniques such as optimization and Monte

Carlo simulation. AIMMS can also handle large data sets efficiently by exploiting sparse data structure. AIMMS has a web-enabled graphical user interface and can be used as an in-house or cloud application. The disadvantage of AIMMS may be that it has a high entry barrier for non-mathematicians. To overcome this handicap, tRBS offers a shell around AIMMS' mathematical programming language that closely follows the seven-step strategic decision-making process. The user just has to capture what is said during the stakeholder dialogue and the strategic dialogue in a number of non-technical screens. Simple simulation models can be specified by non-experts via one database table, without the need to make any programming effort in AIMMS. When the importance of the decision at hand justifies an investment in a more advanced model, a data scientist may be needed. To quote Einstein, things should be made as simple as possible, but not simpler. Even then, the focus in our approach is to create transparency around the assumptions behind the more advanced parts of the simulation model by a number of pre-programmed visual displays.

Next to the AIMMS implementation, there is also an open-source version of the calculation engine behind tRBS in Python available on GitHub. We expect that – given the growing number of Python programmers – this version fulfils the needs of organizations that want to run and adopt the model themselves independently. Finally, there are free cloud-based demos including user interfaces available for both AIMMS and Python. Check the companion resources of this book for the access details.

It may still happen that the simulation model becomes so complex that the decision maker does not have a solid grasp of the main assumptions in the model. In this case, we see two possible solutions. First, the expert responsible for these complex model parts should reduce complexity by breaking down the calculations into smaller sub-steps, for which it is possible to communicate the main assumptions to the decision maker. Again we quote Einstein: 'Complexity is a lack of understanding.' Second, a less complex model should be preferred in order to mitigate the risk that a decision is taken based purely on a black box and thus not thoroughly understood by the decision maker. One should also realize that – no matter how complex the simulation model becomes – every model is a limited representation of reality. In our view, it is better to have a business dialogue around well-understood assumptions and risk appetite, by using a number of comprehensive scenarios, than to be in the hands of the designer of the black box.

In summary, the Responsible Business Simulator reveals the power and beauty of mathematics to the business world by combining and disclosing analytical insights from various disciplines and putting these in the context of the decision at hand.

The added value of combined research methodologies

The method we propose, combining advanced computational techniques with interactive action learning sessions, removes the vague assertions and false choices about sustainability from strategic decision making and from the accompanying investments.

By assigning values and weightings to both financial and non-financial key outputs during the interactive sessions, and thereby indicating how important a particular key output is in comparison with any other, the input for the strategy becomes transparent. Even more importantly, the entire process helps create support for the strategic choices. That is an important factor, because experience shows that strategies that are imposed from the top down hardly ever work. Interaction is important to people, particularly to professionals, so that they feel they have had some say in bringing the strategy about. If people, not only from within the organization but also stakeholders from outside, have been able to make an active contribution, and that contribution is visible in the strategic choices, the strategy is far more likely to be accepted. The chance that the strategy is actually going to be implemented increases in equal measure. The return on the explicit involvement of employees and management alike in interactive action learning sessions will be a greater flexibility during the implementation of the strategy. This is one important benefit of the Responsible Business Simulator approach.

Besides recruiting support as the foundation of the strategic decision-making process, tRBS also ensures that the input is objectified. It quantifies the key outputs and visualizes the weightings that are chosen by the team members. Repeating the sessions a couple of times allows fine-tuning to be effected on the basis of data and dialogue. This just serves to reinforce the probability of the outcomes. As far as the decision making by the Board of an organization is concerned, this means that a proposal for sustainable investments or for a strategic choice can be tabled that is not only 'hard' in terms of outcomes but also well supported by all concerned. For decision making, it also means that the software makes the outcomes of the process crystal clear – whether an enterprise is only pursuing profit and ignoring the other Ps, or whether it is making efforts to ensure a well-chosen balance between the Ps of people, planet and profit. This avoids the phenomenon known as 'greenwashing': acting as if the enterprise is really sustainable while, in reality, sustainability is being used as a marketing tool to portray the enterprise as greener and more socially responsible than it really is.

The strategic decision-making process allows no scope for manipulating sustainability or social factors in a 3P context. This is relevant in the context of the evolution towards fully integrated reporting. In recent years, we have seen that businesses are increasingly supplementing their mandatory annual reports with a social and sustainability annual report. An ever-growing group of pioneers is turning to fully inclusive reporting, a concept that revolves around transparency, ensuring that what is expressed in the enterprise's strategy is also put into practice (Eden and Huxham, 1996). The Responsible Business Simulator puts sustainability to the litmus test and enterprises and organizations can use the method to arm themselves proactively.

References

AIMMS (2023) Advanced Integrated Multidimensional Modeling System, www.aimms.com (archived at https://perma.cc/F4YC-TQKD)

Audit Excel (nd) Spreadsheet testing tool, www.auditexcel.co.za (archived at https://perma.cc/AQJ4-28ZY)

Baskerville, RL (1999) Investigating information systems with action research, *Communications of the AIS*, **2** (3), 4

Baskerville, RL and Wood-Harper, AT (1996) A critical perspective on action research as a method for information systems research, *Journal of Information Technology*, **11** (3), 235–46

Boonstra, J (2012) *Actie-onderzoek, leren en veranderen*, Presentatie Sioo/ Universiteit van Amsterdam

Buecheler, T, Füchslin, RM, Pfeifer, R and Sieg, JH (2010) Crowdsourcing, open innovation and collective intelligence in the scientific method: a research agenda and operational framework, *ALIFE*, 679–86

Davenport, TH and Patil, DJ (2012) Data scientist: the sexiest job of the 21st Century, *Harvard Business Review*, October

Davenport, TH and Patil, DJ (2022) Is data scientist still the sexiest job of the 21st Century?, *Harvard Business Review*, July, https://hbr. org/2022/07/is-data-scientist-still-the-sexiest-job-of-the-21st-century (archived at https://perma.cc/55WA-NSFV)

Dick, B (2002) Action research: action and research, www.aral.com.au/ resources/aandr.html (archived at https://perma.cc/YBQ7-A8ZN)

The Economist (2010) Data, data everywhere, 25 February, www.economist.com/node/15557443 (archived at https://perma.cc/ QW27-CDA7)

Eden, C and Huxham, C (1996) Action research for management research, *British Journal of Management*, **7**, 75–86

European Spreadsheet Risks Interest Group (2022) EuSpRIG Horror stories, eusprig.org/research-info/horror-stories/ (archived at https:// perma.cc/UWB6-H8US)

Gregg, DG (2010) Designing for collective intelligence, *Communications of the ACM*, **53** (4), 134–38

Horton, J, Kumar, DK and Wood, A (2020) Detecting academic fraud using Benford law: The case of Professor James Hunton, *Research Policy*, **49** (8), www.sciencedirect.com/science/article/abs/pii/ S0048733320301621 (archived at https://perma.cc/MS6D-ZYQB)

Lewin, K (1946) Action research and minority problems, *Journal of Social Issues*, **2** (4), 34–46

Mohrman, SA and Winby, S (2018) Working toward sustainable development, in *Research in Organization Change and Development*, AR Shani and DA Noumair (eds), **26**, Emerald Press, London

Operis (nd) Operis Analysis Kit, www.operisanalysiskit.com/ (archived at https://perma.cc/XB3S-GQLT)

Palisade Corporation (nd) The future in your spreadsheet, www.palisade. com/risk/ (archived at https://perma.cc/YJ9E-Q4X7)

Reason, P and Bradbury, H (2001) *Handbook of Action Research: Participative inquiry and practice*, SAGE Publications Ltd, Thousand Oaks, CA

Roobeek, AJM (1996) Strategic management from the bottom up, in *Beyond Theory: Changing organizations through participation*, eds S Toulmin and B Gustavsen, John Benjamins Publishing Company, Amsterdam/Philadelphia

Schaltegger, Sl, Hörisch, J and Freeman, RE (2019) Business cases for sustainability: A stakeholder theory perspective, *Organization & Environment*, **32** (3), 191–212, doi-org.ezproxy.library.wur.nl/ 10.1177/1086026617722882 (archived at https://perma.cc/9DBR-3GSW)

Shani, ABR and Coghlan, D (2021) Action research in business and management: a reflective review, *Action Research*, **19** (3), 518–41, doi.org/10.1177/1476750319852147 (archived at https://perma.cc/ UK3P-7JD4)

Tromp, C (2006) Action research als relevante vorm van interventieonderzoek, *Sociale Interventie*, **4**

Tuthil, S (1990) *The Data Hierarchy*, 3M, MN

Wilmsen, C (2006) Participation, reciprocity, and empowerment in the practice of participatory research, University of California, Berkeley, nature.berkeley.edu/community_forestry/Workshops/2006/WCAR%20 2006%20final%20draft%20Wilmsen.pdf (archived at https://perma.cc/ RV6N-E5GS)

Woolley, AW, Chabris, CF, Pentland, A, Hashmi, N and Malone, TW (2010) Evidence for a collective intelligence factor in the performance of human groups, *Science*, **330** (6004), 868–88

Using the Responsible Business Simulator

07

Making strategic decisions to benefit People, the Planet and Profits is an interactive process with stakeholders that addresses both financial and non-financial aspects. It comprises a seven-step process that leads to a clear strategic choice. The process is empowered by unique modelling software named the Responsible Business Simulator (tRBS). The seven-step process has been described extensively in Chapter 5 and is illustrated in Figure 7.1. This chapter focuses on the practical use of tRBS to execute these steps.

The Responsible Business Simulator code is available in two languages: Python and AIMMS. Users may choose to compile and run the source code themselves or use a plug-and-play version including a rich user interface hosted in the cloud. For the details specific to these versions, we refer to the user guides on the companion site of this book. In this chapter we conceptually describe what input data is needed for each step by tRBS to select the best decision maker's option under various scenarios, given the strategic priorities of the organization. We also explain how the graphical user interface supports the interactive dialogue per step.

For the simulation model to work, at each step of the process relevant information needs to be stored in a database. We allow the user to provide the data in an SQL Server database, a JSON file, an MS Excel sheet or tRBS's internal database that can be filled via the graphical user interface (GUI). For each strategic decision-making

Figure 7.1 The decision-making process: three phases and seven steps

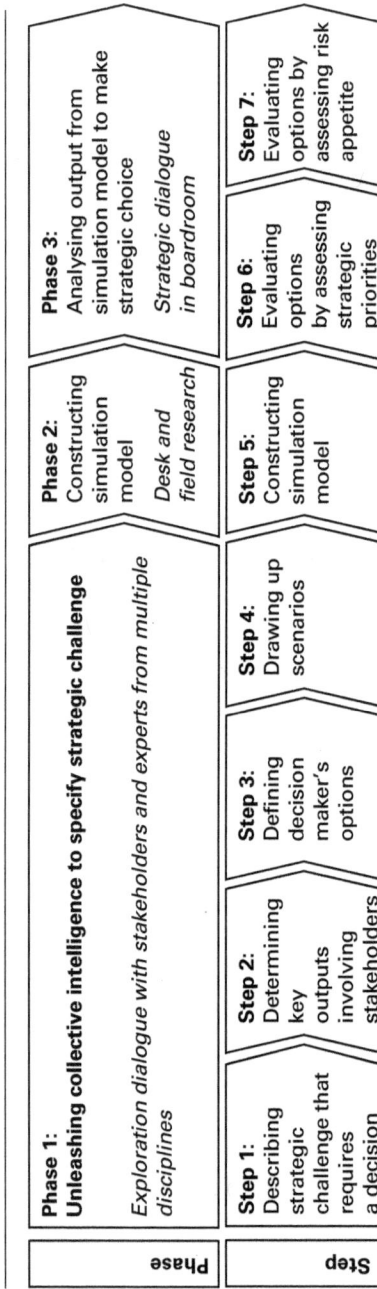

Phase	**Phase 1:** Unleashing collective intelligence to specify strategic challenge			**Phase 2:** Constructing simulation model	**Phase 3:** Analysing output from simulation model to make strategic choice	
	Exploration dialogue with stakeholders and experts from multiple disciplines			*Desk and field research*	*Strategic dialogue in boardroom*	
Step	**Step 1:** Describing strategic challenge that requires a decision	**Step 2:** Determining key outputs involving stakeholders	**Step 3:** Defining decision maker's options	**Step 4:** Drawing up scenarios	**Step 5:** Constructing simulation model	**Step 6:** Evaluating options by assessing strategic priorities	**Step 7:** Evaluating options by assessing risk appetite

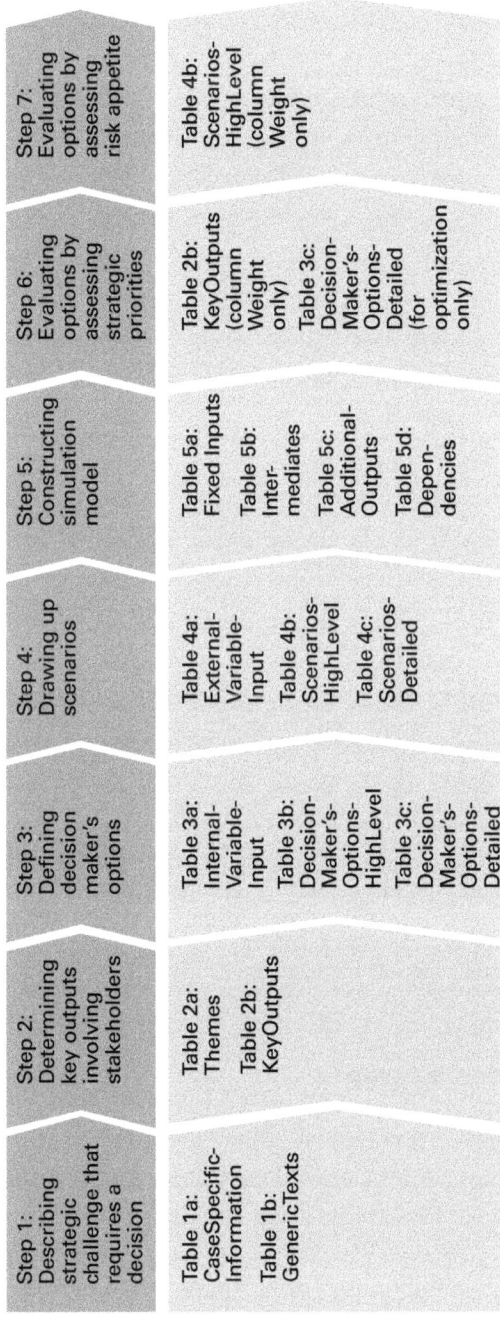

Figure 7.2 The tables in the database connected to the steps of the decision-making process

Step 1: Describing strategic challenge that requires a decision	Step 2: Determining key outputs involving stakeholders	Step 3: Defining decision maker's options	Step 4: Drawing up scenarios	Step 5: Constructing simulation model	Step 6: Evaluating options by assessing strategic priorities	Step 7: Evaluating options by assessing risk appetite
Table 1a: CaseSpecific-Information	Table 2a: Themes	Table 3a: Internal-Variable-Input	Table 4a: External-Variable-Input	Table 5a: Fixed Inputs	Table 2b: KeyOutputs (column Weight only)	Table 4b: Scenarios-HighLevel (column Weight only)
Table 1b: GenericTexts	Table 2b: KeyOutputs	Table 3b: Decision-Maker's-Options-HighLevel	Table 4b: Scenarios-HighLevel	Table 5b: Inter-mediates	Table 3c: Decision-Maker's-Options-Detailed (for optimization only)	
		Table 3c: Decision-Maker's-Options-Detailed	Table 4c: Scenarios-Detailed	Table 5c: Additional-Outputs		
				Table 5d: Depen-dencies		

case, a new database with case-specific information has to be provided. As in previous chapters, we will follow the stepwise process to explain what information needs to be inserted into tRBS. Figure 7.2 displays the tables that eventually make up the database. In every step, up to four database tables are filled. The first two phases of the decision-making process (Steps 1 to 5) support the completion, validation and visualization of input data. The third phase (Steps 6 and 7) is less data intensive: only the weights of the key outputs (reflecting the organization's strategic priorities) and the weights of the scenarios (reflecting the organization's risk appetite) will be added to previously created database tables when these weights are documented during the boardroom dialogue. In case the user wants to optimize their decision, the decision maker's option settings will be overwritten in this phase as well.

Within the GUI the database tables can be inspected via various displays. As well as providing a description of the information that needs to be inserted into these tables, this chapter will highlight some examples of the many graphical visualizations designed to create transparency around the simulation model. There will also be some attention paid to the mathematics within and reasoning behind the model. (NOTE: to avoid confusion between database tables and chapter Tables, a 'database table' will be referred to simply as 'database' in the rest of this chapter.)

For the purpose of explaining the use of tRBS in a consistent way, we have formulated the following fictional case that will be used through each step of the process.

Beerwiser example

We are decision makers at the fictional Australian beer brewery Beerwiser. Just like other brewers we use a lot of water during the heating process as well as in the cleaning of bottles and kegs. On average our brewery uses five pints of water to produce one pint of beer. We are outperformed by competitors like Heineken and Carlsberg who respectively were using 4.8 and 3.3 pints of water per pint of beer in 2012 (Appleyard, nd).

At the same time, injuries among people working on brewery shop floors, which are reported to the Bureau of Labour Statistics, have been on the rise, increasing from 160 in 2011 to 530 in 2014 (Roth, 2016). This is also an issue at our brewery. Therefore, our strategic challenge is to know which investments we need to make for a more sustainable brewing process.

We want to create transparency towards our most important stakeholders around the potential value to our organization of reducing water consumption and accidents.

Step 1: describing the strategic challenge that requires a decision

The first step of the decision-making process is to describe the strategic challenge that requires a decision. The strategic challenge for us as decision makers is 'how to brew more sustainably'. The main stakeholders to be accounted for in this specific case are the Board of the organization (as every decision needs their approval), the employees and the customers. The purpose of tRBS is not only to make better decisions, but also to document the whole decision-making process to inform external stakeholders, e.g. to comply with the Corporate Sustainability Reporting Directive discussed in previous chapters. To achieve this second aim it is crucial to supply enough contextual information to help external stakeholders understand how the decision was made, without the need to consult any other sources. To that end, it may be useful to incorporate, for example, the Mission Statement of the organization in database 1a.

The second table of this step, database 1b, serves to communicate in a language that resonates with internal and external stakeholders. This can take two forms. The first form refers to the main language used in the organization (e.g. English). Currently, the user interface supports English, German, Italian, Spanish and Dutch as main languages. Adding a language, e.g. Portuguese, comes down to providing a Portuguese dictionary of approximately 100 words to get a GUI in

Table 7.1 The two databases completed (1a and 1b) after Step 1 for Beerwiser example

Table name	Description
1a Case-specific information	Scalar information to tailor generic settings to the strategic decision-making case at hand, such as: • the name of the organization ('Beerwiser') • the mission statement ('Brew the best beer, with respect for people and planet') • the strategic challenge ('How to brew more sustainably') • the date of analysis ('20 February 2023').
1b Generic texts	Text to be displayed per keyword in the user interface. This gives the user the opportunity to add their own language to the user interface.

Portuguese. The second form deals with the terminology that the organization wants to use in their communication to stakeholders. For example, although the organization communicates in English, it may prefer to use the term 'key performance indicators' instead of 'key outputs', which is the default term used in tRBS's standard English dictionary.

The information collected in this step is restricted to two databases, which are described in Table 7.1

Step 2: defining key outputs involving stakeholders

Before we can determine the best possible decision, we need to define what 'good' looks like in the eyes of the stakeholders. Therefore, in this step we shortlist all important stakeholders and ask them which measurable outcomes resulting from the decision would determine whether they were satisfied.

Once the strategic challenge of the decision maker and organization-specific information have been inserted, the key outputs on which the decision maker will base their decision and corresponding themes are formulated. This boils down to completing two databases.

In this simple example, the key outputs are water use reduction, accident reduction and unit production cost reduction.

Database 2a: themes

Recall that in the context of responsible business decision making, it may be important that not only the financial effects (Profit) of the decision are made visible, but also any non-financial effects, such as the effect on society (People) and on the natural environment (Planet). In this database the themes relevant to the decision maker are formulated. People, planet and profit are the default themes, but of course it is also possible to use just two themes instead of three, to add themes, or to alter the default themes. For example, the healthcare organization in Chapter 11 focusing on sustainable employability only uses the themes people and profit, whereas the SDG case outlined in Chapter 8 employs nine themes, where each theme represents a material SDG. For the Beerwiser example, the applicable themes are the default themes people, planet and profit.

Database 2b: key outputs

Next, the defined key outputs are to be inserted into the database. The first column in Table 7.2 shows the key outputs that result from the explorative dialogue with stakeholders for the Beerwiser case. To each key output characteristics such as corresponding theme, weight and unit of measurement are added. The weight per key output as displayed in Table 7.2 is typically initially set to the value one in Step 2. The reason for this is that Step 2 is part of the explorative dialogue phase, in which many stakeholders should take part. It hampers the inclusiveness of the dialogue if the decision maker already determines how important these stakeholders are to them. Therefore, strategic priority setting is postponed to the boardroom dialogue in phase 3 and documented, but may be altered during Step 6.

The remaining columns in database 2b serve to specify how key outputs should be appreciated. There are three ways for the user to appreciate key outputs, all by means of an *appreciation function*.

Table 7.2 Database 2b (key outputs) completed for Beerwiser example

Key output	Theme	Weight	Unit	Automatic	Monetary	STB	Linear	Start	End
Water use reduction	Planet	1	hl/year	√			√		
Accident reduction	People	1	#/year	√			√		
Production cost reduction	Profit	1	%	√					

Appreciation functions translate what a particular score on a key output means to the decision maker, such that the key outputs can be compared. The easiest and most commonly used option is the option to allow tRBS to estimate the appreciation functions automatically. Another option allows the user to control all characteristics per appreciation function manually. And last but not least, the user has the option to specify their own function indicating the simultaneous appreciation of key outputs. This will require some case-specific programming outside of the database and is part of Step 5.

For the first two options, the decision maker should indicate whether a key output is to be Smaller The Better (STB) or not. Key outputs that are labelled STB are those the decision maker wants to minimize. An example of a key STB output could be CO_2 emissions. Key outputs that are not categorized as STB are those that the decision maker wishes to maximize, such as accident reduction and unit production cost reduction.

The user can also indicate whether they want a key output to be appreciated in a Linear fashion or not. In the non-linear case tRBS uses an appreciation function that employs the law of diminishing marginal gains. If the binary characteristic Automatic is switched on, the domain of the appreciation function is determined as the interval containing all values between the minimum and maximum of the key output values across the decision maker's options and scenarios. If it is not switched on, the user has to specify the domain via the Start and End characteristic. If the binary characteristic Monetary is switched on, the corresponding key output is appreciated using a linear function with a slope that is based on the Start and End characteristic. Consequently, all key outputs that are set to Monetary, will be appreciated in the same way. In other words, the euro, dollar or pound of every monetary key output is appreciated equally. Technical details on defining advanced appreciation functions, which include so-called Nominal-the-Best functions and functions that employ a threshold, can be found in the online user guides.

For the Beerwiser example, there are no monetary key outputs and we have decided to use the option to allow tRBS to estimate the appreciation functions automatically. This is indicated in the corresponding database, which is displayed in Table 7.2.

In the case of automatic appreciation, tRBS calculates the appreciation functions based on the characteristics described in Table 7.2. The extremes of the key outputs over all the decision maker's options and scenarios are calculated as the so-called Start and End points of the appreciation functions. These points are connected with each other via a straight line when a key output type is set to monetary or linear, or via a (transformed) sinusoid when a key output's type is set to non-linear.

The automatically generated appreciation function for key output production cost reduction is depicted in Figure 7.3.

In Figure 7.3, the horizontal axis displays the minimum and maximum attainable value of the key output and every value in between, and the vertical axis displays the appreciation. Start is displayed in the bottom left corner, while End is displayed in the bottom right corner. If key outputs are modelled manually, the user needs to define a Start and End point. Using automatic or manual estimation of the appreciation functions, all key outputs are at all times appreciated independently. This may not always be realistic, since the appreciation

Figure 7.3   Example of a non-linear (non-monetary), non-STB appreciation function for Beerwiser example

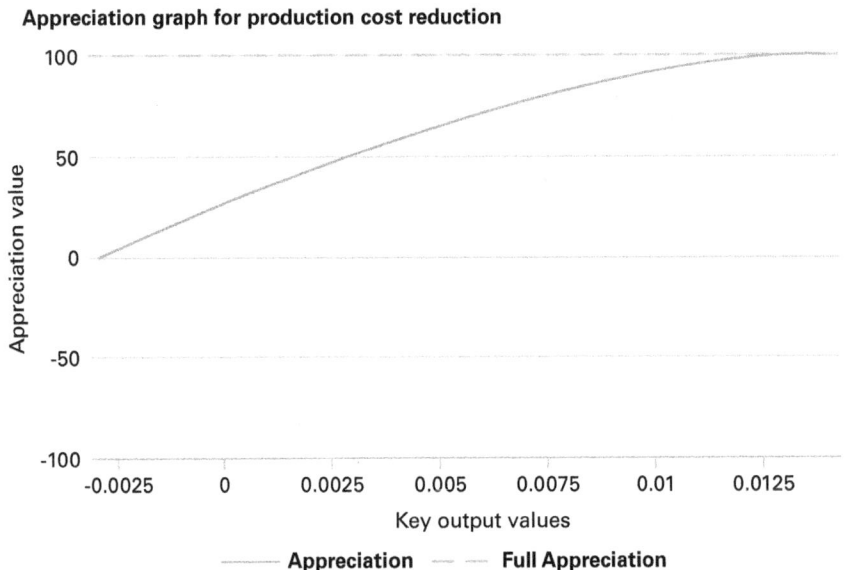

Appreciation graph for production cost reduction

of one key output may depend on whether another output has reached a certain level as a bare minimum. For these cases, the user has the option to specify their own functions indicating the simultaneous appreciation of key outputs. In that case they should switch off the setting of independent appreciation in the database and program the appreciation functions in Step 5.

Step 3: determining decision maker's options

When selecting the best possible decision, there should of course be a choice of potential decisions. In this step, we define the options the decision maker has. We do this by first defining all degrees of freedom for the decision maker and then attaching values for these degrees of freedom for each option.

Now that general information on the strategic challenge and characteristics of the key outputs have been inserted into the first four databases, data regarding the decision maker's options will be inserted. In this step we fill three additional databases.

Database 3a: internal variable inputs

Internal variable inputs are inputs to which the decision maker can assign values, the so-called endogenous variables, decision variables or in-control inputs. The pieces of information that are captured in database 3a are the names of the internal variable inputs and – optionally – information on saturation points, accessible populations and probabilities of success in case the internal variable inputs represent investments. In practice, values of the latter three optional characteristics of the internal variable inputs are often collected during Step 5 in the decision-making process, when more detailed information is specified via desk research.

As can be seen in Table 7.3, the internal variable inputs for the Beerwiser example do represent investments, namely those in

Table 7.3 Database 3a (internal variable inputs) completed for Beerwiser
example

Internal variable input	Saturation point	Accessible population	Probability of success
Invest in training of employees	$300,000	95%	90%
Invest in water recycling	$275,000	100%	100%

training of employees and those in water recycling. Investing in the training of employees refers to educating the employees on the safety regulations surrounding beer production, with the purpose of reducing the number of accidents. Investing in water recycling refers to investing in systems like membrane filtration or reverse osmosis systems. For simplicity, all investments in this case are assumed to be annual expenditures.

The Saturation Point indicates the maximum effective investment, or the ceiling above which further investment has no additional effect. In other words, it indicates to which maximum value an internal variable input can be increased in order to remain effective. For example, if a decision maker decides to invest a total amount of $350,000 in the training of employees and the saturation point is $300,000, then the last $50,000 does not have additional impact and could be invested more usefully elsewhere. The Accessible Population is the part of the population on which the investment will have an effect. In the case of a decision maker wanting to invest in training employees, this intervention will only reach those employees that are capable of following the training. The Probability of Success is the likelihood that the investment will prove to be successful. From the employees that form part of the accessible population, not everyone will experience the intended impact. The probability of success determines which percentage of the target group will be impacted as intended by the training. We consider the values entered in this table to be fixed inputs, i.e. inputs that do not change throughout the decision-making process.

Database 3b: decision maker's options high level

A combination of internal variable input settings is called a decision maker's option and these are formulated in database 3b. It is recommended that the names of the decision maker's options reflect the combination of internal variable inputs that form each option.

For the Beerwiser example, we have formulated three options:

- Focus on water recycling: where a decision maker invests $250,000 in water recycling and $50,000 in training.

- Focus on training: where a decision maker invests $50,000 in water recycling and $250,000 in training.

- Equal spread: where a decision maker invests $150,000 in water recycling and $150,000 in training.

Database 3c: decision maker's options detailed

Database 3c is linked to databases 3a and 3b: for every decision maker's option in 3b, all the non-zero internal variable inputs in 3a will be assigned a value. Table 7.4 illustrates how this database table looks for the options defined above.

Table 7.4 Database 3c (decision maker's options) completed for Beerwiser example

Decision maker's option	Internal variable input	Value
Focus on water recycling	Invest in water recycling	$250,000
Focus on water recycling	Invest in training of employees	$50,000
Focus on training	Invest in water recycling	$50,000
Focus on training	Invest in training of employees	$250,000
Equal spread	Invest in water recycling	$150,000
Equal spread	Invest in training of employees	$150,000

Step 4: drawing up scenarios

Next to the degrees of freedom the decision maker has, there are also a lot of external factors that influence the outcome of the decision. In Step 4 we structure these factors by defining scenarios that contain coherent settings for these external factors. In order to be able to draw up scenarios, three additional databases have to be filled with data, in a way that is analogous to Step 3, but the internal variable inputs are now replaced by external variable inputs and the decision maker's options by scenarios.

Database 4a: external variable inputs

External variable inputs are the inputs that are not in the hands of the decision maker and hence also known as exogenous variables or out-of-control factors. Each external variable input can be thought of as a single aspect of external uncertainty affecting the outcome of the decision in scope.

For Beerwiser the external variable inputs are the cost of a safety accident and the effectiveness of the water recycling investment. The latter represents a factor of conservatism by which the expected effect of investing in water recycling on the use of water is multiplied.

Database 4b: scenarios high level

A scenario is defined by assigning a single value to each external variable input. Since there is typically more than one external variable input, a scenario can be thought of as a coherent combination of future developments, where every single aspect of external uncertainty is represented by choosing a single value for the corresponding external variable input. Thus, scenarios are used to account for a decision maker's risk appetite. It is recommended that the names of the scenarios reflect what the values of the external variable input imply. Typical names for scenarios are:

- 'Base case', representing the scenario reflecting most likely outcomes for the external variable inputs. A risk-neutral decision maker may want to put most weight on this scenario.

- 'Optimistic', representing the scenario reflecting potential outcomes for the external variable inputs that are deemed to have a positive effect on the key outputs. A decision maker with a relatively high risk appetite may want to put most weight on this scenario.

- 'Pessimistic', representing the scenario reflecting potential outcomes for the external variable inputs that are deemed to have a negative effect on the key outputs. A risk-averse decision maker may want to put most weight on this scenario.

To create robust decisions, the decision maker may want to give equal weights to all these scenarios.

It is possible to alter the default scenario names as well as to add or delete scenarios. Typical scenarios that may be added on top of the three scenarios listed above are stress scenarios in which severe shocks are applied to one or more external inputs or scenarios reflecting the personal view of one of the stakeholders or experts taking part in the explorative dialogue. The scenario names are stored in database 4b. For the Beerwiser example we stick to the three default scenario names.

Database 4c: scenarios detailed

Database 4c is linked to databases 4a and 4b: for every scenario in 4b, all non-zero external variable inputs in 4a will be assigned a value. Table 7.5 shows what the scenarios look like for the Beerwiser example.

Recall from Chapter 5 that additional desk and field research may be needed in Step 5 to complete the scenario definitions. Historical data may be involved, and/or other experts may be consulted. In this example we used expert opinions to determine the values of the external variable inputs per scenario.

Step 5: constructing the simulation model

In order to construct the simulation model, we first need to specify the elements it will contain, then validate the model by checking

Table 7.5   Database 4c (scenarios) completed for Beerwiser example

Scenario	External variable input	Value
Base case	Cost of accident	$15,000
Base case	Effectiveness water recycling	98%
Optimistic	Cost of accident	$12,000
Optimistic	Effectiveness water recycling	100%
Pessimistic	Cost of accident	$20,000
Pessimistic	Effectiveness water recycling	90%

Figure 7.4   Calculation flow within the Responsible Business Simulator

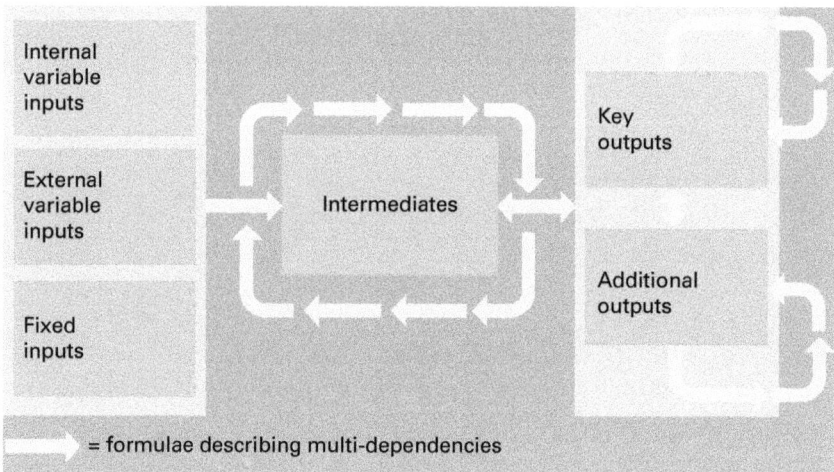

= formulae describing multi-dependencies

NOTE Arrows indicate the formulae describing dependencies

and reviewing the sensitivities, outputs and dependencies. Typically this involves more than just taking into account internal variable inputs, external variable inputs and key outputs. Additional model elements may be required, e.g. extra inputs in the form of *fixed inputs*, *intermediates* in order to create more transparency in the modelling process, and *additional outputs* for supplementary insights. After specifying the additional elements, all model elements are linked by specifying so-called dependencies. The calculation flow is shown in Figure 7.4.

We see that intermediates, key outputs and additional outputs may depend on all other model elements. The only distinction between intermediates, key outputs and additional outputs is that intermediates are not reported in the summary page, and key outputs are made mutually comparable by means of appreciation functions. Model elements from which arrows originate are referred to as *drivers*, while model elements to which arrows are directed are referred to as *destinations*.

Specifying simulation model

All the necessary information required to complete the specification of the simulation model that is in addition to the information specified in the previous Steps is collected through four databases, 5a, b, c and d. We will first discuss the contents of these databases and then explain the Responsible Business Simulator's functionality to validate and visualize the simulation model.

Database 5a: Fixed inputs

Fixed inputs are inputs in addition to previously defined internal and external variable inputs and are often needed to model the relationship between the variable inputs and key outputs. For brewery Beerwiser these fixed inputs are water unit cost, number of employees, current water use, current production cost and current number of accidents. Their values are listed in Table 7.6.

Although the term 'fixed' suggests that these inputs can have only one value, in practice we see that it can sometimes be difficult to get

Table 7.6   Database 5a (fixed inputs) completed for Beerwiser example

Fixed input	Unit	Value	Source
Water unit cost	$/hl	0.050	(Every Little Drop, nd)
# employees		500	Company information
Current water use	hl/year	15,000,000	Company information
Current production cost	$/year	7,500,000	Company information
Current # accidents	#/year	51	Company information

a reliable value for certain inputs. Two different situations can be identified. First, the input may be in the control of the decision maker, e.g. number of employees. If it is important to study the effects of various sizes of the workforce, then this input could be promoted to internal variable input. Second, the input may not be in the decision maker's control. In this case it may be wise to promote this input to external variable input and try out several values. However, this means that the number of trials is limited to the number of scenarios.

For this reason, tRBS enables fixed inputs to be generated by Monte Carlo simulation. Monte Carlo simulation, ascribed to Stanislaw Ulam (Ulam et al, 1947), is a sampling method that can be used to simplify a complex reality. It involves the random sampling from a probability distribution such that a specified number of trials (or iterations) is generated. By evaluating the simulation model for each trial, the probability distribution of key output values can be determined. The higher the number of trials, the higher the level of precision (Vose, 2000). Whether one should use scenarios or Monte Carlo simulation to deal with uncertain input also depends on the sensitivity of the key output for this input. If it turns out that the key output is rather insensitive for variations in the input, which means that the probability distributions of the key outputs are rather narrow, then it may be of limited added value to promote this input to variable input or to use Monte Carlo simulation. Later in this chapter we will discuss how sensitivity can be analysed graphically.

Monte Carlo simulation has been applied in the Rimetaal case described in Chapter 13. A commonly used process in Monte Carlo simulation is a Poisson process, which is a random counting process that is memoryless, as there is a constant and continuous opportunity for an event to occur (Kingman, 1992; Mikosh, 2008). The Poisson distribution is often used to model accidental breakdowns (Vose, 2000).

Database 5b: intermediates

The model will become more transparent by breaking down complex formulae into a number of steps, thereby generating a set of intermediates. For example, instead of calculating the production unit cost reduction, it may be wise to first break this key output down into the decrease in production cost due to a decrease in water use and to a decrease in accidents, then to calculate these components separately, and finally aggregate them. All intermediates are stored in database 5b.

For the Beerwiser example the intermediates are the relative reduction in accidents, the relative water use reduction when effective, relative water use reduction and the production cost reduction in dollars.

Database 5c: additional outputs

Besides key outputs it may be useful to compute additional outputs in order to create complementary insights and/or simple validation possibilities. The additional outputs are stored in database 5c.

In the Beerwiser example, besides the decrease in water consumption, the decision maker is interested in the new number of safety-related accidents, the new water consumption and the cost of training per employee.

Database 5d: dependencies

Dependencies refer to the relations that the six types of model elements (three types of inputs, intermediates and two types of outputs) mutually have. Many of the simulation models that we have developed do not require any programming by the user but can be specified via the database. Recall from the description of Figure 7.4 in the previous section that model elements from which arrows originate are called *drivers*, while model elements to which arrows are directed are referred to as *destinations*.

Filling out database 5d is the most technical part of the whole process and here a data science expert may be required. However, users with only limited modelling expertise but some experience in working with formulae will be able to specify relatively simple simulation models themselves based on the following guidance.

Let us first look at simulation models in which every destination can be written as the sum of the product of two model elements that are either inputs or destinations that have already been computed. In that case no programming is required. We will now explain how a user can specify these simulation models via database 5d:

1 Let x be the vector containing p elements that stacks the three types of inputs in any order. Let y denote the vector containing q elements that stacks all intermediates, key outputs and additional outputs. Note that x contains only drivers, and that y may contain both drivers and destinations. Since all model elements that are used in a formula need to be calculated before they can be used as input into this formula, the order in which the intermediates, key outputs and additional outputs appear in the vector y has to be as follows: all destinations are sorted such that every destination appears after the destination on which it depends.

2 Then the formula for y_1, the first destination, is relatively simple because it only depends on x. It may be written as follows:

$$y_1 = \sum_{j=1}^{p} x_{l(1,\,j)} * x_j$$

(1)

Here $l(1,\,j)$ can be interpreted as the index of the element in the vector x that contains the slope of the linear relationship between y_1 and x_j. Consequently, $1 \leq l(1, j) \leq p$.

3 The formula for y_i, where $2 \leq i \leq q$, looks somewhat more complicated since it may depend on other destinations as well:

$$y_i = \sum_{j=1}^{p} x_{l(i,\,j)} * x_j + \sum_{k=1}^{i-1} x_{m(i,\,k)} * y_k + \sum_{l=1}^{i-1} y_{n(i,\,l)} * y_l$$

(2)

Here, $l(i,\,j)$ can be interpreted as the index of the element in the vector x that contains the slope of the linear relationship between y_i and x_j, so $1 \leq l(i, j) \leq p$. Similarly, $m(i,\,k)$ can be interpreted as the index of the element in the vector x that contains the slope of the linear relationship between y_i and y_k, so $1 \leq m(i, k) \leq p$. Finally, $n(i,\,l)$ can be interpreted as the index of the element in the vector y that contains the slope of the linear relationship between y_i and y_l, so $1 \leq n(i, l) \leq j - 1$.

4 Based on this notation, the first three columns of database 5d can now be specified. These three columns are: Driver, Destination and Slope. Every term in the formulae above is specified by one row in database 5d as follows. The model elements x_j are inputs and drivers. Although y_k and y_l can be both drivers and destinations (these may be intermediates, key outputs or additional outputs), they take the role of driver in formula (1). Similarly, y_i may be drivers as well, but in formula (2) they take the role of destinations. The model elements $x_{l(i,j)}$ and $x_{m(i,k)}$ are inputs and drivers that take the role of slope and, finally, $y_{n(i,l)}$ may be drivers and destinations, but take the role of drivers, and – more specifically, the role of slope – in Formula (2). When completing the database, keep in mind that the order of the model elements inserted into the vectors is crucial for correct calculations, as can be seen from the ranges for $l(i, j)$, $m(i, k)$ and $n(i, l)$.

5 If the destinations can be calculated by the formulae above, then the operator simply reads '*'. However, tRBS also supports expressions for destinations that take the same form as the formulae above, but use other operators than '*', such as '–*', '/', 'min' or 'max'. In those cases, the corresponding operator is put in the fourth column of database 5d called Operator.

6 To ensure that destination values remain within their natural range, database 5d also contains two columns called Minimum and Maximum. After every iteration of formulae (1) and (2), the formula (3) is applied as post-processing. Of course, this formula is only executed when these columns in the corresponding rows are non-empty. If only the Minimum column is non-empty, then the max operator is omitted and vice versa:

$$y_i = \max(\min(y_i, Maximum_i), Minimum_i)$$

$$(3)$$

Table 7.7 allocates the model elements in the formulae above into the first four columns of database 5d.

Note that in many cases, the formulae for y_i will contain a lot of terms in which the slopes are simply 1, thereby simplifying the specification of dependencies considerably.

Table 7.7 Database 5d columns (model elements) for Beerwiser example

Destination	Driver	Slope	Operator
y_i	x_j	$x_{l(i,\,j)}$	*
y_i	y_k	$x_{m(j,\,k)}$	*
y_i	y_l	$y_{n(j,\,l)}$	*

If the calculation of the destination is more complicated than this, the user will have to do some programming. In the Operator column of database 5d they can then specify the operator as Other, and program the corresponding expression manually in Python or AIMMS. In that case, the advantage of not having to involve a programmer when using tRBS has to be sacrificed.

It is worth noting that the column named Maximum in database 5d often follows directly from the definition of the model element; e.g. the relative production cost reduction is by definition capped at 100 per cent. However, it can often be substantiated by using desk research as well. This is especially the case in the context of effects that result from investments for which saturation points, accessible population and probabilities of success have been defined in database 3b. Together they form the inputs to the calculation of effects of drivers on destinations. When this type of capping is applied, the Operator column in database 5d needs to be set to Squeezed*.These effects are calculated in case the dependency operator inserted in database 5d is Squeezed*. In that case the following formula is applied, where i refers to the driver that affects destination j:

$$\text{Direct effect}_{ij} = \text{Accessible population}_i * \text{Probability of success}_i$$
$$* \frac{\min(\text{Investment amount}_i, \text{Saturation Point}_i)}{\text{Saturation Point}_i} * \text{Maximum effect}_{ij}$$

For the Beerwiser example, there is no need for additional programming regarding the dependencies.

A capped or squeezed effect in the Beerwiser example is the effect that can be attained on water consumption reduction by investing in water recycling systems. We learnt that with the right device, 50 per cent of the waste water can be recycled (Appleyard, nd). We also learnt that investing in training can decrease safety-related incidents by a maximum of 48 per cent (Burke et al, 2006).

For the Beerwiser case, we have now completed database 5d, which has resulted in Table 7.8. Note that water use reduction and accidents reduction appear both as intermediate and as key outputs.

Validating simulation model

After the simulation model has been constructed via storing and processing all the information gathered in the foregoing steps of the decision-making process the simulation model can then be validated. The Responsible Business Simulator has several (visual) functionalities to help users with this. There is an option to review the dependencies visually, or users can also investigate key output scores, their appreciations, both in tabular and graphical format. Investigating sensitivities is an activity that users are encouraged to do as well.

Checking dependencies

Since Table 7.8 may seem rather technical, we have created dependencies graphs, generated by tRBS to visualize dependencies as programmed in the simulation model. Figure 7.5 shows the dependencies for the Beerwiser case. The thick arrows refer to links between drivers and destinations, and the thin arrows refer to links between slopes and destinations. Along the arrows it is stated which operator is used. The user can select a specific dependency graph for one single driver or destination as well, by clicking on the node corresponding to the output or intermediate of interest. Clicking on an arrow results in an overview of all data involved in the corresponding dependency.

The user may also perform a dependency check on circular definitions, and to see whether all model elements inserted into the database are used somewhere in the simulation model and – vice versa – whether

Table 7.8   Database 5d columns completed for Beerwiser example

Destination	Driver	Slope	Operator	Maximum effect
Accidents reduction %	Invest in training of employees	1	Squeezed *	0.48
Water use reduction % when effective	Invest in water recycling	1	Squeezed *	0.5
Water use reduction %	Water use reduction % when effective	Effectiveness water recycling	*	
Accidents reduction	Current # accidents	Accidents reduction %	*	
Water use reduction	Water use reduction %	Current water use	*	
Production cost reduction $	Invest in training of employees	1	-*	
Production cost reduction $	Invest in water recycling	1	-*	
Production cost reduction $	Water use reduction tmp	Water unit cost	*	
Production cost reduction $	Accidents reduction tmp	Cost of accident	*	
Production cost reduction	Production cost reduction $	Current production cost	/	
Cost of training per employee	Invest in training of employees	# employees	/	
New # accidents	Current # accidents	1	*	
New # accidents	Accidents reduction	1	-*	
New water use	Current water use	1	*	
New water use	Water use reduction	1	-*	

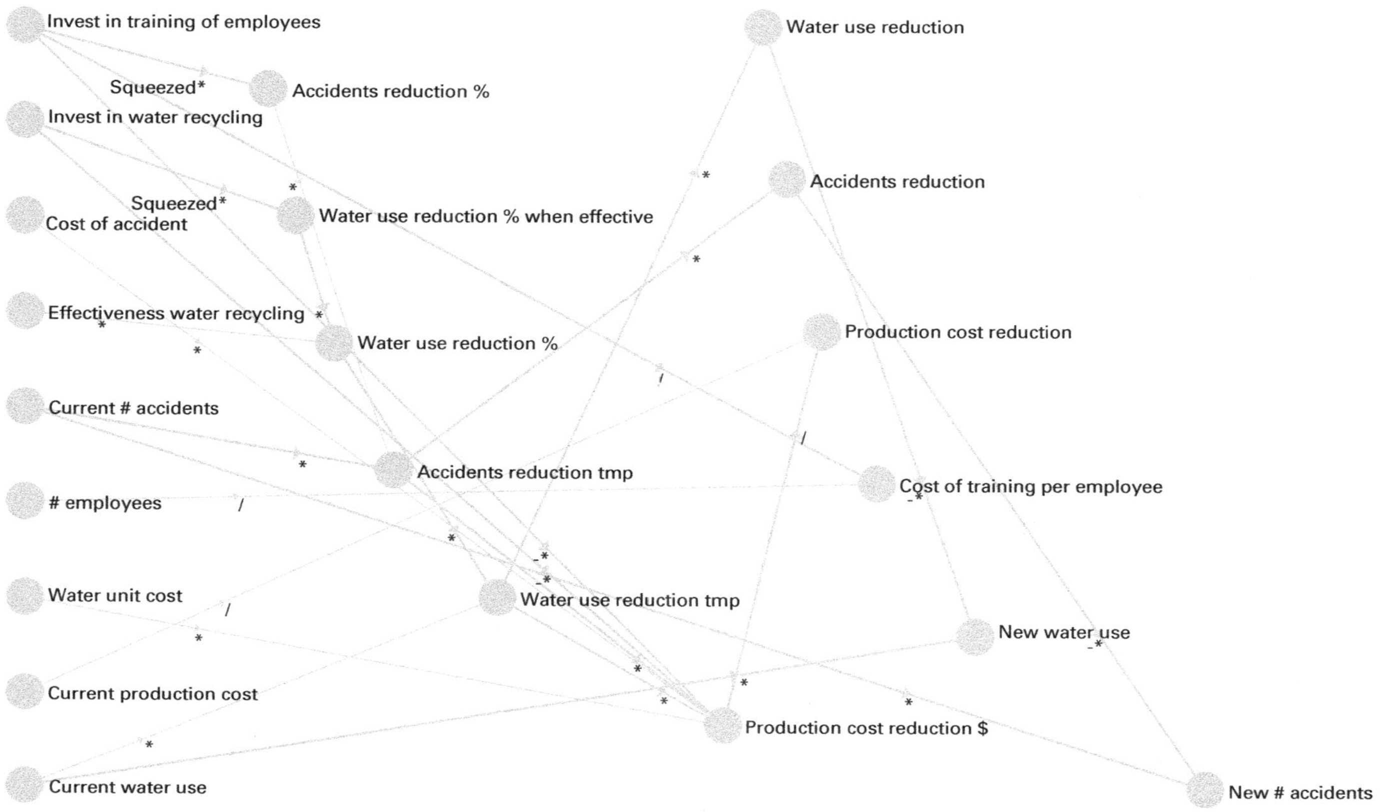

Figure 7.5 Dependencies as displayed in Step 5 of the strategic decision-making process for Beerwiser example

all model elements needed to compute other model elements are inputs or calculated from inputs. Some of these checks are already performed as warnings or blocking errors upon importing the database.

Comparing key outputs

A simple table containing all key output values and their appreciations for each decision maker's option and for each scenario is available as well.

Analysing sensitivities

Sensitivities can be used to understand graphically how a destination reacts upon changes in a driver via a so-called sensitivity curve. In this curve, the horizontal axis displays the driver value and the vertical axis displays the destination value. The curve itself indicates the sensitivity of the destination to changes in the driver.

To illustrate this, let us consider again our Beerwiser example. Suppose that, as a decision maker, we decided to invest in water recycling systems and that we want to know the direct effect of our investment on the water consumption reduction. In Step 3 we learnt that the accessible population and the probability of success are both 100 per cent. In Step 5 we learnt that with the right device, 50 per cent of the waste water can be recycled. The direct effect of our investment in water recycling systems therefore causes a reduction of water consumption of 100% × 100% × 50% = 50%. This implies that water consumption can be decreased by 50 per cent via this intervention.

This, however, is only the case if a decision maker invests the maximum effective amount or the saturation point. Based on company-specific information we learnt that the saturation point of investing in water recycling is $275,000. In this case, all Beerwiser's available water is recycled. Let us assume now that we only have an available budget of $250,000. The direct result would then be:

$$50\% \times (250{,}000/275{,}000) \cong 45\%$$

This is exactly what can be inferred from Figure 7.6, which shows this sensitivity curve for the Beerwiser example. On the horizontal axis the invested amount in water recycling is displayed. On the vertical axis the attainable reduction of the water consumption is shown without the factor of conservatism. The water consumption reduction varies from 0 per cent up to 50 per cent, and takes its maximum at the saturation point. Of course this example sensitivity curve is a fairly simple one because we specified it ourselves directly via the maximum effect and the saturation point. However, when one selects, for example, a fixed input as driver and a key output that is computed through a sequence of intermediates, the sensitivity curve often turns out to be non-linear. For large sensitivities one might rethink whether one is really sure about the value of this fixed input. If not, one might 'promote' the fixed input to an external variable input to test its effect on the optimal decision maker's option. The opposite may also happen: if one selects an external variable input as driver, and the sensitivity is quite flat for all key outputs, then one may 'demote' the external variable input to fixed input.

How to adjust the advanced settings of this sensitivity curve (minimum value and the maximum value as well as the number of points plotted in the sensitivity curve) is explained in the online user guides.

The sensitivity plot discussed so far allows the user to select one driver and one destination. It is also possible to inspect the sensitivity of the appreciations of all key outputs simultaneously for one selected

Figure 7.6 Sensitivity of 'water consumption reduction' to changes in 'invest in water recycling' for Beerwiser example

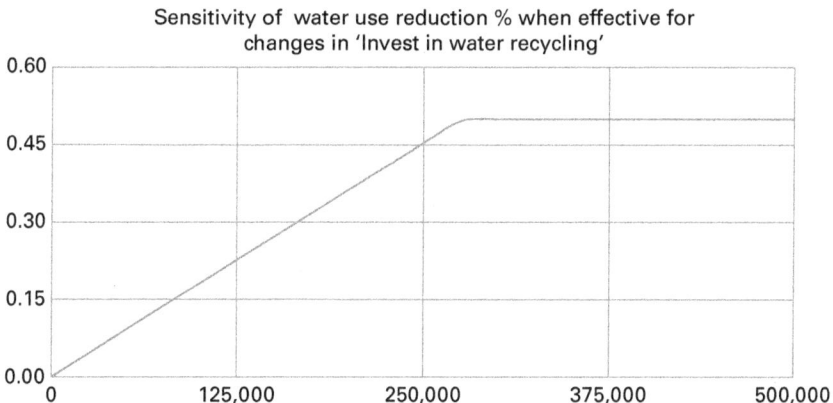

Sensitivity of water use reduction % when effective for changes in 'Invest in water recycling'

driver. This functionality makes it easy to find out which drivers primarily drive the key outputs.

Now that tRBS is specified and validated, the key output scores can be calculated and we can proceed to the selection of the best strategic choice. For that, two steps remain: assessing the strategic priorities (Step 6) and assessing the risk appetite of the decision maker (Step 7).

Step 6: evaluating options by assessing strategic priorities

Now that we have a validated simulation model that converts all inputs to outputs, we can study these outputs to compare the decision maker's options and select the best one.

Strategic priorities can be indicated by assigning weights to key outputs. Weights can be freely chosen and will be automatically calibrated and made mutually comparable (i.e. transformed to relative weights) in the back end. The Responsible Business Simulator also allows for assigning weights to themes. This depends on the set-up chosen when starting the modelling process. When assigning weights to themes, key output weights are used to determine how important a key output is within a theme. As described earlier in this chapter, key output weights can be altered in database 2b or in the GUI for Step 6 or in the summary page within tRBS. Extra information on the contribution of each output's appreciation to the overall appreciation per decision maker option is available in the GUI as well. Note that Step 6 focuses on comparing the decision maker's options for one selected scenario.

Optimization is an additional feature that enables the decision maker to let tRBS determine an optimal combination of settings for internal variable inputs. This presumes a predefined scenario and predefined strategic priorities. The pre-programmed (constrained) optimization engine currently only works when all internal variable inputs represent investments. All the decision maker needs to do is to insert the maximum amount of total investment. The optimization engine will then search for a breakdown of this maximum investment over the

Figure 7.7 Comparison of decision maker's options when more focus is put on reduction of accidents in the base-case scenario for Beerwiser example

Total appreciation

☐ Water use reduction ☐ Accidents reduction ▨ Production cost reduction

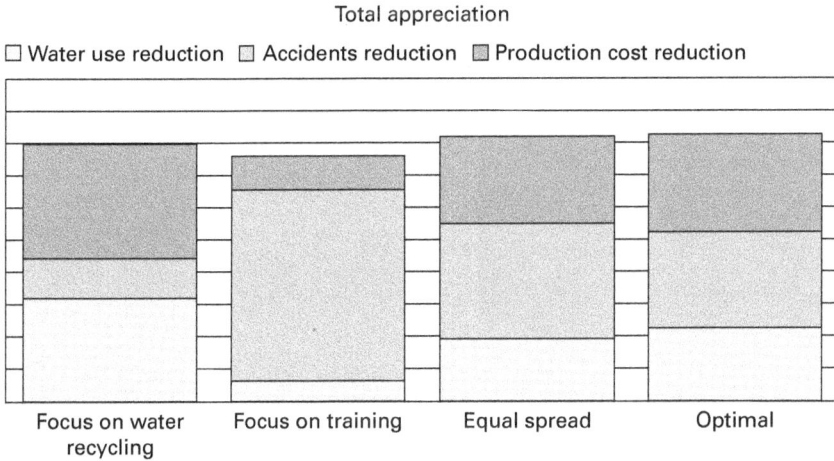

Focus on water recycling   Focus on training   Equal spread   Optimal

internal variable inputs such that the total appreciation is maximized. The decision maker's option in which this breakdown is stored is called Optimal by default. How to calibrate the solver and create logs of the optimization process is explained in the online user guides.

For the Beerwiser case, Figure 7.7 shows the comparison of the three options that we defined ourselves, plus the Optimal option calculated by tRBS for the neutral scenario when the weights assigned to reduction of accidents, reduction of water use and reduction of production costs are 2, 1 and 1 respectively. In this case the optimal decision maker's option slightly outperforms the integrated approach, by spending $124,170.70 on training and $175,829.30 on water recycling. This setting is only optimal for this specific strategic priority setting and in the base-case scenario. How it performs under other scenarios will be the subject of the next section.

Step 7: evaluating options by assessing risk appetite

In the previous step, we kept all external factors fixed in one scenario. Now we want to go one step further and understand the impact of different scenarios, which allows us to compare the decision maker's options, including variations in external factors.

Analogous to Step 6, in which weights are assigned to key outputs to reflect strategic priorities, risk appetite can be indicated by assigning weights to scenarios. The scenario weights depend on the risk appetite of the decision maker, who might have a high or low risk appetite, or may be neutral in this respect. As described in Step 4, scenario weights can be altered in database 4c or via the GUI for Step 7. The best option depends on the decision maker's risk appetite.

Figure 7.8 illustrates this for the Beerwiser case. In the optimistic scenario, the focus on water recycling option scores best, because in that scenario less cost for accidents is expected, and therefore the return on investment in training to avoid accidents is smaller. In this scenario, the effect of water recycling is also deemed higher. In the pessimistic scenario it is better to focus on training followed by the equal spread option. Here, the effect of training is higher because of the high expected costs of accidents.

In order to identify a robust scenario, the decision maker can search for an option that performs well when accounting for all scenarios. The decision maker can assign weights to the scenarios and let tRBS calculate one aggregated score per option over the scenarios.

Figure 7.8 Comparison of decision maker's options when more focus is put on reduction of accidents for all scenarios for Beerwiser example

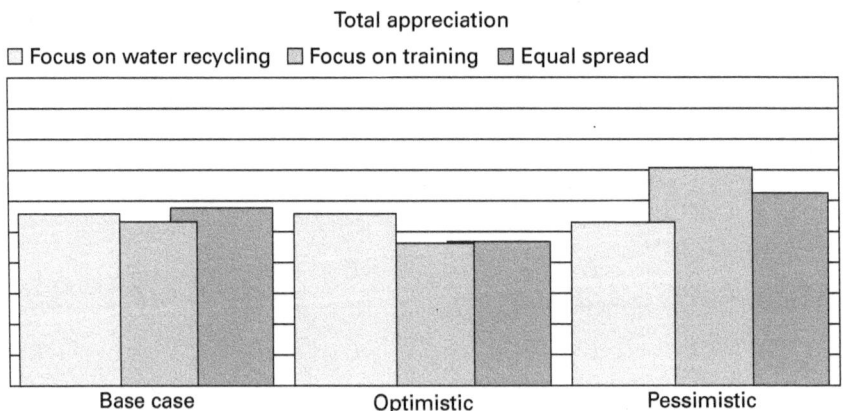

Total appreciation
□ Focus on water recycling ■ Focus on training ■ Equal spread

Base case   Optimistic   Pessimistic

Figure 7.9 Comparison of decision maker's options when all scenarios have equal weights for Beerwiser example

Total appreciation

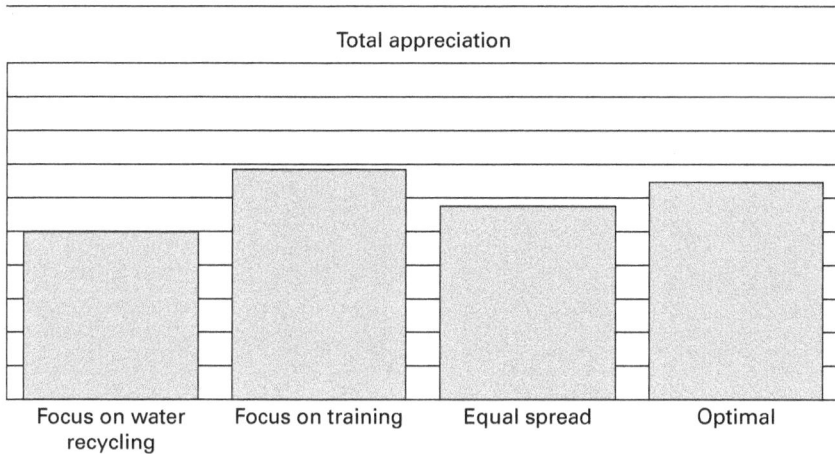

| Focus on water recycling | Focus on training | Equal spread | Optimal |

This means that we aggregate the scenarios based on the weight that is assigned to them and then conclude what the best option is.

For the Beerwiser case, if the decision maker looks for a robust option in the sense that they put equal weights to all three scenarios, then it turns out that the focus on training would be the winning option, as shown in Figure 7.9.

References

Appleyard, D (nd) Brewing up change in water treatment technology, *Waste & water International*, www.waterworld.com/articles/wwi/print/volume-29/issue-1/technology-case-studies/industrial-water-treatment/brewing-up-change-in-water-treatment-technology.html (archived at https://perma.cc/8YAF-W8Z5)

Burke, MJ, Sarpy, SA, Smith-Crowe, K, Chan-Serafin, C, Salvador, RO and Islam, G (2006) Relative effectiveness of worker safety and health training methods, *American Journal of Public Health*, **96** (2), 315–24

Every little drop (nd) The Cost of Water, everylittledrop.com.au/knowledge-center/the-cost-of-water/ (archived at https://perma.cc/SM4K-7WTY)

Kingman, JF (1992) *Poisson processes*, Clarendon Press, Oxford

Mikosh, T (2008) *Elementary Stochastic Calculus with Finance in View*, World Scientific Publishing, Singapore

Roth, B (2016) As safety accidents increase, so do conversations about safety, *All About Beer Magazine*, allaboutbeer.com/brewery-safety/ (archived at https://perma.cc/9VRW-NKAU)

Ulam, S, Richtmyer, D and Neumann, J v (1947) Statistical methods in neutron diffusion, *LAMS-551*

Vose, D (2000) *Risk Analysis: A quantitative guide*, John Wiley & Sons Ltd, West Sussex

PART THREE
Practical applications

Using SDGs to develop and deliver professional services

08

The UN Sustainable Development Goals (SDGs) were established in 2015 and define global priorities and aspirational goals for the year 2030. They seek to mobilize global efforts around a common set of goals and targets and call for worldwide action among governments, businesses and societies to end poverty and create a life of dignity and opportunity for all, within the boundaries of the planet (SDG Compass, 2015). In the publication *State of Progress: Business contributions to the SDGs* (Global Reporting Initiative (GRI), 2022), GRI and Support the Goals evaluated over 200 companies worldwide and found that four out of five companies assessed in 2020 included a commitment to the SDGs in their sustainability reports, yet fewer than half set measurable targets for how their actions would contribute towards fulfilling the goals:

- 83 per cent state that they support the SDGs, recognizing the value of aligning their reports with the goals.

- 69 per cent of companies articulate which goals are most relevant to their business, with 61 per cent specifying how their actions support the SDGs.

- 40 per cent of companies set measurable commitments for how they will help achieve the SDGs, while 20 per cent include evidence to assess their positive impacts.

This chapter illustrates how the Responsible Business Simulator (tRBS) was used to gather insights into PwC's performance against the Sustainable Development Goals. The main challenge for PwC was how to measure their current impact against SDGs, then implement appropriate actions to achieve its strategic objective. We will therefore start by introducing PwC in the context of its organization's strategic objective: 'to build trust and solve important problems'. Then we address the issue of 'wicked problems' and how SDGs can be used to meet PwC's challenges. Next, we show how tRBS was applied to fit PwC's case, and how data was applied to create transparency and generate the insights necessary to guide the business going forward.

About PwC

PwC is an international professional services group of firms, operating as partnerships under the PwC brand. The organization offers clients a range of professional business services, including accounting, tax, and strategy or management consulting. It is among the largest professional services firms in the world, and considered one of the Big Four accounting firms along with Deloitte, EY and KPMG. At the time of writing, PwC employs over 300,000 people across 688 cities in 152 countries and realized a global revenue of $50.3 billion in 2021 (PwC, 2022a).

PwC's objective is 'to build trust in society and solve important problems'. PwC Netherlands (PwC NL) considers the SDGs to be in line with its objective as well as supportive of its ambition to become a purpose-led and values-driven organization, and links the SDGs to policies and activities (PwC, 2022b). It is exactly within this context that PwC NL has applied tRBS, using it to provide insights into PwC's contribution to achieving the SDGs. Currently, they measure the impact of their business operations on achieving the SDGs and report on the outcomes in their annual report. These outcomes form the basis for a dialogue on policies, activities and next steps.

Wicked problems and SDGs

Environmental, social and governance (ESG) issues such as anthropogenic climate collapse, exponential biodiversity loss and failing global gender equity or justice mechanisms, are becoming increasingly relevant in both the public and private arenas, as well as in political debate (United Nations, 2015). This set of interconnected ESG challenges are described as wicked problems: problems which are difficult or impossible to solve because of their complex and interconnected nature, and which are characterized by incomplete, contradictory and unstable requirements under ever-increasing time pressures (Marshall, 2008: Rittel and Webber, 1973). In *Principles of Sustainable Business*, the authors have made an extensive analysis of how SDGs can be used as a framework for resolving wicked problems and corporate actions (van Tulder and van Mil, 2023). It is in this context that decision makers face the most difficult challenge; deciding the future direction of their organization, the economy or society at large (Hák et al, 2012). The decision makers' first requirement is a metric with which to measure the degree of sustainability within their processes, products, services, organizations or institutions. These metrics of sustainability are needed to assess progress, encourage participation, assess trade-offs, meet or anticipate new requirements, reward excellence or confer benefits.

Across the academic, public and private sectors, however, there is no consensus on the definition and scope of *sustainability measurement*. Instead, it has been left to politicians to define its parameters, thus excluding any measures other than the political or economic. Moreover, sustainability metrics are still in their infancy, and are primarily focused on physical processes associated with product creation, rather than on services provided. These metrics are typically indicators, benchmarks, audits, sustainability standards and certification systems like Fairtrade, indices and accounting, as well as assessment, appraisal and other reporting systems, and are applied over a wide range of spatial and temporal scales.

Recognizing the wickedness of ESG issues as well as the disputes surrounding definition and scope, the SDGs represent a holistic approach to sustainable development. They are widely recognized as encompassing the interdependence of human and natural systems. Combined with the standardized, target-focused and uncontested definitions of sustainable development provided by the SDGs (as opposed to ESG metrics that are not globally standardized and process-focused), this recognition has resulted in roughly 40 per cent of the world's biggest companies currently adopting the SDGs in (part of) their reporting processes (McKenzie, 2021; LexisNexis, 2021). This includes organizations like ING, Heineken, Pfizer, Samsung, Telefónica, Triodos and Vodafone.

The SDGs are a collection of 17 interlinked global goals designed to be a blueprint to achieve a better and more sustainable future for all (United Nations, 2017). The SDGs, established in 2015 by the General Assembly of the United Nations, are intended to be achieved by 2030.

The 17 SDGs

1 No poverty

2 Zero hunger

3 Good health and wellbeing

4 Quality education

5 Gender equality

6 Clean water and sanitation

7 Affordable and clean energy

8 Decent work and economic growth

9 Industry innovation and infrastructure

10 Reduced inequalities

11 Sustainable cities and communities

12 Responsible consumption and production

13 Climate action

14 Life below water

15 Life on land

16 Peace, justice and strong institutions

17 Partnerships for the goals

SOURCE United Nations, 2022

The goals are broad and interdependent, and in 2017 they were made more 'actionable' by a UN Resolution adopted by the General Assembly (UN, 2017). The Resolution identifies specific targets for each goal, along with indicators to measure progress towards each target. The year by which the target is meant to be achieved is usually between 2020 and 2030. For some of the targets, no end date is given.

The strategic decision-making process

PwC strives to look beyond financial results only. The organization seeks to integrate financial and non-financial insights to steer and report on them, and the SDG framework is being used to facilitate this transformation, as all 17 goals can be classified into the People, Planet or Profit (PPP) category. The Responsible Business Simulator was used to put the SDGs into operation for PwC.

The results of applying tRBS are insights into the financial and non-financial performance of the company as a whole, in the form of positive, neutral or negative impacts. Therefore, it was extremely important to incorporate all the areas in which PwC is active. This led to the involvement of various internal stakeholders drawn from across the firm who would provide input into strategic dialogues and facilitate the data collection process. With the help of these stakeholders and decision makers, we measured the impact of over 34 indicators (and over 200 sub-indicators), the results of which have been shared in PwC's annual report on a yearly basis since 2021 as 'SDG Impact Measurement'. The Board as well as individual departments use the insights for steering purposes. In the following section we take a deep dive into the steps that were taken to get to these results.

Describing the strategic challenge that requires a decision

As PwC's strategic objective is to build trust in society and solve important problems, the decision makers in this case (board of management, the chief sustainability officer and the transformation lead) wanted to have insights into and be totally transparent about PwC's contribution to society. Based on these insights steering decisions were made. The decision makers were well aware that 'objective' goes beyond solely profit-related elements and has a much broader perspective. The SDG framework can give meaning to this because it encompasses all PPP criteria. For reasons of efficiency, it was decided that the impact measurement would consider the nine most relevant and material SDGs, of which four would form the main focus. The process of selecting the SDGs on which to focus is outside the scope of this case study, but PwC's methodology can be found on their website (PwC, 2022d) In 2022, the SDGs selected were (focus goals in bold):

- SDG4: quality education
- **SDG5: gender equality**
- SDG7: affordable and clean energy
- **SDG8: decent work and economic growth**
- **SDG10: reduced inequalities**
- SDG12: responsible consumption and production
- **SDG13: climate action**
- SDG16: peace, justice and strong institutions
- SDG17: partnerships for the goals

The decision makers used the results of the SDG impact measurement to evaluate their performance on (non-)financial indicators and to enter into strategic dialogue with the business units about the areas that required most attention. The strategic challenge for PwC was formulated as follows: 'How to increase our contribution to the SDGs throughout the organization.'

The strategic challenge that we address in this chapter is primarily internally focused. Consequently, this resulted in a longlist of relevant internal stakeholders, as many internal departments as well as the leads of many industries and services were involved.

Defining key outputs involving stakeholders

To reflect PwC's SDG impact, the key outputs had to cover the most important elements of the business. For a company that has substantial activities across many services and industries it was crucial to formulate key outputs that represented the entire organization. It was also important to find a balance in terms of the number of key outputs, as too few might miss important insights while too many might slow down the key output selection and the data collection process, as well as the guidance and improvement process after the impact is measured.

Therefore, Step 2 of the seven-step framework (selecting and defining the key outputs) was a crucial step. Apart from the overview of targets as adopted by the General Assembly, the UN provides no specific guidelines on how to measure an organization's progress or contribution to the SDGs. Hence, as a starting point we collected all available key performance indicators or key outputs that represented the relevant targets associated with PwC's relevant SDGs (United Nations, 2017). The longlist consisted of over 300 key outputs set by reliable organizations such as the Global Reporting Initiative (GRI), Organisation for Economic Co-operation and Development (OECD) and World Economic Forum (WEF). As this was a generic list, not specifically designed for PwC, we worked with internal PwC experts to convert these general key outputs into customized key outputs with definitions that suited PwC's operations as well as the industries and services in which the business operates. The longlist of 300 key output definitions was reduced to a shortlist by scoring each key output against the following five criteria:

1 relevance of the key output for PwC
2 contribution of the key output to one of the nine selected SDGs

3 influenceability of PwC on the key output

4 independence between the selected key outputs

5 availability of data to measure the key output

In collaboration with the stakeholders and internal experts, scores were assigned to each criterion. The stakeholders provided input on their relevance and the experts on the data availability. One of our aims in selecting the final shortlist was to ensure that the key outputs represented PwC in its totality, and showed both the positive and the negative impacts of the company's actions. Involving multiple stakeholders from different departments of the business made it possible to get a representative set, and approaching the key outputs from the SDGs and their targets made it possible to include the most relevant indicators without pre-judging how PwC would score against them, and selecting only those SDGs against which PwC performs well.

This resulted in a pre-shortlist which was approved by the Board. The shortlist consisted of 34 key outputs which are shown in Table 8.1.

Table 8.1   Overview of key outputs per SDG

SDG	Key Output	Definition
4	Training equality	Average training hours per FTE of female colleagues over average hours of training per FTE of male colleagues (#)
	Training hours	Average training hours per FTE by job level (#)
	Education through PwC Academy	Total hours booked on design, development and delivery of education to clients through the PwC Academy (#)
	Evaluation score PwC Academy training	Average evaluation score of clients on education delivered through the PwC Academy (#)
	Academic education	Number of PwC colleagues officially registered as teacher at academic educational institutions (#)
	Engagement contribution to education	Total number of hours booked on (job) engagements for clients in the education sector (#)

(continued)

Table 8.1 (Continued)

SDG	Key Output	Definition
5	Gender pay gap	1. Difference in average salary between male and female colleagues (by job level) over average salary male colleagues (#) 2. Difference in average bonus between male and female colleagues (by job level) over average bonus male colleagues (#)
	People Engagement Index (PEI)	PEI female colleagues over PEI male colleagues (by job level) (#)
	Gender diversity	1. Female colleagues in the workforce over total workforce (by job level) (%) 2. Intake female colleagues over total intake (by job level) (%) 3. Employee turnover female colleagues over employee turnover male colleagues (by job level) (#) 4. Promotion rate female colleagues over promotion rate male colleagues (by job level) (#)
	Gender diversity in leadership	Female members of the Board of Management and Supervisory Board over total number of members in Board of Management and Supervisory Board (%) Female partners over total number of partners (%)
	Gender diversity in (job) engagement teams	Percentage of female colleagues on (job) engagements (%)
7	Energy efficiency	Energy efficiency in buildings (in kWh per m2) Building energy (heat, gas, electricity) use per m2 during the reporting period
	Renewable energy use	Energy sourced from renewable sources (e.g. biomass, geothermal, solar, water and wind energy sources) either purchased or self-generated as a percentage of total energy consumption (%)
	Renewable electricity generation	Percentage of total electricity use covered by renewable electricity generated by PwC (%)
	Renewable electricity use	Percentage of total electricity use that is sourced from renewables either purchased or self-generated *Definition of renewable electricity according to RE100 requirements*

(continued)

Table 8.1 (Continued)

SDG	Key Output	Definition
8	Financial results	Average yearly revenue growth per FTE over the past three reporting periods (%)
	Wellbeing	Wellbeing by gender, job level and cultural background: 1. Percentage of sick leave (%) 2. Percentage of colleagues with a favourable score* on the four PEI-related questions in the Global People Survey (GPS) (%) 3. Percentage of colleagues with a favourable score* on the seven flexibility and wellbeing related questions in the GPS (%) * favourable score is 4 or 5
	Digitization and innovation	1. Intake of colleagues with STEM (science, technology, engineering and mathematics) profile (%) 2. Revenue obtained by wide applicable digital assets (in type 1 and type 2a) [UN Target 8.2]
	People involved in corporate sustainability (CS) projects	1. Hours booked on pro bono engagements (jobs) for social enterprises (and other organizations with the goal to create shared value [social, ecological and economic]) (#) 2. Colleagues involved in engagements (jobs) for social enterprises (and other organizations with the goal to create shared value [social, ecological and economic]) as a percentage of the total number of colleagues (%)
10	Global People Survey (GPS) scores Inclusion & Diversity (I&D)	Percentage of colleagues with a favourable score on I&D in one group* over percentage colleagues with a favourable score on I&D in other groups for the following categories: 1. Job level (#) 2. Cultural background (#) 3. Age group (#) 4. Sexual orientation (#) * favourable score is 4 or 5

(continued)

Table 8.1 (Continued)

SDG	Key Output	Definition
	Cultural diversity	1. Colleagues by cultural background over total workforce (by job level) (%) 2. Intake of colleagues by cultural background over total intake (by job level) (%) 3. Equality in employee turnover between colleagues with different cultural backgrounds (by job level) (#) 4. Equality in promotion rate between colleagues with different cultural backgrounds (by job level) (#)
12	Supplier science-based targets	Percentage of our suppliers that have science-based targets for emissions reduction
13	GHG emissions	1. Scope 1: Direct emissions from owned/controlled operations (tCO_2e) 2. Scope 2: Indirect emissions from the use of purchased electricity, steam, heating and cooling (tCO_2e) 3. Scope 3: Indirect upstream and downstream emissions (tCO_2e)
	Carbon offsetting and removals	1. Carbon offsetting (%): Total GHG emissions offset by PwC NL as a percentage of total GHG emissions emitted 2. Carbon removal offsetting (%): Total GHG emissions offset by PwC NL through removals as a percentage of total GHG emissions emitted
	Environmental spend	Environmental spend as a percentage of internal carbon pricing (%)
	Taking Action on environmental impact	GPS score on Taking Action on environmental impact
16	Integrity	1. Complaints filed to the Complaints Committee (#) 2. Notifications submitted to the Business Conduct Committee (#)
	GPS score leadership effectiveness (transparency)	Percentage of colleagues with a favourable score* on the question 'The leaders I work with make a point of being transparent with information' in the GPS (%) * favourable score is 4 or 5

(continued)

Table 8.1   (Continued)

SDG	Key Output	Definition
	Reputation	Percentage of favourable media coverage for PwC NL (%)
	Stakeholder dialogue on purpose	Percentage of stakeholders that consider PwC contribute to a large or very large extent to its objective (%)
17	Number of social enterprises supported	Number of pro bono engagements for social enterprises (and other organizations with the goal to create shared value [social, ecological and economic]) (#)
	Sponsorships by PwC	1. Number of sponsorship agreements (#) 2. Total contractual value of all sponsorship agreements (€) 3. Percentage of long-term (at least three years) sponsorships (%)
	Investing in financial, volunteering and pro bono services	GPS score on investing in financial, volunteering and pro bono services
	Thought leadership and partnership to help solve important problems	GPS score on thought leadership and partnership to help solve important problems

Constructing the simulation model

After defining the key outputs, tRBS constructed the model. In the case of PwC, there were no decision maker's options or scenarios formulated, as policies and activities would be developed later on, based on the outcomes and relevant dialogues. The focus of this impact measurement case study was on the process of calculating key outputs, comparing them to a threshold, calculating an overall impact score per SDG, and developing a meaningful dialogue on the results afterwards.

Before evaluating the results of the calculation, let us consider how the model was constructed.

Setting thresholds

PwC explicitly requested a transparent impact measurement process in which positive, neutral and negative contributions were all incorporated. This means that for all key outputs, thresholds were set so that for each key output value it could be determined whether the result contributed positively, neutrally or negatively to a certain SDG.

To develop these thresholds for each indicator, a three-step approach, as visualized in Figure 8.1, was developed.

The thresholds developed, from the most to the least preferable, were:

1 The first and most preferred threshold was based on the absolute, quantitative threshold presented in the SDG itself or its sub-targets. For example, SDG 5 aims to 'achieve gender equality by ending all forms of discrimination, violence and any harmful practices against women and girls in the public and private spheres' (Eurostat, 2022). When comparing the salaries of male and female employees within this context, it can be concluded that anything other than equal pay for equal work is discriminatory and therefore has a negative impact.

2 If the SDGs do not directly imply a quantitative threshold, then another external source must be used to set thresholds. This source may be informed by SDGs, but this is not a requirement. For example, SDG 13.2 states that entities must 'integrate climate change measures into national policies, strategies and planning'. This is not enough to set a threshold. In PwC's case, we used information from the Science Based Targets Initiative (SBTI) (Science Based Targets, 2019). As the name implies, this is an initiative that uses science to provide a clearly defined pathway for companies to reduce emissions in line with scientific models. Current models state that emissions must reach net zero no later than 2050. Therefore, the threshold relating to CO_2 emissions was set at net zero, as this is the desired state.

Figure 8.1 Three-step approach to establishing thresholds

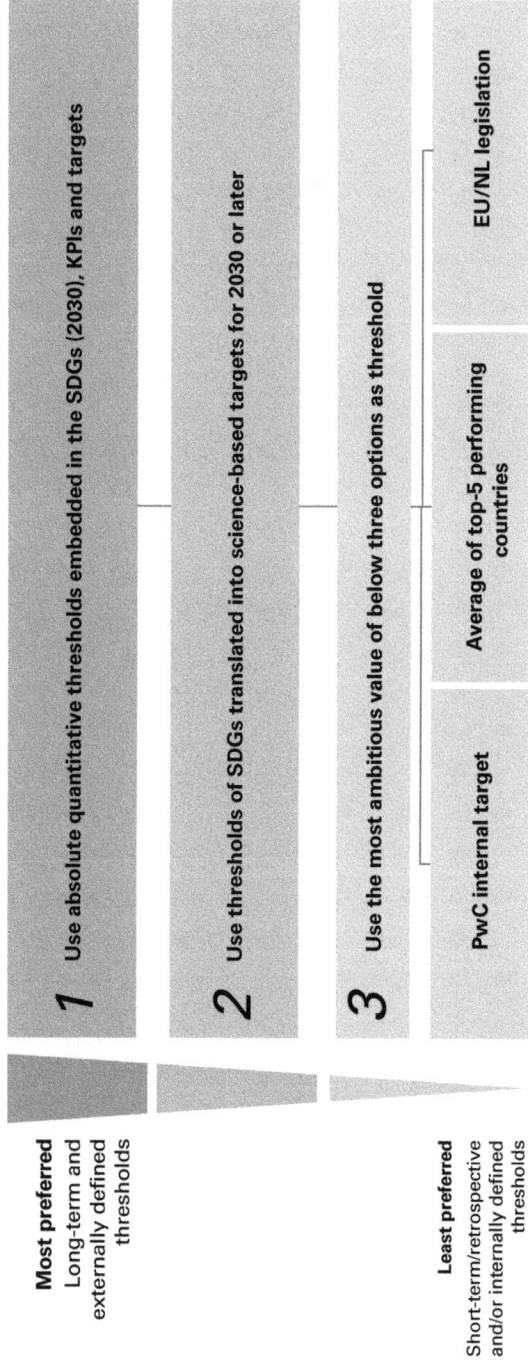

Most preferred
Long-term and externally defined thresholds

1 Use absolute quantitative thresholds embedded in the SDGs (2030), KPIs and targets

2 Use thresholds of SDGs translated into science-based targets for 2030 or later

3 Use the most ambitious value of below three options as threshold

PwC internal target

Average of top-5 performing countries

EU/NL legislation

Least preferred
Short-term/retrospective and/or internally defined thresholds

3 If setting thresholds through externally, science-based sources is also not possible, the final step can be used. In this third step, three different values were researched, of which the most ambitious value is accepted. The values used in this case were: (a) PwC's internal targets on the selected SDG, KPI or target; (b) the average from the top five best-performing countries based on the latest Sustainable Development Report; and (c) EU or NL legislation on the topic. This step was used, for example, in the calculation of training hours (SDG 4). Legislation states that at least 40 hours/year must be spent on education; the top five countries had values around 15 hours/year; and PwC NL does not have a target per function level. Therefore, the threshold for this indicator was placed at 40 hours.

Drawing up curves

Once all thresholds were set, the appreciation curves could be further defined. Appreciation curves for impact measurement differ slightly from the appreciation curves discussed in Chapters 5 and 7 as they allow for negative, neutral and positive appreciations. The values of the key outputs are therefore not standardized into a score between 0 and 100, but the standardized score ranges from –100 to 100. To draw the appreciation curves, the direction, shape, minimum value and maximum value have to be determined per key output.

For example, we wanted to highlight a key output formulated for SDG 12: Percentage of suppliers that have science-based targets for emissions reduction. We had set a threshold of 50 per cent, in line with the science-based target. The impact would be negative if the percentage was lower than 50 per cent and positive if the key output value exceeded 50 per cent. This implies a 'larger the better' curve, as a higher percentage leads to higher appreciation.

Now we needed to determine whether the shape of the curve was linear or non-linear. In this example it was linear since each increase in percentage is appreciated the same. The appreciation graph therefore looks like an upward sloping straight line, represented in Figure 8.2 by the red line. In order to map the values of the key output to the

Figure 8.2   Appreciation curve percentage of suppliers that have science-based targets for emissions reduction

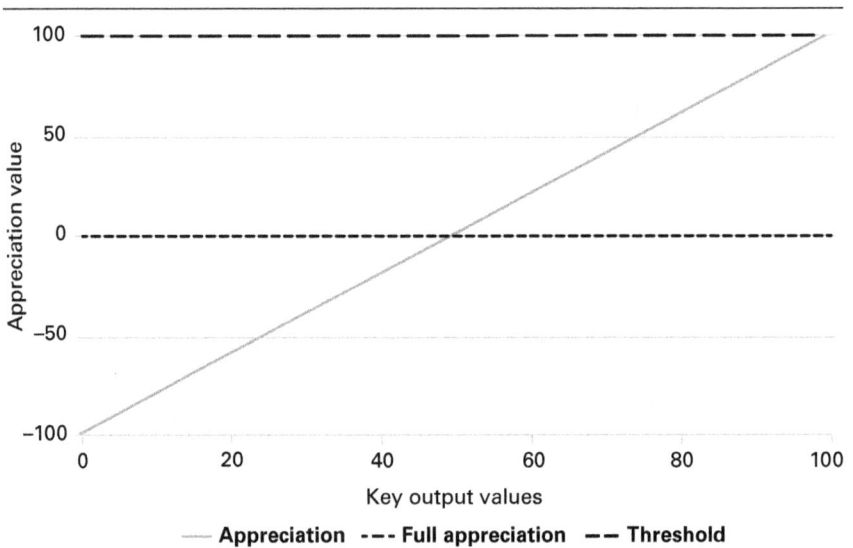

standardized scores we needed to set a minimum and a maximum value. In this case the minimum value was set at zero, and at this value appreciation was the lowest. The maximum value was set at 100, the highest percentage attainable.

Note that even though we draw a full graph, the impact attained is mapped onto three outcomes: positive (>50%), negative (<50%) or neutral (=50%).

Using comprehensive desk research and in collaboration with experts and stakeholders, the thresholds and appreciation functions were set following the above steps.

Dependencies

As can be seen earlier in Table 8.1, with the exception of SDG 12, each SDG consisted of multiple key outputs. In order to determine to what extent the impact of PwC on each SDG was positive, negative or neutral, these key outputs need to be aggregated. In this case we gave each key output equal weight.

For example, SDG 8 consisted of the key outputs: Financial results, Wellbeing, Digitization and innovation, and People involved in CS projects. They all got a weight of 1 when aggregating.

Many key outputs consisted of multiple underlying indicators, so called sub-key outputs. These were assigned equal weights as well. For example, key output Wellbeing (in SDG 8) was calculated by aggregating:

- percentage of sick leave (%)
- percentage of colleagues with a favourable score on the four People Engagement Index (PEI)-related questions in the Global People Survey (GPS) (%)
- percentage of colleagues with a favourable score on the seven flexibility and wellbeing-related questions in GPS (%)

evaluated by gender, job level and cultural background.

Weights were assigned based on the sub-key output with the largest number of indicators, in this case, sub-key outputs 2 and 3. Sub-key output 1, percentage of sick leave, was evaluated only by gender and cultural background, while sub-key outputs 2 and 3 were also evaluated by job level.

Job level was divided into five categories, cultural background into three and gender into two. (There are three categories of gender: male/female/nonbinary. As the n of nonbinary is too low to be included in the calculation, we work only with the categories male and female.) Job level is therefore leading to determine weights. Weights were then calculated based on this largest number. Let's take a look at the percentage of colleagues with a favourable score on PEI-related questions in GPS:

- function level consists of five categories, with each category having weight 1; this results in a total of $5 \times 1 = 5$
- gender consists of two categories, with each category having weight 5/2; this results in a total of $2 \times (5/2) = 5$
- cultural background consists of three categories, with each category having weight 5/3; this results in a total of $3 \times (5/3) = 5$
- the total weight = $5 + 5 + 5 = 15$

Using this analogy we obtained the same weights for percentage of colleagues with a favourable score on the seven flexibility- and well-being-related questions in GPS and calculated the weight of percentage of sick leave as follows:

- gender consists of two categories, and each category has a weight of $(15/2)/2 = 3.75$; this results in a total of $2 \times 3.75 = 7.5$
- cultural background consists of three categories, and each category has a weight of $(15/2)/3 = 2.5$; this results in a total of $3 \times 2.5 = 7.5$
- total weight $= 7.5 + 7.5 = 15$

Results

After setting the thresholds, drawing up curves and aggregating the key outputs, the data was collected, and the impact calculated for each SDG. The results for each material SDG are displayed in Figure 8.3. For each SDG the impact can be identified as positive, negative, neutral or not calculated. 'Not calculated' means that we document the key output value, but that there is no threshold set. This is, for example, the case for SDG 16: there was no threshold set for the number of complaints filed to the Complaints Committee. The reason for this is that it is hard to establish an optimal number of complaints. Zero complaints might sound optimal but might also indicate that people do not feel free to speak freely rather than the fact that there are no complaints.

When interpreting the results, it is important to keep in mind the aggregation as explained in the previous paragraph. For example, SDG 12 consisted of only one key output: the percentage of suppliers that have science-based targets for emissions reduction. With the threshold set to 50 per cent – an SBTI target – and a current value of 16 per cent of suppliers with science-based targets, the impact on SDG 12 was fully negative. When more key outputs are allocated to an SDG, for example SDG 4 that has six key outputs and more sub-key outputs, a negative value on one key output and positive values on other key outputs immediately looks less extreme. PwC could

Figure 8.3　SDG impact measurement results

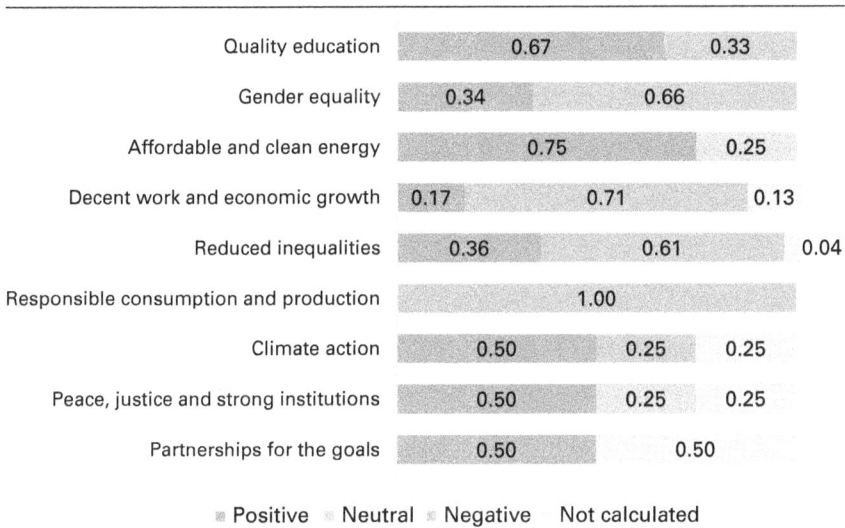

	Positive	Neutral	Negative	Not calculated
Quality education	0.67		0.33	
Gender equality	0.34	0.66		
Affordable and clean energy	0.75		0.25	
Decent work and economic growth	0.17	0.71	0.13	
Reduced inequalities	0.36	0.61		0.04
Responsible consumption and production	1.00			
Climate action	0.50	0.25	0.25	
Peace, justice and strong institutions	0.50	0.25	0.25	
Partnerships for the goals	0.50	0.50		

■ Positive　Neutral　■ Negative　Not calculated

have easily added a key output to SDG 12 where it had a positive impact to make results look better, but decided not to.

The other SDG that has a more negative than positive impact is SDG 8, Decent work and economic growth. SDG 8 consists of Average revenue growth, Wellbeing, Digitization and innovation, and Supporting social enterprises. In the latter two categories PwC performed no better than the thresholds it set for itself. Here again, PwC could have adjusted thresholds as there are no SDG thresholds or science-based targets available, but again decided to be ambitious. The rationale behind this strict approach is that PwC has set its ambitions for 2030, and against that perspective, we could say they are on the right track.

We commend PwC for being this open and for adhering strictly to its genuine, actual results, especially in times when greenwashing is commonly practised by large organizations.

In conclusion, current results indicate that PwC's contribution to achieving the SDGs is not (yet) fully positive for any material or focus SDG. PwC's impact is mainly positive on SDGs 4, 7, 13 and 16, while the other SDGs require more attention. Based on this information PwC can annually evaluate its policies and formulate its future activities.

Reflections

The results of this research have been published in PwC's 2020 and 2021 Annual Reports (PwC, 2021; PwC, 2022c) and will be replicated each reporting year. These results provide insights for PwC's Board to help them make the right decisions to execute their strategy. PwC can therefore be called a true frontrunner because of this level of transparent and integrated reporting.

The Corporate Sustainability Reporting Directive (CSRD) was adopted on 10 November 2022 (European Parliament, 2022). It is an EU law that requires large companies to disclose information related to ESG indicators. This development confirms the relevance of this way of reporting and this (type of) legislation can catalyse organizations' contributions to the SDGs.

Since the current focus has been on the operations of PwC, we see an opportunity to include the impact of PwC's service delivery into the SDG impact measurement. This is something we recommended, and since then PwC have started to develop an approach to implement the recommendation. What is good to know is that *indirect impact* is becoming increasingly important and often has a much larger impact than direct impact (Impact Institute, 2022; Metabolic, 2018). This implies *chain responsibility* throughout the whole service delivery chain, and because of the increasing complexity of value chains, both upstream and downstream segments should be evaluated. In this analysis we only evaluated the number of suppliers with science-based targets, but obviously its indirect impact is larger than that and definitely worth looking into.

In addition, current analysis and results will be more meaningful when the actual extent of the impact is measured, rather than just whether it is positive, negative or neutral, and this is on PwC's wish list for future development.

The application of the Responsible Business Simulator in this way shows the flexibility of the framework. Going forward, it will be valuable for the business to move from reporting to decision making and adding Steps 3, 4, 6 and 7 to the research. This would enable PwC to develop a strategy based on the impact of its actions, and underpin its decisions by quantitative measures.

References

European Parliament (2022) Sustainable economy: Parliament adopts new reporting rules for multinationals, www.europarl.europa.eu/news/en/press-room/20221107IPR49611/sustainable-economy-parliament-adopts-new-reporting-rules-for-multinationals (archived at https://perma.cc/PS55-YBYR)

Eurostat (2022) SDG Gender Equality: Achieve gender equality and empower all women and girls, ec.europa.eu/eurostat/statistics-explained/index.php?title=SDG_5_-_Gender_equality (archived at https://perma.cc/7WMJ-QBUD)

Global Reporting Initiative (2022) State of progress: business contributions to the SDGs – A 2020–2021 study in support of the Sustainable Development Goals, www.globalreporting.org/media/ab5lun0h/stg-gri-report-final.pdf (archived at https://perma.cc/74F4-ZVW2)

Hák, T, Moldan, B and Dahl, A (2012) *Sustainability Indicators: A scientific assessment*, Washington, Covelo, Island Press, London

Impact Institute (2022) More than 90% of companies' impact is indirect. Do you have a grip on your investments' value chain?, www.impactinstitute.com/indirect-value-chain-impact (archived at https://perma.cc/7CC9-S3WG)

LexisNexis (2021) SDGs vs ESGs: What is the Better Measure of Sustainability? November 23, www.lexisnexisip.com/resources/sdgs-vs-esgs-what-is-the-better-measure-of-sustainability (archived at https://perma.cc/3UE6-R7FH)

McKenzie, M (2021) Reporting the SDGs: How to get it right – Business has an important role to play in helping to achieve the SDGs, home.kpmg/xx/en/home/insights/2020/01/reporting-sdgs-how-to-get-it-right.html (archived at https://perma.cc/V9JD-JG25)

Marshall, T (2008) Wicked problems, in *Design Dictionary*, eds M Erlhoff and T Marshall, Board of International Research in Design, Birkhäuser, Basel, doi.org/10.1007/978-3-7643-8140-0 (archived at https://perma.cc/U4EH-S277)

Metabolic (2018) Why indirect impacts are indeed your business, www.metabolic.nl/news/why-indirect-impacts-are-indeed-your-business (archived at https://perma.cc/W34R-6KLC)

PwC (2021) PwC Annual Report 2020/2021, www.pwc.nl/nl/onze-organisatie/jssrbericht2021/documents/pwc-annual-report-2020-2021.pdf (archived at https://perma.cc/7KER-SPWS)

PwC (2022a) Global Annual Review 2022, www.pwc.com/gx/en/about/global-annual-review-2022.html (archived at https://perma.cc/9ZAW-FWZT)

PwC (2022b) Sustainable Development Goals, www.pwc.nl/en/onze-organisatie/corporate-sustainability/sustainable-develoment-goals.html (archived at https://perma.cc/Y8LZ-KTTN)

PwC (2022c) PwC Annual Report 2021/2022, www.pwc.nl/nl/onze-organisatie/jaarbericht2022/documents/pwc-annual-report-2021-2022.pdf (archived at https://perma.cc/QA4P-NH8D)

PwC (2022d) Getting started with SDGs – our story, www.pwc.nl/nl/onze-organisatie/corporatesustainability/documents/our-sdg-journey.pdf (archived at https://perma.cc/A2DM-5U4H)

Rittel, H and Webber, M (1973) Dilemmas in a general theory of planning, *Policy Sciences*, 155–59

Science Based Targets (2019) Foundations of science-based target setting, sciencebasedtargets.org/resources/?tab=background#resource (archived at https://perma.cc/K3VP-ECDB)

SDG Compass (2015) Learn more about the SDGs, sdgcompass.org/sdgs (archived at https://perma.cc/Y7HV-2RXB)

United Nations (2015) Transforming our world: The 2030 Agenda for Sustainable Development, Resolution adopted by the General Assembly on 25 September 2015, www.un.org/en/development/desa/population/migration/generalassembly/docs/globalcompact/A_RES_70_1_E.pdf (archived at https://perma.cc/U83Z-5YMP)

United Nations (2017) Statement on the Adoption of the Global Indicator Framework for SDGs, www.un.org/pga/71/2017/07/06/statement-on-the-adoption-of-the-global-indicator-framework-for-sdgs/ (archived at https://perma.cc/KQJ8-62HB)

United Nations (2022) Sustainable Development: The 17 Goals, Department of Economic and Social Affairs, sdgs.un.org/goals (archived at https://perma.cc/7WZK-5BYD)

van Tulder, R and van Mil, E (2023) *Principles of Sustainable Business: Frameworks for corporate actions on the SDGs*, Routledge (See also their interactive website with many tools, formats and cases: www.principlesofsustainablebusiness.nl/ (archived at https://perma.cc/WB7M-782M)

Accommodating Ukrainian refugees 09

By the end of 2021, according to UNHCR's Global Trends Report (UNHCR, 2022a), 89.3 million people were on the run from war, violence, prosecution or human rights violations. This was 8 per cent more than the year before and more than double the number compared to 10 years ago.

The Russian invasion of Ukraine on 28 February 2022 (Reuters, 2022) caused many Ukrainians to leave their homes and find shelter elsewhere. At the same time, the Netherlands is still struggling to accommodate the refugees and economic migrants that entered the country in 2014–15.

Under international law, countries have obligations towards refugees. The ongoing war situations in Ukraine and Syria, and the unstable and unsafe situation in other countries in the Middle East and Central Asia, have resulted in many casualties. With continuing threats and dozens of cities demolished, many people have fled their countries, which has resulted in more than a million people from different nations, nationalities and cultures fleeing from war zones to seek shelter in Europe. It is the third time in recent history that this kind of displacement has taken place. During the late 1990s, Europe had an influx of refugees fleeing civil war in the former Yugoslavia.

During the first months of the Ukrainian refugee influx in the Netherlands, Ukrainians were invited into citizens' homes. This was in contrast to what happened in 2014–15, when most citizens were against refugees being accommodated in their own towns, let alone in their homes (de Witte, 2022). When it comes to non-Ukrainian refugees, xenophobia and stigmatization of foreigners appears to be more acceptable than when directed towards Ukrainian refugees (Esposito, 2022). Frequently heard complaints about the arrival of and the offering of shelter to non-Ukrainian refugees are that criminality and unemployment increase and economic growth decreases (Noack, 2015; BBC News, 2015; Robins-Early, 2015). However, taking a closer look at crime rates, it turns out that if age, gender, marital status and whether or not someone receives social benefits are all taken into account, then an increase in crime cannot be ascribed to ethnic background (Engbertsen et al, 2015). In this highly complex arena, we see Europe struggling between humanitarian impulses, wanting to offer a helping hand and shelter, and political opportunism, blaming 'foreigners' and newcomers for problems in society. At the same time, the Ukrainian refugee influx is affecting other refugees and displaced people worldwide (Norwegian Refugee Council, 2022).

In this chapter we focus on strategic decision making at the regional level in the case of the Ukrainian refugee influx. The chapter focuses on the situation in the Netherlands, but can easily be applied to regions in other countries in Europe. In this sphere, politicians, civil servants, authorities, refugee organizations, employers and volunteers are the actors who have to handle the influx, integration and perspective on a new future for the newcomers from Ukraine as well as from other countries. Taking into account what was learnt from previous refugee streams, what could and should be done better this time? And what opportunities are created by the refugee influx? Since Europe in 2022 is not the same as Europe of 5 or 20 years ago, this will be done by considering the economic crisis, which still exists in parts of Europe, and the many reforms (e.g. on development cooperation, financial and monetary policy, open borders and fighting crime) that are underway, causing unrest and instability (Government of the Netherlands, 2023). Nowadays, populist parties are part of the political system in many democratic countries in Europe and sometimes form part of the government. Therefore, it is crucial that their points of view are addressed in the decision-making process, just like any other point of view.

It is not easy to come to a consensus at a national, regional or local level. At the same time there are many parties to consider when making strategic decisions. What can the Responsible Business Simulator (tRBS) do and how can it add value to the strategic decision-making process? By giving all stakeholders a voice in the debate and translating these voices into numbers, we have been able to facilitate politics based on facts. Creating a level playing field by using the facts based on the data we researched, we opened the door to more and better choices at regional level to allocate budgets for the integration of Ukrainian refugees and simultaneously consider local inhabitants and refugees from other countries.

About the Ukrainian refugee influx

According to the European Central Bank (ECB) the war in Ukraine has triggered the largest displacement of European citizens since the Second World War, with women and children accounting for the vast majority of refugees. The United Nations High Commissioner for Refugees (UNHCR) states that by 31 May 2022 around 7 million people had already crossed Ukraine's borders (2022, ECB). In the Netherlands, nearly 75,000 Ukrainian refugees were registered in August that year.

Dutch municipalities and regions mostly have to reinvent the wheel themselves regarding the reception and accommodation of Ukrainians. Whereas in the initial phase of the Russian invasion, Ukrainian refugees could count on a great deal of involvement from Dutch citizens, for example in the form of home shelter, after the first months more and more stories came out about struggles between host families and their guests. Meanwhile, six months after the war began, over 1,000 Ukrainians were still arriving in the Netherlands every week, with fewer and fewer reception places available. As at August 2022, for example, nearly 75,000 Ukrainian refugees were registered in the Netherlands and only 3,322 beds were available. Besides accommodating Ukrainian refugees, the Netherlands struggles with the hosting of non-Ukrainian refugees that have entered the country since 2014–15 due to the ongoing war in Syria and unstable and unsafe countries in the Middle East and Central Asia. From 2022, Dutch municipalities were legally obliged to shelter asylum seekers (Rijksoverheid, 2022a).

In August 2022, Hubert Bruls, chairman of the Netherlands Security Council, warned that if the war continues and more refugees come to the Netherlands, it may even become a serious problem to receive more refugees in the area (ANP, 2022). This is because local authorities have to deal with an extensive list of tasks which are new to them, but for which they do not have the necessary experience, manpower or expertise. Moreover, many different interests within the municipality or the region play a part in the reception of Ukrainians, such as integrating Ukrainian refugees while simultaneously considering non-Ukrainian refugees and local residents.

For many reasons, such as the perceived similarities with and fraternal feelings for Ukrainians, the willingness to accommodate Ukrainian refugees differs greatly from that witnessed for earlier refugees (Esposito, 2022). Also, the starting point for arrival is very different. Just like the refugees from former Yugoslavia in the 1990s, the European Commission has offered Ukrainian refugees temporary protection, which means residence grants and working rights for Ukrainians fleeing conflict (Government of the Netherlands, 2022). This makes the decisions that have to be made, and thus the determination of policy, very complex.

Matching refugees with host municipalities

According to the Dutch Knowledge Platform 'Integration and Society' (Kennisplatform Integratie & Samenleving, 2019) in which over 200 Dutch municipal authorities are represented, 60 per cent of non-Ukrainian refugees have a chance to work only after following an educational programme or by doing voluntary work, whereas 30 per cent of refugees are seen as impossible to direct towards (paid) work. Since the burden for social costs falls mainly on municipalities, it is in their interests to know more about the background of the refugees in order to guide them through the integration processes that will have a more positive impact. In 2016 only 16 per cent of municipalities said they knew enough about the background of the accepted and licensed refugees to guide them towards the right sort of work (Razenberg and De Gruijter, 2016). The more refugees are active in work, the better it is for both refugees and for municipalities and society at large (*The Economist*, 2015).

The Dutch Employee Insurance Agency (UWV) reports that in November 2022 more than 46,000 notifications of employment of Ukrainian refugees were received. Most of them found work in the catering industry through employment agencies and mostly in the areas of Groot Amsterdam and the Hague (UWV, 2022). From this, it can be deduced that not all refugees find a job that matches their skills or previous education. The Dutch yearly monitor *Work for Refugees* reported in 2020 that 17 per cent of the refugees arriving after 2014–15 had found a job (Kennisplatform Integratie & Samenleving, 2019). The working group 'Working and Integration' of the Ministry of Social Affairs carried out this research and advised the use of early screenings and assessments of refugees' work experience and educational qualifications and skills as soon as they arrive. The goal is to make matches between municipalities with specific industries and their need for skilled labour.

A city like Eindhoven, for example, can be a better place for refugees with ICT work experience than for refugees with a farming background. Early screening can also guide refugees more quickly to education and jobs in those places where they have the best opportunity to integrate into society. The advantage of early screening and assessment is that municipalities get a much better idea what kind of refugees they will have to find housing for and what kind of jobs could be sought. This adds value to the waiting time between arrival in the asylum centres or short-term-stay locations and their departure to towns and cities for a longer stay. In the meantime, more focused activities can be organized for them in terms of acquiring general knowledge about the new country, participating in voluntary work, learning the language, or preparing for education and internships to get more work experience. From mid-2016, screening and assessment has been started in one of the asylum centres and it is expected this approach will be expanded to many more places. These types of policy will ultimately increase the effectiveness of the measures taken at municipal level, and which will be discussed in this chapter.

Special attention for young refugees

Not much research has been done so far into the position of young asylum seekers and their integration via education and work. The Verwey-Jonker Institute undertook an exploratory research study commissioned by Movisie about young refugees in the Netherlands (Stavenuiter et al, 2016). The main conclusions were that young asylum seekers in the age group 13 to 23 years, and with a licence to stay, represent a pool of underutilized talent. Due to limited fluency in the language, many young refugees are placed at education levels lower than their abilities. This can lead to frustrations, particularly among those with higher intellectual capabilities. Additional language programmes provided by educational institutions are highly regarded, as fine-tuning of the language is an important ticket into the labour market. Peer coaching during education is an additional support for youngsters. Providing access to networks that can be useful for internships, temporary work experience, or professional work is an important asset for integration. Getting to know local people and making contacts is necessary for taking the first steps towards work; lack of it is an obstacle to integration. The resulting waste of talent of these young refugees in host countries stresses the need for a more fact-based dialogue concerning their integration.

Finding the best allocation of budgets for integration of refugees

Since 2022, municipalities and regions in the Netherlands have been legally tasked with the reception and accommodation of asylum seekers (Rijksoverheid, 2022b). It is therefore crucial for decision makers to base their actions on factual information. Quantifying the effects of their actions facilitates a constructive dialogue, where opinions are traded for facts and figures, and resistance to mutual understanding diminishes. In this complex setting, a decision maker needs to obey the law and at the same time address citizens' concerns and the opinions of differently minded politicians. It should be no surprise that these concerns and opinions are not always aligned and cause conflicts of interest.

Several regions try out a mix of activities consisting of language programmes, voluntary work, learning activities and helping in the daily routines of the temporary asylum centres or shelters, like cleaning, cooking and playing with children. The recommendation is to keep refugees busy in a meaningful way and to lower the risk of frustration and increase the feeling of safety in the community. Notwithstanding the many positive initiatives at the regional level, it remains very difficult to decide what to do and when – and which has the greatest impact.

As municipalities and regions are the main governmental actors in accommodating and integrating refugees, we approached several local governments to try out the Responsible Business Simulator techniques in making strategic decisions on the refugee issue.

The simulation model discussed in this chapter has been developed for policymakers at municipal or regional level. The focus of the model lies on the interventions for Ukrainian refugees, but also takes into account the impact on non-Ukrainian status-holders and local inhabitants. The purpose of the tRBS's application in this context is to support policymakers in their decision-making process regarding their response to the refugee crisis and the dialogue around it. In the simulation model, effects that have already been researched are disclosed and combined so that policymakers are provided with quantitative insights that facilitate the decision-making process and enable fact-based dialogue.

The strategic decision-making process

In order to develop the strategic decision-making process, we worked with a team of experts from academia, charity and refugee organizations, and local and national governments. The expertise comprised strategy, data analytics and communication. Experts from central and local governments were consulted throughout different stages of the process. In various workshops the inputs for and the outputs of the strategic decision-making process were validated. The model builds on knowledge and experience that was developed by the authors to address the 2014–15 influx (Roobeek, de Swart and van der Plas, 2018).

Describing the strategic challenge that requires a decision

As mentioned in the introduction to this chapter, policymakers have a lot of stakeholders with different interests to take into account when they are deciding what actions are best for their region or municipality to enable them to deal with the refugee influx. The potential actions are formulated with a focus on the most recent refugee influx, namely Ukrainian refugees. However, as mentioned before, the model will also consider the effect of these actions on non-Ukrainian refugees and local inhabitants. The strategic challenge for a decision maker is, therefore, formulated as 'how to balance scarce resources among refugees in their region'. In the remainder of this case study the region evaluated is the province of Utrecht, in which the decision maker typically is a specially appointed officer.

Defining key outputs involving stakeholders

In order to address the strategic challenge, key stakeholders are identified as:

- Ukrainian refugees who are allocated to or have arrived in a region
- non-Ukrainian refugees that are allocated to or already reside in the region
- the region's inhabitants
- local entrepreneurs
- local employers

Inhabitants' political preferences, as reflected in their opinions towards the arrival of the refugees and their actions regarding Ukrainian and non-Ukrainian refugees, come in all colours. The refugees, in turn, are affected by the sentiments and attitudes of their neighbours and the actions that a region takes. Arguments raised for and against the housing of refugees can be considered aspects that policymakers should take into account when deciding upon an action. These arguments concern the quality of life, unemployment and economic growth. Based on these topics and the experience of policymakers of different municipalities, we have formulated and validated six key outputs. These key outputs can be allocated to two themes: economy and society. Table 9.1 gives an overview of these key outputs, to which theme they relate and a brief description.

Table 9.1 Key output definitions for Refugees case

Key output	Unit	Theme	Description
Unemployment reduction Ukrainian refugees	%	Society	Decrease in unemployment of Ukrainian refugees due to policymaker's actions
Unemployment reduction non-Ukrainian refugees	%	Society	Decrease in unemployment of non-Ukrainian refugees due to policymaker's actions
Unemployment reduction inhabitants	%	Society	Decrease in unemployment of inhabitants due to policymaker's actions
Economic impact	€	Economy	Economic growth due to policymaker's actions, calculated by the investments made, and the resulting effects on social benefits needed and income acquired
Quality of life Ukrainian refugees	.	Society	Increase in the quality of life of Ukrainian refugees due to policymaker's actions
			Quality of life is impacted through feelings of safety, (physical and mental) health, social cohesion and financial security

(continued)

Table 9.1 (Continued)

Key output	Unit	Theme	Description
Quality of life non-Ukrainian refugees	.	Society	Increase in the quality of life of refugees due to policymaker's actions
			Quality of life is impacted through feelings of safety, social trust and financial security
Quality of life inhabitants	.	Society	Increase in the quality of life of inhabitants due to policymaker's actions
			Quality of life is impacted through feelings of safety and financial security

---

Quality of life

To measure the quality of life we follow the definition as formulated by the World Health Organization (WHO, 2012):

> An individual's perception of their position in life in the context of the culture and value systems in which they live and in relation to their goals, expectations, standards and concerns.

In the WHOQOL (2012) the UN describes quality of life as a broad-ranging concept that incorporates a person's physical health, psychological state, level of independence, social relationships, personal beliefs and relationships to salient features of the environment in a complex way. For our model we have formulated the following indicators to measure most of the elements described: health, employment, education, social participation, social trust, social cohesion, jealousy, safety, financial security and income.

Determining decision maker's options

The arrival of refugees may have both positive and negative effects on key outputs. Local decision makers want to mitigate or neutralize the negative effects as far as possible and exploit the positive effects as much as they can. Based on discussions with refugee experts from several municipalities, five possible actions or internal variable inputs have been formulated.

There are two internal variable inputs that are considered to be important regarding addressing the strategic challenge, but which, after careful consideration, have not been added to the set of internal variable inputs in this model:

1 Psychological support: even though the mental wellbeing of refugees is considered to be very important, the cost of treatment of serious mental illnesses like post-traumatic stress disorder (PTSD) is assumed to be reimbursed through health insurance and is therefore not considered as an action or responsibility for local decision makers.

2 Housing: making houses available can speed up integration, but may cause envy among the group that is not being assigned a house at the same time. As the action comes with a different budget and an unpredictable probability of success, we recommend modelling this issue as a separate case.

The internal variable inputs that are incorporated into the model are displayed in Table 9.2.

Table 9.2 Internal variable input definitions for Refugees case

Internal variable input	Description
Tertiary education	An investment in one year of tertiary education with the purpose of increasing refugees' chances on the labour market
Sport and associations	An investment in membership of sports clubs or associations to improve the wellbeing of refugees as well as their integration into the community
Language and integration	An investment in language and integration courses to ease the integration process, to improve social cohesion and increase chances in the labour market
Employment creation and matching	An investment in coaching regarding job finding and the application process with the purpose of decreasing unemployment among refugees
Access to transport	An investment in access to public transport or a bicycle to improve social cohesion and access to the labour market

Since this case is evaluating a budget allocation decision, in the remainder of this chapter we refer to 'internal variable inputs' as 'investments'. All investments refer to the allocation of budget to interventions concerning Ukrainian refugees. To illustrate the practical application of the simulation model, the Dutch province of Utrecht has been selected. Dutch regions or municipalities receive a budget of €1,250 per year per asylum seeker (RTL Nieuws, 2022). For Ukrainian refugees there is no given budget, but municipalities or regions will be compensated by the Dutch authorities for expenses incurred sheltering Ukrainians. We therefore set an investment amount to be allocated of €1,250 per Ukrainian refugee. For the province of Utrecht, that currently shelters 5,175 Ukrainian refugees, this leads to a total budget of €6,468,750, uniformly distributed over the refugees.

The province of Utrecht formulated the following decision maker's options. The budget is provided per Ukrainian refugee:

- *Mix:* €250 is spent on each internal variable input.
- *Employment and Language:* €625 of the budget is spent on language and integration, €625 on employment.
- *Employment and Education:* €625 of the budget is spent on employment, €625 on education.
- *Sport and Language:* €750 of the budget is spent on language and integration, €500 on sport.

Drawing up scenarios

Besides the inputs that are controlled by the decision maker, external variable inputs have been formulated in order to account for exogenous uncertainties. This enables us to draw up scenarios. We consider five sources of uncertainty that we want to monitor for their influence on key outputs. From Table 9.3 it can be deduced that four of them refer to the monthly salary that an inhabitant or refugee earns if jobs are created because of investments in one of the internal variable inputs. If a decision maker decides to invest in one or more of the options to accommodate refugees as listed in Table 9.2, these options need to be facilitated and this creates jobs for the inhabitants or refugees. Even though we are aware that jobs in sport and associations as well as in language and integration may be partially carried out by volunteers, we did not include this assumption in our model.

The remaining external variable input concerns the minimum investment in language and integration that is necessary for a full employment effect to be realized for a refugee. The assumption is that successful language and integration courses are crucial for the refugees in the job search process. If the investment in language and integration courses is too small, then a significantly lower effect is expected from the investment in employment. We will explore this so-called 'interaction phenomenon' later in this chapter. As we have used expert opinion to determine the minimum investment, we offer the decision maker the opportunity to assess the impact of variations in this value.

We have formulated three scenarios. Since all but one external variable input refers to labour (it is important to stress that the first four relate to labour created for local inhabitants as well as for the Ukrainian and non-Ukrainian refugees), we have named these scenarios labour optimistic, base case and labour pessimistic. In a labour optimistic scenario, the decision maker expects lower salaries

Table 9.3 Specification of scenarios for Refugees case

| External variable input | Scenarios | | | Source |
	Labour optimistic	Base case	Labour pessimistic	
Salary higher education	€36,972	€43,512	€50,052	(Loonwijzer.nl, nd)
Salary sport and associations	€21,384	€25,332	€34,332	(Loonwijzer.nl, nd)
Salary language and integration course	€27,084	€34,872	€40,776	(Loonwijzer.nl, nd)
Salary employment and matching	€26,796	€30,492	€34,080	(Loonwijzer.nl, nd)
Minimum investment in language and integration for full employment effect	€500	€500	€1,000	Expert opinion

for inhabitants, thus increasing the return on a given investment. At the same time, the minimum investment needed in language and integration to create the full employment effect for refugees is expected to be smaller in the labour optimistic scenario. The opposite is the case in the labour pessimistic scenario. The specifications of the scenarios are given in Table 9.3.

Constructing the simulation model

The information collected so far has been inserted into tRBS. However, for the simulation model to provide accurate and clear insights for the decision maker, a large amount of additional information is required. Via comprehensive desk research and in collaboration with the stakeholders, we collected the missing information and completed the simulation model. This information can be broken down into inputs related to a municipality, those related to direct effects and those to indirect effects.

Input related to a region

For each region, characteristics with regard to refugees that distinguish them from other regions are needed to calculate the key outputs. Table 9.4 specifies the most important characteristics for the province of Utrecht. These inputs are necessary for the calculation of the inhabitants' unemployment rate reduction, their quality of life and the economic impact.

Input related to direct effects

The effects that investments have on key outputs are modelled in various steps. In the first step, the direct effect is calculated. Typically, this first step models the effect of an investment on one or more intermediates and does not yet model the impact of an investment on a key output. A good example is 'quality of life', which consists of multiple factors. In the first step, we model the effect that investments may have on these factors.

Table 9.4   Specification of fixed inputs for the region of Utrecht for Refugees case

Fixed input	Value	Description
Number of Ukrainian refugees	5,175	Current number of Ukrainian refugees in the region (UNHCR, 2022b, Rijksoverheid, nd d)
Number of Ukrainian refugees in the potential workforce	3,105	Current number of Ukrainian refugees in the region that has no job or is looking for a job that better fits its qualification* (NL Times, 2022)
Number of non-Ukrainian refugees in the potential workforce	1,532	Current number of non-Ukrainian refugees in the region that is unemployed (Utrecht Monitor, 2022)
Number of inhabitants in the workforce	24,000	Current number of inhabitants in the region that is unemployed (Provincie Utrecht, 2021)
Social benefits Ukrainian refugees	3,120	Living money Ukrainian refugees receive on a yearly basis [€260/month] (Rijksoverheid, nd a)
Social benefits non-Ukrainian refugees	3,120	Living money non-Ukrainian refugees receive on a yearly basis [€60/week] (Rijksoverheid, nd b)
Social benefits inhabitants	14,352	Social welfare per single person or single parent (Rijksoverheid, 2022a)

NOTE *We assume that the percentage of Ukrainian refugees with jobs perfectly fitting their qualifications is negligible

Table 9.5 displays four characteristics of the investments that are taken into account when modelling the direct effects of the investments.

The first three inputs in Table 9.5 only relate to the type of investment. Their values and – if available – references to their sources are listed in Table 9.6. If no source is listed, experts have been consulted. As described earlier, the decision maker has the opportunity to add an uncertainty to these expert opinions via the use of scenarios.

As explained in Table 9.5, the maximum possible effects of investments do not only depend on the type of investment, but also on what they impact. These can be key outputs and intermediates, where intermediates refer to variables that are calculated to break down the modelling process into several steps. Here, the only key output that is directly impacted by investments is the reduction in the refugees' unemployment rate. The intermediates are mostly used in the calculation of quality of life improvement, which will be further explained later (Tables 9.8 and 9.9). The values of the maximum possible effects are listed in Table 9.7, again including – if applicable – their reference. If a cell contains no value, this means that no relevant research or expert opinion could be found and we assume, conservatively, that there is no effect. The effects are applicable to inhabitants,

Table 9.5 Definitions of fixed inputs related to direct effects for Refugees case

Fixed input	Description
Eligible population	Percentage of the population that is eligible for the investment: statistics primarily based on desk research
Probability of success	Likelihood that the investment will prove to be successful: statistics partially based on expert knowledge
Saturation point	Maximum effective investment, or the ceiling above which further investment has no further effect: statistics primarily based on desk research
Maximum possible effect	Maximum effect obtained when investing an amount greater or equal than the saturation point. Since an investment may have more than one direct effect, for each investment, various maximum possible effects need to be specified: statistics primarily based on desk research

Table 9.6 Values of fixed inputs related to direct effects for Refugees case

Internal variable input	Eligible population	Probability of success	Saturation point
Higher education	21% (Central Intelligence Agency, 2016; Unicef, 2016)	71% (Central Bureau of Statistics, 2007)	€12,674 (OECD, 2014)
Sport and associations	63% (Central Intelligence Agency, 2016)	70%	€500 (Bremmer, 2008)

(continued)

Table 9.6 (Continued)

Internal variable input	Eligible population	Probability of success	Saturation point
Language and integration course	57% (Central Bureau of Statistics, 2022)	70% (Maastricht University, 2014)	€2,694 (Sagenn, nd)
Employment and matching	63% (Central Intelligence Agency, 2016; Engbertsen et al, 2015)	60%	€2,500 (SEO Economisch Onderzoek, 2010)
Public transport	94% (Central Bureau of Statistics, 2022)	66%	€3,128 (9292, 2021)

Ukrainian and non-Ukrainian refugees, unless specified otherwise. NOTE: future references to 'refugees' will refer to both Ukrainians and non-Ukrainians.

Combining the information from Tables 9.6 and 9.7 with the invested amounts, the direct effect of each investment can be calculated. The direct effect of an investment i on intermediate or key output j, where i and j refer to the rows and columns of Table 9.7, respectively and k refers to the eligible population for a specific internal variable input, is calculated by means of the following formula:

$Direct\ Effect_{ij}$

$$= Probability\ Of\ Success_i \frac{\min\left(\frac{Investment\ amount_i}{Eligible\ population_k * Population}, Saturation\ Point_i\right)}{Saturation\ Point_i}$$

$\times Maximum\ Possible\ Effect_{ij}$

In this formula we assume that the effect of all investments increases in a linear fashion up to the saturation point and that investments larger than this saturation point do not result in any additional effect. Please note that the formula slightly differs from the formula described in Chapter 7, as we work with an eligible population per investment which means that we assume that the investment amount is only used for a subset of the total population.

Table 9.7 Specification of maximum possible effects* of internal variable inputs for Refugees case

Internal variable input	Affected intermediates or key outputs						
	Language acquisition Ukrainian refugees	Tertiary education level Ukrainian refugees	Social cohesion Ukrainian refugees	Social participation Ukrainian refugees	Jealousy inhabitants or non-Ukrainian refugees	Health Ukrainian refugees	Unemployment reduction Ukrainian refugees
Tertiary education		47% (UAF, 2016)					
Language and integration course	65% (van Tubergen, 2010)						22.9% (Lang, 2022)
Sport and associations	42% (van Tubergen, 2010)		12% (Toepoel, 2013)			22% (Giron, 2012)	
Employment and matching							68% (UAF, 2021)
Public transport			1.4% (Du et al., 2022)	53.7% (Mott MacDonald, 2013)			
Any intervention					100% (Sadjad, 2022)		

NOTE *Some values have been transformed to correct for scale differences and log functions

To illustrate this mechanism, let us consider a decision maker who wants to invest in employment and matching. Suppose we want to know the direct effect that this investment has on the unemployment rate reduction among refugees. From our desk review of the literature, we have learnt that 63 per cent of the refugees are eligible for employment and matching (i.e. the accessible population = 63 per cent), that employment and matching can reduce unemployment by 68 per cent (i.e. the maximum possible effect = 68 per cent) and from experts we have learnt that investing in employment and matching has a desired effect on 60 out of 100 participants (i.e. probability of success = 60 per cent). The direct effect of this investment on unemployment is therefore a reduction of at most $63\% \times 68\% \times 60\% = 25.7\%$.

This is the case if a decision maker invests the maximum effective amount or the saturation point. From desk research, we have learnt that the saturation point for investing in employment and matching is €2,500. Let us assume now that the decision maker has an available budget of €500, which is considerably lower than the saturation point. The direct result would then be: $25.7\% \times (500/2,500) = 5.14\%$. By investing €500 per refugee in employment and matching, a municipality or region could therefore reduce the unemployment rate of the refugees by 5.14 per cent.

Figure 9.1 illustrates the rationale described above. On the horizontal axis the amount invested in employment and matching is displayed (for the full population), and the vertical axis shows the attainable reduction in the unemployment rate of the refugees. The curved line indicates the sensitivity of the unemployment rate reduction to changes in higher education (with a maximum of 25.7 per cent), the straight line is at the intersection of the investment of €500 per refugee (or €2,587,602 in total) with the sensitivity. This intersection indicates a reduction of 5.14 per cent which is in line with the calculation above.

Input related to indirect effects

From Table 9.7 we know that except for the reduction in refugee unemployment, key outputs are not directly affected by any one of the internal variable inputs. The internal variable inputs have an

Figure 9.1   Sensitivity of 'unemployment rate reduction refugees' to changes in 'employment and matching' for Refugees case

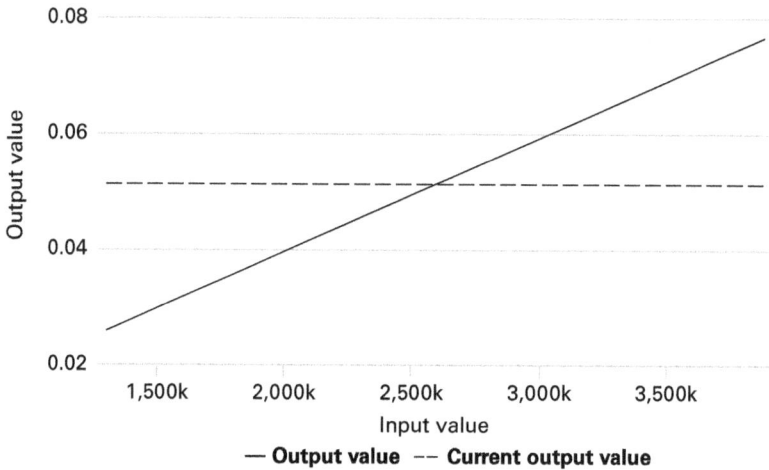

effect on several variables that in turn affect the key outputs, the so-called intermediates. Both the effects that intermediates have on other intermediates and key outputs, and the effects key outputs have on each other, are called indirect effects. Their maximum values are displayed in Table 9.8 (the effects intermediates and key outputs have on intermediates) and Table 9.9 (displays the effects intermediates and key outputs have on key outputs). Tables 9.7, 9.8 and 9.9 build upon each other's values.

For example, from Table 9.7 it can be seen that an investment in sport and associations (internal variable input) has, among others, a maximum effect of 12 per cent on social cohesion of Ukrainian refugees (intermediate). Following on from this, Table 9.8 then shows that the maximum possible effect social cohesion has on crime reduction (intermediate) is 26 per cent. Crime reduction in turn, as can be seen from the same table has a maximum effect of 29 per cent on safety feelings (intermediate). Finally, in Table 9.9 we see how 'safety feelings' has a maximum impact on key output quality of life of 82 per cent. By following the data, we can therefore incorporate all the research literature into our model.

Table 9.8 Specification of maximum indirect effects on intermediates for Refugees case

Intermediate or key output	Intermediate							
	Income (purchasing power) Ukrainian refugees	Income (purchasing power) non-Ukrainian refugees	Income (purchasing power) inhabitants	Financial security	Safety feelings	Social cohesion refugees	Social trust refugees	Crime reduction refugees
Language acquisition Ukrainian refugees	15.5% (Bach et al, 2017)					2.2% (Hannafi and Marouani, 2022)		
Tertiary education level Ukrainian refugees	70% (OECD, 2014)				26.7% (Visser et al, 2013)			
Social cohesion Ukrainian refugees								26% (Beuningen et al, 2013)
Unemployment reduction	81% (Rijksoverheid, nd c)	81% (Rijksoverheid, nd c)	37% (Rijksoverheid, nd c)				1% (Stone and Hulse, 2007)	
Income (purchasing power)				0.7% (Mätha et al, 2011)				
Crime reduction refugees					29% (Boers et al, 2008)			26% (Beuningen et al, 2013)

Table 9.9   Specification of maximum indirect effects on key outputs for Refugees case

Key output		
Intermediate or key output	**Unemployment reduction refugees**	**Quality of life**
Language acquisition Ukrainian refugees	22.9% (Bach et al, 2017)	
Tertiary education level	15.8% (de Vroome and van Tubergen, 2010)	
Social cohesion Ukrainian refugees		24.6% (Beuningen and Kloosterman, 2011)
Social participation Ukrainian refugees		39.1% (Beuningen and Kloosterman, 2011)
Jealousy inhabitants or non-Ukrainian refugees		−5% (Fazaldad et al, 2020)
Health Ukrainian refugees		112% (Beuningen and Kloosterman, 2011)
Unemployment reduction		26.6% (Beuningen and Kloosterman, 2011)
Financial security		46% (Howell et al, 2012)
Safety feelings		82% (Węziak-Białowolska, 2016)
Social trust refugees		20.9% (Beuningen and Kloosterman, 2011)

Effects on economic impact are excluded from Tables 9.8 and 9.9. This is because the value of this key output is calculated based on the changed income of refugees and inhabitants due to a change in the unemployment rates caused by (a combination of) the investments.

For reasons of caution, we assume that effects of investments are limited to one year. In reality, a refugee or inhabitant can experience positive effects of investments for a far longer period. Limiting the shelf-life of internal variable inputs to just one year reduces the risk of overestimating the effective period.

Evaluating options by assessing strategic priorities

Having inserted all required information into the Simulator, the decision maker can easily evaluate which of the options defined earlier is the 'best' by setting strategic priorities via assigning weights to key outputs. By default, all key outputs are assigned equal weights.

We will now compare the decision maker's options as formulated before under the assumption that the region, Utrecht, deems all key outputs equally important. Figure 9.2 illustrates how each decision maker's option performs under this assumption. We deduce that the overall recommended strategy is to invest in 'sport and language'. Considering all key outputs to be equally important could for instance be a strategic priority of a municipality or region with divergent opinions and preferences in their town council.

To evaluate other perspectives as well, we have inserted a political preference that only focused on the economic impact of the interventions and one that focused on all key outputs except quality of life.

Figure 9.2 Comparison of decision maker's options when all key outputs have equal weights in base-case scenario for province of Utrecht for Refugees case

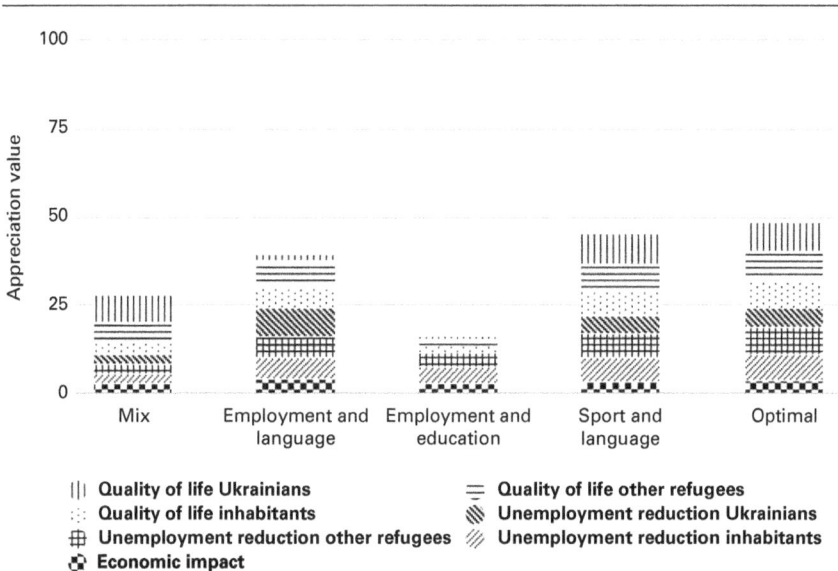

Legend:
- ||| Quality of life Ukrainians
- ::: Quality of life inhabitants
- ⊞ Unemployment reduction other refugees
- ⚙ Economic impact
- ═ Quality of life other refugees
- ▨ Unemployment reduction Ukrainians
- ▨ Unemployment reduction inhabitants

Having one of those preferences, it turns out to be best to invest in 'employment and language'.

Additionally, we used the optimization mechanism within the Responsible Business Simulator. Details of the workings of this optimization are described in Chapter 7. Optimizing the decision maker's options, given that all key outputs are deemed equally important, shows that the four options considered so far are suboptimal. Spending a budget of €1,250 and considering Utrecht's desire to perform well on all key outputs, the optimization engine recommends a different investment combination, namely €739 in 'employment and matching' and €511 in 'sport and associations'.

Evaluating options by assessing risk appetite

Up until now we have not accounted for the uncertainties that go hand in hand with the modelling process. However, we earlier distinguished three scenarios – base case, labour optimistic and labour pessimistic. In terms of risk appetite, the risk-averse person would pay more attention to the risk of high salaries for staff needed to execute the interventions. Therefore, this person would put more weight on the labour pessimistic scenario. Conversely, the person with a larger risk appetite would put more weight on the labour optimistic scenario. Figure 9.3 shows that, given equal weights, regardless of the risk appetite, 'Optimal' is the preferred option, but in the labour optimistic scenario 'Sport and language' and 'Optimal' do not differ that much. If we exclude both from the evaluation, we see that 'Employment and language' is the preferred option in the base and labour optimistic cases, but 'Mix' is the preferred option in the labour pessimistic scenario.

If we exclude the optimization and adjust weights as in the previous paragraph (only weights on Unemployment reduction and Economic impact), we see that in the base case and labour optimistic scenarios, the preferred option is 'Employment and language'; however, in the labour pessimistic scenario we see that this option is outperformed by the 'Sport and language' option.

Figure 9.3 Four decision maker's options evaluated under three scenarios for the province of Utrecht for Refugees case – all weights equal

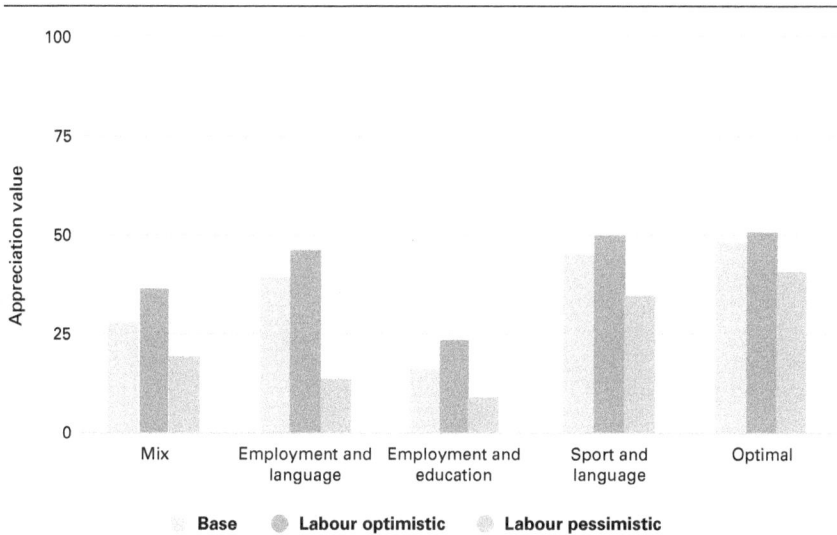

This change in preferred option due to change in risk appetite can be explained when recalling that a labour pessimistic person has set a higher minimum threshold on investing in language and integration than a labour optimistic person. When the minimum threshold is not met, which is the case for the 'Employment and language' decision maker's option for the risk-averse person, the effectiveness of investing in employment will be decreased. Therefore, the 'Sport and language' option outperforms the 'Employment and language' option as it still 'scores' on other aspects, while 'Employment and language' does less. Since the threshold of the risk-loving person is set much lower, capping on the effectiveness of investing in employment will not take place in the labour optimistic scenario, but it will in the labour pessimistic scenario, and this explains the difference. Figure 9.4 illustrates this.

Evidence in practice for mixed allocations

In practice, the regions, local councils and volunteers can all count on additional support from outside organizations in their efforts to help

Figure 9.4   Four decision maker's options evaluated under three scenarios for the province of Utrecht for Refugees case

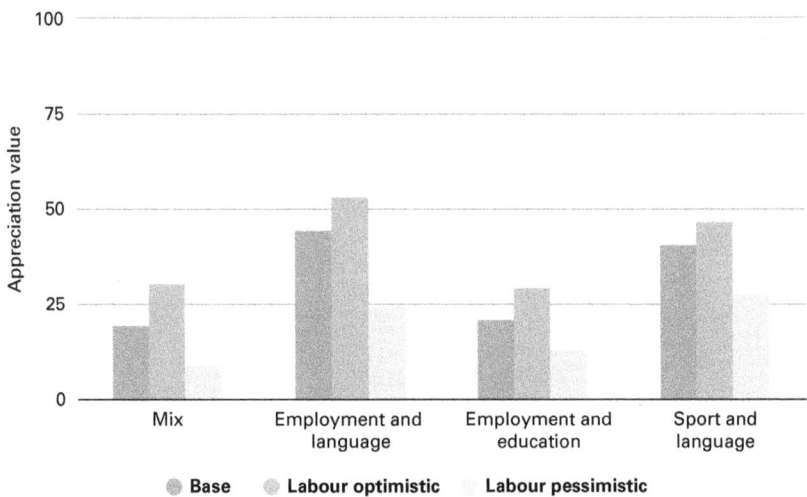

NOTE Weights only on 'Unemployment reduction' and 'Economic impact'

Ukrainian refugees. For example, (temporary) free phone calls from the Netherlands to Ukraine offered by Dutch phone providers KPN, Vodafone and t-Mobile; (temporary) free public transport (all Dutch public transport organizations and Nederlandse Spoorwegen); and job offerings. Dutch municipalities and regions are taking an innovative and more diversified approach to stimulate the integration process of Ukrainian and non-Ukrainian refugees with a permit to stay. The municipality of Utrecht, for example, at the end of 2022, gave status-holders a priority position for three weeks to get access to social housing. And in Leiden, a renowned university town, the medical university, which is in close proximity to the asylum accommodation, started giving special lectures to refugees with a higher level of education, like doctors, engineers and economists, after the 2014–15 influx. These lectures cover a wide range of topics, not just the standard culture and language classes as taught to many refugees, but aimed at offering these educated refugees entertainment and a chance to build their networks, for example, through lectures delivered in museums in Leiden. This brought together refugees from different backgrounds, stimulated content-rich conversations and approached higher-educated people at a level that was stimulating and aspiring. This contributes to better wellbeing for refugees.

The municipality of Haarlem had to deal suddenly with accommodating large groups of refugees in 2014–15. Although this was initially a shock to some inhabitants and administrators, solidarity with the humanitarian aspects of the situation prevailed. In order to start the integration process for a specific group of refugees quickly, a plan was made to mix the refugees with students. Housing with students had the advantage that the refugees were not placed in an isolated location. This helped those refugees to meet locals immediately and possibly even become motivated to start studying themselves. A sign of the attitude with which Haarlem received the refugees is that the largest problems that arose were not created by refugees, but were due to the fact that so many people wanted to go by the asylum accommodation to drop off goods for the benefit of refugees that it created traffic jams! It demonstrated the warmth of the welcome for the refugees, and as a positive outcome, most of the refugees that received a permanent residency permit chose to stay in Haarlem. As for the current situation (2022), which includes sheltering non-Ukrainian refugees that cannot be housed at the general asylum centre (Ter Apel), Haarlem offers, among others, accommodation in ships and, with help from the locals, in guest families.

In the municipality of Amstelveen, in 2015, the mayor went against the national government's standard policy, which is to provide sober initial accommodation for refugees that have just arrived (i.e. a bed, bath and bread). The mayor and her staff, however, wanted to treat the refugees from day one as if they would never leave and chose to treat them as citizens of the municipality. Instead of segregating them, they started immediately offering language courses, activities and gatherings with locals. Also, on top of catering services, they made sure the refugees had their own kitchens and were given the opportunity to volunteer, immediately giving them a meaningful way to keep busy. Lastly, against national protocol, multiple entrepreneurs stayed with their companies in the building that housed the refugees. This mix created even more interaction between the existing and new inhabitants of Amstelveen. The engagement with the inhabitants actually resulted in a situation in which the number of volunteers helping refugees became larger than the number of refugees themselves. It shows the degree of willingness in society to take an active part in the integration process, which is often not mentioned in the wave of negative publicity in the media.

Reflections

The objective of the strategic decision-making process as developed in this case study is to support policymakers in their decisions concerning the accommodation of Ukrainian refugees in their municipality or region, as well as in the allocation of budgets available to stimulate the integration of the newcomers into society. At the same time, it is important to be aware of the impact of taking action for Ukrainians on non-Ukrainian refugees as well as on local inhabitants. The element of jealousy plays a role, as non-Ukrainians and (some) local citizens are also in need of support. The strategic decision-making process has been introduced to multiple regions of different sizes and with different strategic priorities as well as in a round-table meeting with model experts, content experts and policymakers from different municipalities.

During the strategic dialogues that took place as part of this process, we observed that the majority of the municipalities determine the allocation of the proposed budgets from their functional departments instead of allocating them based on predicted impact for a successful integration. The Simulator played a crucial role in the shift from 'budget-thinking' with the sole focus on language training inside the refugee centres towards 'impact-thinking' for integration. Listening to refugees, learning from other refugee influxes in the 1990s and in 2014–15 as well as making use of the many volunteering citizens that want to make the life of refugees more meaningful, led to the proposition of a different type of allocation. The Responsible Business Simulator shows that a combination of 'Sport and associations' with 'Employment and matching' within the same budget has a greater effect than focusing on one specific intervention. This mix represents the natural process of communicating, meeting people, and trying to understand each other in different situations. This is a more stimulating way for refugees to get to know the new environment in which they are living, working and studying, than staying isolated in refugee centres.

A variant of this model was used for meaningful dialogues in 2014–15 on the accommodation of mostly Syrian refugees within the Business Refugee Action Network. National and international discussions have indicated a need for this model as well as its international applicability for each region that wishes to accommodate refugees. In our discussions with regional decision makers we learnt that the generic strategic decision-making concept applied in this case is fit to support several other policy decisions as well.

References

9292 (2021) Bus, tram and metro tickets, Abonnementen bus, tram en metro, 9292.nl/prijzen-en-abonnementen/stads-en-streekvervoer/abonnementen#Netabonnement (archived at https://perma.cc/HX4Y-F68Z)

ANP (2022) Municipalities run up against borders when helping Ukrainians, Binnenlands Bestuur, www.binnenlandsbestuur.nl/bestuur-en-organisatie/gemeenten-hebben-extra-handjes-nodig-bij-hulp-aan-oekrainers (archived at https://perma.cc/3KYW-92DZ)

Bach, S, Brücker, H, Haan, P, Romiti, A, van Deuverden, K and Weber, E (2017) Refugee integration: A worthwhile investment, *DIW Economic Bulletin*, ISSN 2192-7219, Deutsches Institut für Wirtschaftsforschung (DIW), Berlin, 7 (3/4), 33–43

BBC News (2015) Migrant crisis: Finland's case against immigration, BBC News Europe, www.bbc.co.uk/news/world-europe-34185297 (archived at https://perma.cc/T6YG-NY2Y)

Beuningen, J v and Kloosterman, R (2011) Subjectief welzijn: welke factoren spelen een rol?, Centraal Bureau van de Statistiek, Den Haag/Heerlen

Beuningen, J v, Smeets, H, Arts, K and Riele, St (2013) De samenhang tussen etnische diversiteit en criminaliteit: de rol van sociaal kapitaal, Centraal Bureau van de Statistiek, Den Haag

Boers, J, Steden, R v and Boutellier, H (2008) Het effect van positieve en negatieve factoren op veiligheidsbeleving, Tijdschrift voor Veilighe

Bremmer, D (2008) Kind op sport, wat kost dat?, 11 August, www.geldenrecht.nl/artikel/2008-08-11/kind-op-sport-wat-kost-dat (archived at https://perma.cc/DB2Y-2KKW)

Central Bureau of Statistics (2007) Jonge vrouwen hoger opgeleid dan mannen, 7 March, www.cbs.nl/nr/exeres/20F7E2BC-6E02-4F71-A668-2AEC94FA2EF3.htm (archived at https://perma.cc/58D9-3GER)

Central Bureau of Statistics (2022) Mainly women and children from Ukraine registered, www.cbs.nl/en-gb/news/2022/14/mainly-women-and-children-from-ukraine-registered (archived at https://perma.cc/7BP8-LGY5)

Central Intelligence Agency (2016) Syria, *The World Factbook*, 22 February, www.cia.gov/library/publications/the-world-factbook/geos/sy.html (archived at https://perma.cc/D762-KKSY)

Du, Y, Sun, G, Choe, EY and Kwan, M-P (2022) Mediation effects of social isolation on pathways connecting public transport use with subjective wellbeing among older people, *Journal of Transport & Health*, **25**, doi.org/10.1016/j.jth.2022.101378 (archived at https://perma.cc/2QRP-HNXB)

Engbertsen, G, Dagevos, J, Jennissen, R, Bakker, L, Leerkes, A, Klaver, J and Odé, A (2015) Geen tijd verliezen: van opvang naar integratie van asielmigranten, WWR - Policy Brief 4, Wetenschappelijke Raad voor het Regeringsbeleid, Den Haag

Esposito, A (2022) The limitations of humanity: Differential refugee treatment in the EU, *Harvard International Review*, 14 September, hir.harvard.edu/the-limitations-of-humanity-differential-refugee-treatment-in-the-eu/ (archived at https://perma.cc/3W2M-S884)

European Central Bank (2022) The impact of the influx of Ukrainian refugees on the euro area labour force, *ECB Economic Bulletin*, Issue 4/2022, www.ecb.europa.eu/pub/economic-bulletin/focus/2022/html/ecb.ebbox202204_03~c9ddc08308.en.html (archived at https://perma.cc/6T3Q-7T2W)

Fazaldad, G, Iqbal, S and Hassan, B (2020) Relationship between jealousy and subjective happiness among university students: Moderating role of self-esteem, *Pakistan Journal of Psychological Research*, **35**, 393–409, 10.33824/PJPR.2020.35.2.21 (archived at https://perma.cc/X6G4-BNZ4)

Girón, P (2012) Determinants of self-rated health in Spain: differences by age groups for adults, *European Journal of Public Health*, **22** (1), February 2012, 36–40, doi.org/10.1093/eurpub/ckq133 (archived at https://perma.cc/NY4Z-DWB4)

Government of the Netherlands (2022) European Commission extends Temporary Protection Directive, 14 October, www.government.nl/latest/news/2022/10/14/european-commission-extends-temporary-protection-directive (archived at https://perma.cc/GWE4-EEWT)

Government of the Netherlands (2023) The Netherlands and EU Policy areas, 21 January, www.government.nl/topics/european-union/the-netherlands-and-the-eu-policy-areas (archived at https://perma.cc/4UMN-WYVH)

Hannafi, C and Marouani, MA (2022) Social integration of Syrian refugees and their intention to stay in Germany, *Journal of Population Economics*, doi.org/10.1007/s00148-022-00913-1 (archived at https://perma.cc/4B5F-TUVB)

Howell, R, Kurai, M and Tam, L (2012) Money buys financial security and psychological need satisfaction: Testing need theory in affluence, *Social Indicators Research*, 110, 10.1007/s11205-010-9774-5 (archived at https://perma.cc/GP7R-J29G)

Kennisplatform Integratie & Samenleving (2019) Monitor gemeentelijk beleid arbeidstoeleiding vluchtelingen 2019, www.kis.nl/sites/default/files/2022-06/monitor-gemeentelijk-beleid-2019.pdf (archived at https://perma.cc/ND94-W5YQ)

Lang, J (2022) Employment effects of language training for unemployed immigrants, *Journal of Population Economics*, **35**, 719–54, doi.org/10.1007/s00148-021-00832-7 (archived at https://perma.cc/B4NL-JD5G)

Loonwijzer.nl (nd) Salaris-check, https://loonwijzer.nl/salaris/salarischeck#/ (archived at https://perma.cc/7MKM-KWX6) (Table 9.3)

Maastricht University (2014) *Feiten & cijfers Geletterdheid*, Stichting Lezen en Schrijven Maastricht (Table 9.6)

Mathä, T, Porpiglia, A and Sierminska, E (2011) The immigrant/native wealth gap in Germany, Italy and Luxembourg, Working Paper Series 1302, European Central Bank

MottMacDonald (2013) Valuing the social impacts of public transport, Department for Transport, assets.publishing.service.gov.uk/government/uploads/system/uploads/attachment_data/file/226802/final-report.pdf (archived at https://perma.cc/2UN8-N94Z)

NL Times (2022) Over 40% of Ukrainian refugees in the Netherlands now employed: Report, 22 August, nltimes.nl/2022/08/22/40-ukrainian-refugees-netherlands-now-employed-report (archived at https://perma.cc/93WP-E8ZG)

Noack, R (2015) This map helps explain why some European countries reject refugees, and others love them, *Washington Post*, 8 September, www.washingtonpost.com/news/worldviews/wp/2015/09/08/this-map-helps-explain-why-some-european-countries-reject-refugees-and-others-love-them/ (archived at https://perma.cc/VLD8-GS2T)

Norwegian Refugee Council (2022) The war in Ukraine is bad news for the world's refugees, 25 March, www.nrc.no/perspectives/the-war-in-ukraine-is-bad-news-for-the-worlds-refugees/ (archived at https://perma.cc/SE9B-4DBD)

OECD (2014) Education at a glance 2014, www.oecd.org/edu/Education-at-a-Glance-2014.pdf (archived at https://perma.cc/V8DF-P3PN)

Provincie Utrecht (2022) Impact coronacrisis: Overzicht economische effecten, www.provincie-utrecht.nl/sites/default/files/2021-10/Monitor%20Impact%20Coronacrisis%20%2319%2C%20oktober%202021.pdf (archived at https://perma.cc/9BPL-2EZP)

Razenberg, I and De Gruijter, M (2016) *Vluchtelingen aan het werk. Enquête onder gemeenten over arbeidstoeleiding van statushouders,* Kennisplatform Integratie & Samenleving, Utrecht

Reuters (2022) Timeline: The events leading up to Russia's invasion of Ukraine, www.reuters.com/world/europe/events-leading-up-russias-invasion-ukraine-2022-02-28/ (archived at https://perma.cc/34GR-TC9T)

Rijksoverheid (2022a) Uitkeringsbedragen per 1 januari 2023, www.rijksoverheid.nl/onderwerpen/bijstand/documenten/publicaties/2022/12/05/uitkeringsbedragen-per-1-januari-2023 (archived at https://perma.cc/4HKU-BZHR)

Rijksoverheid (2022b) Gemeenten en provincies krijgen wettelijke taak tot opvang asielzoekers, www.rijksoverheid.nl/actueel/nieuws/2022/05/25/gemeenten-en-provincies-krijgen-wettelijke-taak-tot-opvang-asielzoekers (archived at https://perma.cc/5C76-RQ3E)

Rijksoverheid (nd a) Werk en inkomen voor vluchtelingen uit Oekraïne, www.rijksoverheid.nl/onderwerpen/opvang-vluchtelingen-uit-oekraine/werk-en-inkomen#:~:text=Vluchtelingen%20uit%20Oekra%C3%AFne%20ontvangen%20leefgeld,officieel%3A%20tewerkstellingsvergunning%20of%20twv (archived at https://perma.cc/GF3V-TL7D)

Rijksoverheid (nd b) Hoeveel geld krijgen asielzoekers in Nederland?, www.rijksoverheid.nl/onderwerpen/asielbeleid/vraag-en-antwoord/ hoeveel-geld-krijgen-asielzoekers-in-nederland (archived at https:// perma.cc/H6YL-45J6)

Rijksoverheid (nd c) Bedragen minimumloon 2022, www.rijksoverheid.nl/ onderwerpen/minimumloon/bedragen-minimumloon/bedragen- minimumloon-2022 (archived at https://perma.cc/Y3CT-LXJF)

Rijksoverheid (nd d) Cijfers opvang vluchtelingen uit Oekraïne in Nederland, www.rijksoverheid.nl/onderwerpen/opvang-vluchtelingen- uit-oekraine/cijfers-opvang-vluchtelingen-uit-oekraine-in-nederland (archived at https://perma.cc/M3WD-GHD3)

Robins-Early, N (2015) 5 Major myths of Europe's refugee and migrant crisis debunked. *Huffington Post*, 16 September, www.huffingtonpost.com/entry/ europe-refugee-migrant-crisis-myths_us_55f83aa7e4b09ecde1d9b4bc (archived at https://perma.cc/BZ5M-MQC3)

Roobeek, A, Swart, de J and Plas, van der M (2018) *Responsible Business: Making strategic decisions to benefit people, the planet and profits*, Kogan Page, London

RTL Nieuws (2022) Aanpak asielcrisis: gemeenten krijgen 2500 euro bonus per opgevangen asielzoeke, 8 November, www.rtlnieuws.nl/ nieuws/politiek/artikel/5345488/gemeente-krijgt-2500-euro-opvang- plek-asielzoekers (archived at https://perma.cc/H4H3-CQRC)

Sadjad, M (2022) Solidarity and 'social jealousy': emotions and affect in Indonesian host society's situated encounters with refugees, *Third World Quarterly 2022*, **43** (3), 543–60, doi.org/10.1080/01436597.2021.1969 228 (archived at https://perma.cc/F4JL-2VFU)

Sagenn (nd) Prijzen. Nederlands leren, Inburgering, Staatsexamen I/II en Alfabetisering, www.sagenn.nl/prijzen (archived at https://perma. cc/4LC9-TXXK)

SEO Economisch Onderzoek (2010) Kosten en resultaten van re-integratie, www.seo.nl/uploads/media/2010-33_Kosten_en_resultaten_van_re- integratie.pdf (archived at https://perma.cc/F48B-3KB6)

Stavenuiter, M, Smits van Waesberghe, E, Noordhuizen, B and Oostrik, S (2016) Onderwijs en doorstroom naar de arbeidsmarkt van jonge nieuwkomers in Nederland, www.verwey-jonker.nl/publicaties/2016/ onderwijs-en-doorstroom-arbeidsmarkt-nieuwkomers (archived at https://perma.cc/35JH-428U)

Stone, W and Hulse, K (2007) Housing and social cohesion: an empirical exploration, www.ahuri.edu.au/media/documents/research-reports/AHURI_Final_Report_No100_Housing_and_social_cohesion_an_empirical_exploration.pdf (archived at https://perma.cc/6LXN-EBMN)

The Economist (2015) Getting the new arrivals to work, 12 December, www.economist.com/news/business/21679791-businesses-could-benefit-and-refugees-integrate-faster-if-newcomers-europe-were-able (archived at https://perma.cc/68GV-LHWN)

Toepoel, V (2013) Ageing, leisure, and social connectedness: How could leisure help reduce social isolation of older people?, *Social Indicators Research*, **113** (1), 355–72

UAF (2016) Vluchtelingen in het hoger onderwijs. UAF in opdracht van de Inspectie van het Onderwijs, www.eur.nl/sites/corporate/files/2019-08/uaf-rapport-vluchtelingen-in-het-hoger-onderwijs.pdf (archived at https://perma.cc/BZ38-PANS)

UAF (2021) Successen, www.uaf.nl/over-ons/successen/ (archived at https://perma.cc/2Q4C-2TPC)

UNHCR (2022a) Global Trends Report 2021, www.unhcr.org/62a9d1494/global-trends-report-2021 (archived at https://perma.cc/K38Z-U4C2)

UNHCR (2022b) Operational data portal, Ukraine Refugee Situation, data.unhcr.org/en/situations/ukraine (archived at https://perma.cc/9B6E-3HBE)

Unicef (2016) At a glance: Syrian Arab Republic, 22 February, www.unicef.org/infobycountry/syria_statistics.html (archived at https://perma.cc/B2AL-KGU3)

Utrecht-Monitor.nl (2022) Huisvesting & integratie vluchtelingen, utrecht-monitor.nl/bevolking-bestuur/bevolking/huisvesting-integratie-vluchtelingen#bookmark5 (archived at https://perma.cc/DP9T-9Y2V)

UWV (2022) Ruim 46.000 meldingen ontvangen van werkenden vluchtelingen uit Oekraïne, www.uwv.nl/nl/persberichten/ruim-46000-meldingen-ontvangen-van-werkenden-vluchtelingen-uit-oekraine#:~:text=Ook%20vinden%20veel%20vluchtelingen%20werk,)%20(13%25)%20een%20baan (archived at https://perma.cc/GSV2-FHCC)

van Tubergen, F (2010) Determinants of second language proficiency among refugees in the Netherlands, *Social Forces*, 89, 10.2307/40984545 (archived at https://perma.cc/TR8W-UQ87)

Visser, M, Scholte, M and Scheepers, P (2013) Fear of crime and feelings of unsafety in European countries: Macro and micro explanations in cross-national perspective, *The Sociological Quarterly*, **54** (2), 278–301, www.jstor.org/stable/24581910 (archived at https://perma.cc/K59N-NW3U)

Vroome, de T and van Tubergen, F (2010) The Employment Experience of Refugees in the Netherlands, *The International Migration Review*, **44** (2), 376–403, www.jstor.org/stable/25740854 (archived at https://perma.cc/C7P4-8QMG)

Węziak-Białowolska, D (2016) Quality of life in cities: Empirical evidence in comparative European perspective, *Cities*, **58**, 87–96

Witte, de M (2022) Ukrainian refugees face a more accommodating Europe, says Stanford scholar, *Stanford News*, 24 March, news.stanford.edu/2022/03/24/ukrainian-refugees-face-accommodating-europe-says-stanford-scholar/ (archived at https://perma.cc/C9RP-5ZRG)

World Health Organization (2012) WHOQOL: Measuring Quality of life, www.who.int/tools/whoqol (archived at https://perma.cc/F83J-HBTQ)

Increasing the social impact of banking

10

This chapter describes the application of the Responsible Business Simulator at Volksbank NV (de Volksbank). The need to bring about social impact within the banking sector has grown tremendously over the past years, which is confirmed by the increase in regulations such as Corporate Sustainability Reporting Directive (CSRD) and the public exposure of banks' behaviour on sustainability. De Volksbank, a medium-sized bank in the Netherlands, is committed to achieving a substantial and measurable positive impact on society.

About de Volksbank

De Volksbank is the fourth largest bank in the Netherlands with a focus on the Dutch retail market. It is the driving force behind four brands: SNS, ASN Bank, RegioBank and BLG Wonen. With their four brands, de Volksbank serves different customer segments in the Netherlands based on a single, central IT platform. It offers simple and transparent mortgages, savings and payment products to private individuals, self-employed people and smaller companies. De Volksbank aims to meet the specific financial needs of their customers in a people-oriented, efficient and sustainable manner. By being a driving force, it aims to contribute to changes at customer and system level. Their mission is 'banking with a human touch'. They plan to achieve this by creating benefits for their customers, improving their business operations by taking responsibility for society, genuinely paying attention to their employees, and also achieving returns to their shareholders.

In this way they strive to optimize 'shared value' rather than shareholder value only. In their strategy (de Volksbank, 2021) for the period 2021–2025, entitled 'Better for each other – from promise to impact' they focus on two major goals:

1 De Volksbank is the bank with the strongest customer relationships in the Netherlands.

2 De Volksbank achieves social impact on the climate and decent living by integrating these themes into their services.

De Volksbank has already been clearly successful in reaching the first goal, given the results of the Dutch Banking Monitor. Three of the four brands of de Volksbank participated in this monitor. Table 10.1 shows that the top three banks in the Netherlands (ING, Rabobank and ABN AMRO Bank) score lower than the three brands of de Volksbank on all four characteristics.

With respect to the second goal, demonstrating the impact that de Volksbank makes on society in a quantitative way is not as simple as

Table 10.1 Results of the Dutch Banking Monitor on a scale from 1–10

	General	Internet & mobile	Costs	Service
RegioBank	9.5	8.8	6.5	8.9
ASN Bank	9.1	8.5	6.5	8.5
Knab	8.4	8.5	6.4	8.4
Triodos Bank	8.3	8.1	5.3	8.2
SNS	8.1	8.4	5.9	8.1
ING	7.0	8.2	5.1	7.3
Rabobank	6.9	8.1	5.3	7.1
ABN AMRO	6.7	8.1	5.1	7.0

SOURCE Consumentenbond, 2022

it may seem since there are several complexities that need to be addressed. Still, de Volksbank has already made major steps in their external reporting on non-financial value (de Volksbank, 2023). At the same time, other banks are catching up quickly under pressure from the Corporate Sustainability Reporting Directive, which forces banks to start reporting on the environmental, social and governance aspects of their operations. De Volksbank has always been the frontrunner in focusing on non-financial impact and has already contributed to the development of indicators to make that impact measurable during an era in which there was not much guidance on how to do it. For example, the Platform Carbon Accounting Financials established to enable financial institutions to measure and disclose greenhouse gas (GHG) emissions of loans and investments was headed by ASN. Since EFRAG (nd) issued draft Environmental & Social Reporting Standards (ESRS), much more guidance is now available. This has meant that de Volksbank has put effort into reporting in formats that turn out not to be required. Also, the development by de Volksbank of non-financial indicators that do turn out to be useful in the context of ESRS may have been done less efficiently than just awaiting the EFRAG guidance. In other words: the challenge of de Volksbank when it comes to reporting on non-financial value is to escape from the so-called head-starter's handicap, also known as first-mover disadvantage or 'dialectics of progress' (Romein, 1935).

However, there are three reasons why being a first mover may still turn to be beneficial for de Volksbank:

- First, it is not the objective of the bank to be the only one that is creating societal value. Given de Volksbank's intrinsic motivation to contribute to the transition to a better world, it is not desirable to have just one 'social' bank. In other words, it is desirable that other banks catch up quickly as well. In fact, de Volksbank wants to be a source of inspiration in this field, e.g. by disclosing the case studies in this chapter as inspiration to other organizations to take similar action, de Volksbank serves as a guide, leading by example for the banking sector.

- Second, irrespective of the efforts to report on non-financial value, the bank's focus on increasing their societal impact should also result in non-financial scores that are simply better than those of other banks. As can be seen from Table 10.1, the focus on the social wellbeing of customers does indeed result in better scores.

- Third, it is important to realize that CSRD entails more than just reporting on environmental and social impact retrospectively. According to ESRS 2, article 46(c), organizations are also required to disclose how their decision making helps them to control the creation of non-financial value. Here, banks that are lagging in this respect will have a harder time to catch up with the first movers than they would have when just collecting data to report retrospectively. In other words, the crux of the matter is to deliberately plan and act to create shared value instead of just waiting to see whether shared value will be created. Figure 10.1 depicts this graphically. In the remainder of this chapter we will address some examples of the upward vertical movement in this graph by consolidating different scales into one metric.

ASN focuses on climate, biodiversity and living wages. The first two focus areas make ASN a green bank. The third focus area shows that ASN addresses social impact as well. De Volksbank (2018) has identified

Figure 10.1   Moving from reports based on multiple measurement scales to strategic plans for shared value

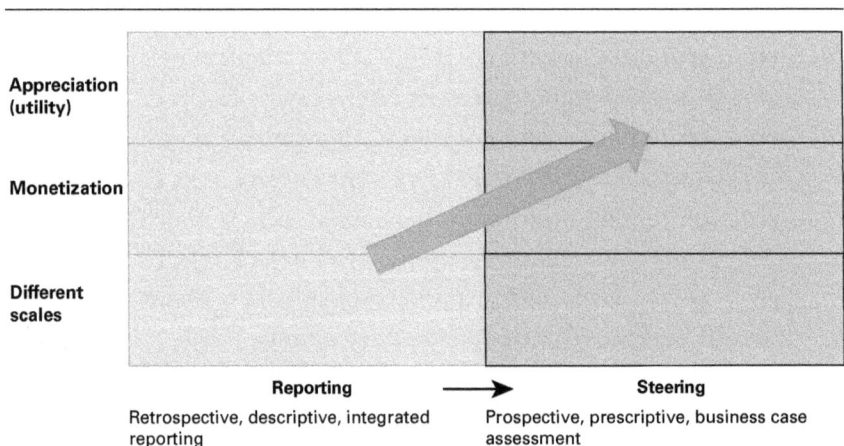

Appreciation (utility)

Monetization

Different scales

Reporting
Retrospective, descriptive, integrated reporting

Steering
Prospective, prescriptive, business case assessment

living wages as one of the five most salient human rights issues related to ASN's Investment Funds. In addition, ASN has already incorporated how companies in which they are considering investing for a long time address human rights.

The other three brands focus on creating social impact. Whereas ASN is an internet bank, SNS, RegioBank and BLG Wonen maintain a rich local network of franchisees and financial advisors. SNS has more than 200 branches. At the time of this case, RegioBank maintains a network of more than 530 branches. BLG Wonen works with more than 3,000 independent financial advisors. This local presence differentiates these three brands from the top three banks in the Netherlands, who have shut down many local branches over the past years. ING have shut down more than 25 per cent of their branches and as at January 2022 had 57 full-service branches and 291 service points. The number of Rabobank's branches decreased from 371 in 2019 to 133 in February 2023. ABN AMRO's branches decreased from more than 1,000 in 1996 to 53 in May 2022.

In this chapter, we will focus on RegioBank and BLG Wonen for two reasons. First, these two brands focus on creating social impact, and there is already a lot of attention in the banking sector on green investments, but not so much on the 'S' in ESG. Second, within these two brands, there have been two recent decision-making cases that are interesting to report on.

Each of these two brands focuses on a specific social theme:

- quality of life in the neighbourhood for RegioBank
- good housing for everyone for BLG Wonen

These two themes are also obvious focal themes from a brand-naming perspective: BLG Wonen and RegioBank are the only Dutch brands that have a residential and regional connotation in their names (*wonen* means living in a residence in Dutch; *regio* is the Dutch equivalent for region).

In the next section, we will provide more context on each of these themes.

About quality of life and good housing

Quality of life in the neighbourhood and good housing for everyone represent a wide range of themes, they have three common denominators. First, the degree to which these two themes have been met are all hard to quantify. Second, from a banking perspective, it requires more than one stakeholder to define a strategy to create an impact on these themes. Third, if an impact has been created, what part of that impact can be attributed to de Volksbank? Because of these similarities, we discuss these in this single chapter. We start with a small introduction for each theme, and from these introductions, most readers will probably conclude that it is a no-brainer to strive for both objectives. However, how to reach these objectives by providing a quantified baseline and creating actionable insights on how to guide the current situation in a positive direction is much harder. In the next section we will sketch what steps in the seven-step framework have been applied to achieve this.

Quality of life in the neighbourhood (RegioBank)

For more than 100 years RegioBank's mission has been to improve the quality of life, the 'liveability', in the neighbourhoods it serves. Everything RegioBank does is aimed at keeping the neighbourhood alive or to making it more attractive as a place to live. Instead of closing local bank branches, RegioBank stays nearby. This way, people not only have the security and (digital) benefits of a large bank, but also have a familiar face around the corner. RegioBank wants to contribute to an environment in which people can enjoy working and living in their homes and neighbourhoods. They want to play a connecting role to stimulate local involvement and solidarity. RegioBank's slogan reads: 'A better society starts in the neighbourhood'. Also, RegioBank coined the Dutch term *Buurtzaam*, which could be translated into English as 'neighbourly' or 'communality'. As we will explain in more detail when discussing the key output definitions in the next section, this notion correlates strongly with the two dimensions 'civic engagement' and 'personal security' in the term 'quality of life' as defined by OECD (2011), which is also promoted and used by the United Nations and RegioBank.

To contribute to the liveliness and satisfaction of residents in the neighbourhood, RegioBank quantifies how satisfied residents are right now with their residences, their jobs and their direct social environment. Based on this information, RegioBank can determine how 'neighbourly' a region is and pinpoint where there is room for improvement in what dimension of regional liveability. This empowers their network of franchisees to take targeted action.

Good housing for everyone (BLG Wonen)

BLG Wonen strives for a housing market where everyone can live where they want. Owning their own home gives people a feeling of security and happiness. To contribute to this theme, BLG Wonen works, among other things, to promote accessibility to the housing market, which we refer to as 'housing accessibility'. As a first step, BLG Wonen measured housing accessibility. De Volksbank's research revealed that there are already various indices that map a range of aspects of the housing market in the Netherlands, but these do not focus on housing accessibility for specific residential segments. Also, they do not distinguish between target groups and do not yet report at the granular postal code 4 level. Given this, it is very hard to make definite statements about current housing accessibility.

To measure this type of accessibility, BLG Wonen has developed a mathematical model. This model represents housing accessibility across various permanent residential segments for specific target groups per area in the Netherlands. This cross-section of residential segment and target group provides insights into where and for whom the housing market in the Netherlands is currently (not) accessible. The insights have been used by BLG Wonen to identify new priorities in their service offering, such as home-seekers who currently spend a large portion of their income on rent. In this way, the model provides a prescriptive analysis, suggesting what the decision maker should do. It turns out that BLG Wonen can play a role in reducing or eliminating some of these issues. In addition to using the model internally for creating insights into residential accessibility per region and its drivers, BLG Wonen has made the model's outcomes available in an intuitive and transparent manner via the Housing Accessibility Monitor (BLG Wonen, nd). This monitor visualizes housing accessibility in the form of a dashboard and can also be used externally in stakeholder dialogues. This allows BLG Wonen to provide insight into residential accessibility from different perspectives.

In summary, the Housing Accessibility Monitor can be used to identify problems in the housing market and serve as a starting point from which to devise and calculate appropriate change strategies to resolve these problems. In this way, the monitor also provides an overview of different actions, thus forming a basis for understanding the housing market and, above all, for achieving social benefits.

The strategic decision-making process

For the two cases presented in this chapter, de Volksbank used the seven-step framework. It is beyond the scope of this book to discuss all these projects in detail. Instead, we sketch each step in the framework for each of the two cases at a high level, where we focus on the main characteristics of the framework: involvement of many stakeholders and experts from various disciplines; the use of data science for quantification and appreciation of non-financial value next to financial value; and selecting the most robust decision maker's option to meet strategic objectives. It is also important to note that this chapter reports on de Volksbank's strategy execution throughout the period 2020–2022. Since early 2023, it has started a strategic reorientation. As such, the purpose of this case is not to discuss de Volksbank's strategy, but to sketch how a bank can operationalize its strategy into concrete decisions, actions and initiatives. New societal developments will probably always require updates before this process has converged completely.

Describing the strategic challenge that requires a decision

Based on the previous paragraph it is possible to word the strategic challenges for each of the brands as follows:

- How can RegioBank and their franchisees increase the quality of life in the neighbourhood?
- How can BLG Wonen design banking products and services that increase housing accessibility?

Defining key outputs involving stakeholders

For each of the strategic challenges, we discuss the key output high-level definitions.

RegioBank

Key outputs have been defined for three purposes: to get a baseline performance, to track this performance in a monitor, and to predict how key outputs will change as a result of interventions.

The hierarchical structure in Figure 10.2 is used to break down the theme 'neighbourliness' into sub-themes. Brainstorming sessions per sub-theme resulted in longlists of potential key outputs.

Table 10.2 shows the results of filtering these longlists based on predetermined selection criteria, e.g. availability of data in terms of update frequency and granularity. The column 'Appreciation' lists whether a key output is Smaller-the-Better or Larger-the-Better. (The acronym COROP stands for Coördinatiecommissie Regionaal Onderzoeksprogramma and refers to a division of the Netherlands for statistical purposes.) Inspection of the Update frequency column reveals that RegioBank is well positioned to provide such a monitor. Acquiring data from commercial data provider EDM, and combining this with open-source data and internal data is unique for a bank with a local presence like RegioBank, and provides insights that cannot be generated by other organizations.

Figure 10.2   Value tree for regional liveability

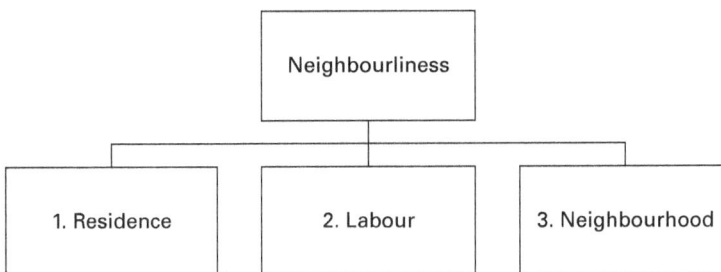

Table 10.2 Key outputs in theme 'Neighbourliness' for RegioBank case

Id	Key output	Scale (unit)	Appreciation	Granularity	Update frequency	Source
1.1	Average residential satisfaction	Likert(1-5)	LtB	Province	Every three years	CBS (WoON, 2023)
1.2	Average distance to bars & restaurants	km	StB	Municipality	Annually	CBS (2022)
1.3	Average distance to groceries	km	StB	Municipality	Annually	Nabijheid voorzieningen CBS (2022)
1.4	Average distance to primary school	km	StB	Municipality	Annually	Nabijheid voorzieningen CBS (2022)
1.5	Average distance to hospital	km	StB	Gemeente niveau	Annually	Nabijheid voorzieningen CBS (2022)
1.6	Membership of associations	%	LtB	Municipality	Annually	Waarstaatjegemeente (2023)
1.7	Average price of a house	€	StB	COROP	Quarterly	NVM (2023)
2.1	Local expenditure	€	LtB	ZIP code	Daily	RegioBank
2.2	Percentage of citizens receiving social welfare benefits	%	StB	Municipality	5 times per year	CBS (2022)

2.3	Number of local jobs per citizen	#	LtB	Municipality	Annually	CBS (2023a)
2.4	Average household income	€	LtB	ZIP code	Annually	EDM (commercial data)
3.1	Feeling of safety	Likert (1-5)	LtB	Province	Annually	CBS (2023b)
3.2	Social cohesion	Likert (1-5)	LtB	Province	Annually	CBS (2022)
3.3	Intention to migrate	%	StB	ZIP code	Twice per year	EDM (commercial data)
3.4	Number of sports accommodation per 10,000 citizens	#	LtB	Municipality	Irregular (last update: 2020)	NOCNSF (2022)

Figure 10.3 shows the Neighbourliness of the Netherlands by region. It is the result of collecting data and applying weights and appreciation functions. We discuss these appreciations in more detail when discussing the construction of the simulation model. The weights are set equally per sub-theme by default, as are the key outputs. The user of this monitor (typically the franchisee) can change these weights according to their interests. By setting all weights to zero except the weight for one key output and its corresponding sub-theme, individual key outputs can be inspected as well.

Next to these 15 key outputs covering the theme Neighbourliness, there is a theme called 'monetary societal impact'. Some of the key outputs in Table 10.2 can be expressed in societal monetary return as well. If so, a monetary counterpart is defined. There are also key outputs reflecting societal monetary return that do not have a counterpart in Table 10.2. An example of such a key output is the societal

Figure 10.3   Neighbourliness monitor of RegioBank

value of volunteer hours, which we will discuss in more detail in the section on constructing the simulation model.

To model the financial effect of decisions to create shared value, outputs of the franchisee compensation model have been added as key outputs as well. One of the components of financial compensation of franchisees is a literal output in terms of the Theory of Change model, since it is partly based on how active a franchisee has been in applying the centrally developed services focusing on regional liveability.

BLG Wonen

BLG Wonen has developed the Housing Accessibility Monitor. In this monitor, housing accessibility is shown as a percentage and is defined as the number of seekers that find a residence within a year divided by the total number of people looking for a residence. This percentage is calculated at a very granular level: per Dutch municipality, and per residential segment (i.e. rental or owner-occupied). By applying the distribution of different target groups to the accessibility percentage per municipality per residential segment level, it is possible to calculate housing accessibility from the perspective of target groups.

The monitor includes 16 different target groups at the time of writing. The different target groups are shown in Figure 10.4. Based on

Figure 10.4   Overview of target groups for Housing Accessibility Monitor

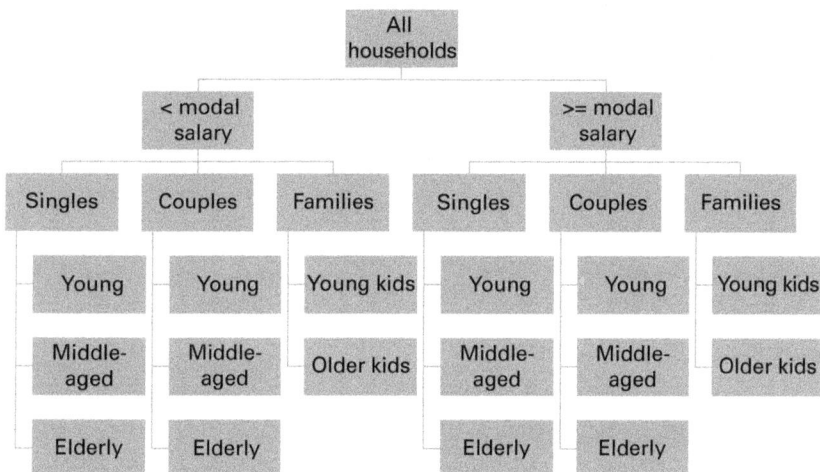

these three cross-sections, target groups, municipalities and residential segments can be compared with each other in the context of housing accessibility and are input for making statements about the frictions and opportunities in the Dutch housing market.

The following six indicators are provided in the monitor to gain insights into how they relate to housing accessibility:

1 outflow

2 waiting time

3 increase house price

4 labour/supply factor

5 affordability

6 demand/supply ratio

Brainstorming sessions about the possible indicators influencing housing accessibility in combination with expert judgement and data availability led to the selection of the indicators above.

Figure 10.5 shows the Housing Accessibility Monitor with the residential accessibility and underlying indicators for a selected municipality.

Just as for the regional Liveability Monitor of RegioBank, BLG has created a unique monitor of the housing market by compiling data from open and commercial data sources (e.g. CBS micro data, EDM, WoON2018) at a granular level. Since it is hard for a bank to influence housing accessibility directly, a statistical analysis has been conducted to understand how these six indicators correlate with housing accessibility. This analysis revealed that there is a statistically significant correlation for two driving indicators for housing accessibility: affordability and demand/supply ratio.

Since this chapter is about designing interventions to improve housing accessibility, we will focus on the latter two indicators as key outputs of a decision to increase housing accessibility. Once BLG Wonen succeeds in making decisions that lead to key output scores that show improvement compared to the baseline scores, the bank can come to a conclusion about the extent to which they contributed to residential accessibility.

Figure 10.5 Residential Accessibility Monitor of BLG Wonen

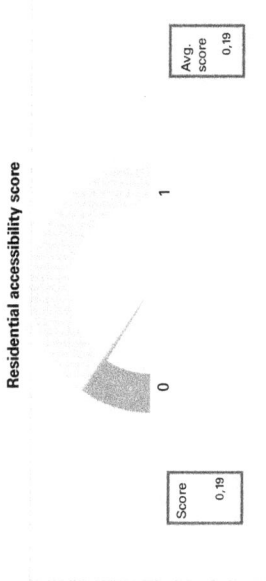

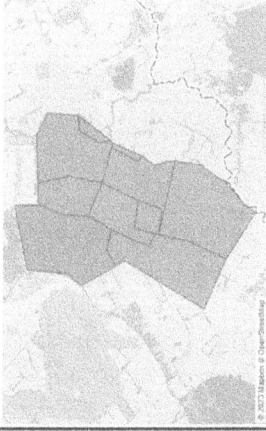

Residential accessibility score

Score 0,19

Avg. score 0,19

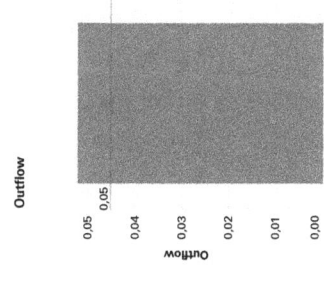

Outflow

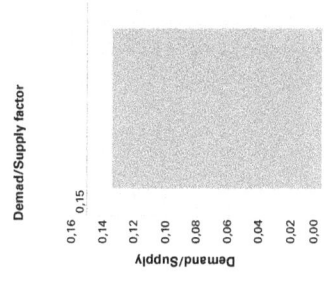

Demad/Supply factor

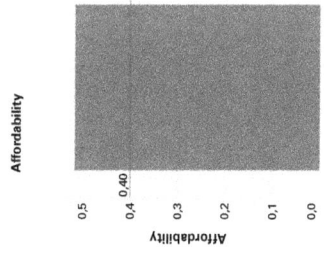

Affordability

Determining decision maker's options

To influence the future key output scores, each of the three brands defined a set of internal variable inputs. In this case, these inputs represent both existing services and ideas for new services. For RegioBank there is an additional variable input reflecting which part of the franchisee compensation is based on how many of these services franchisees have been offering. As such, a decision maker's option consists of a portfolio of services and to what degree a franchisee is receiving an incentive for offering these services. We limit ourselves to detailing the longlists of existing and potential services per label.

RegioBank

- banking awareness course ('EuroWise') in primary schools
- cashier function during Children Savings Week
- organization of sports event
- organization of volunteering day
  - cleaning up the neighbourhood
  - supporting local entrepreneurs
  - fighting loneliness
- organization of activity as part of programme 'NL for each other'
- organization of informative session on RegioBank's social initiatives
- housing improvement programme by local contractors
- education programme for adults
- help with application for subsidy out of two Dutch funds:
  - Oranjefonds (Orange Funds)
  - Samen voor de Buurt (Fund for the Neighbourhood)

BLG Wonen

- help in reconfiguring houses from one-family into multi-occupancy dwellings
- (partially) exclude study debt from equity position in mortgage application process

- create a think-tank consisting of specialists from housing market sector and interested people in order to develop innovative ways to increase housing stock and finance residences (e.g. self-built houses, kangaroo houses (houses with accommodation for two generations))

Drawing up scenarios

It is obvious that many external inputs determine to what degree the decision maker's option will influence the key outputs for all three strategic challenges discussed in this case study. After all, a major part of the simulation model consists of modelling human behaviour and perceptions. Next to that, the economic outlook, and especially the forecasts on interest rates for mortgages and on saving accounts, all play a major role in projecting sales volumes and profitability for a retail bank such as de Volksbank.

The coefficients that are used to model how key outputs related to personal growth, regional liveability and residential accessibility depend on inputs were quantified as 95 per cent confidence intervals. This information was obtained from either secondary data collection (research reports and academic literature) or from primary data collection (surveys and analysis of the impact of fluctuations in de Volksbank's own historical data). The uncertainty is expressed as the width of these confidence intervals. Best- and worst-case scenarios have been defined by assigning lower or upper bounds to each of these coefficients.

Relevant scenarios for the future development of sales volumes were designed together with the franchisees. In the case of RegioBank, the seven steps were used to determine the compensation of the franchisees, thereby generating insight into the franchisees' earnings under various scenarios.

In the case of BLG Wonen, the bounds of the confidence intervals of the coefficients in the statistical model that express the influence of drivers for residential accessibility are suitable inputs for scenarios. Also, future Dutch population forecasts across age categories and household types are available from the Central Bureau of Statistics and are inputs for scenarios.

Constructing the simulation model

When describing the simulation model, it is relevant to distinguish between the simulation of social and financial impacts for each of the two brands.

RegioBank

Figure 10.6 shows an example of how the social monetary return resulting from the organization of a volunteering day is calculated. These calculations are not complex as long as they are broken down in small steps, including sources and assumptions. The Responsible Business Simulator generates visualizations of these breakdowns automatically.

Another potential activity in Step 5 is the calibration of appreciation functions that make key output scores mutually comparable. As explained in Chapter 7, the user can choose automatic determination of these functions based on the variety of absolute key output scores across the decision maker's options and scenarios. However, in this regional liveability case it was deemed important to be in full control of these appreciation functions by defining these manually. As an example, we briefly sketch the reasoning behind the appreciation function of membership of associations. RegioBank has divided the Netherlands into a number of market areas in such a way that each market area is covered by one RegioBank branch. Across these areas, the percentage of citizens who are members of an association is at most 43.6 per cent. Consequently, the appreciation of membership percentages of lower than 13.6 per cent is 0 and that of values higher than 43.6 per cent is 100.

BLG Wonen

Whereas the Housing Accessibility Monitor has evolved into a mature instrument to gain insights into the various frictions in the housing market, including forecasts of which frictions will increase and decrease over time, BLG is still in the process of modelling the relationship between the interventions defined in Step 3 and these frictions. Some of these relationships are straightforward, such as the effect of offering a service to help with reconfiguring houses on the demand/supply ratio. However, modelling the effect that failure to

Figure 10.6 Example of dependency tree in simulation model for RegioBank case

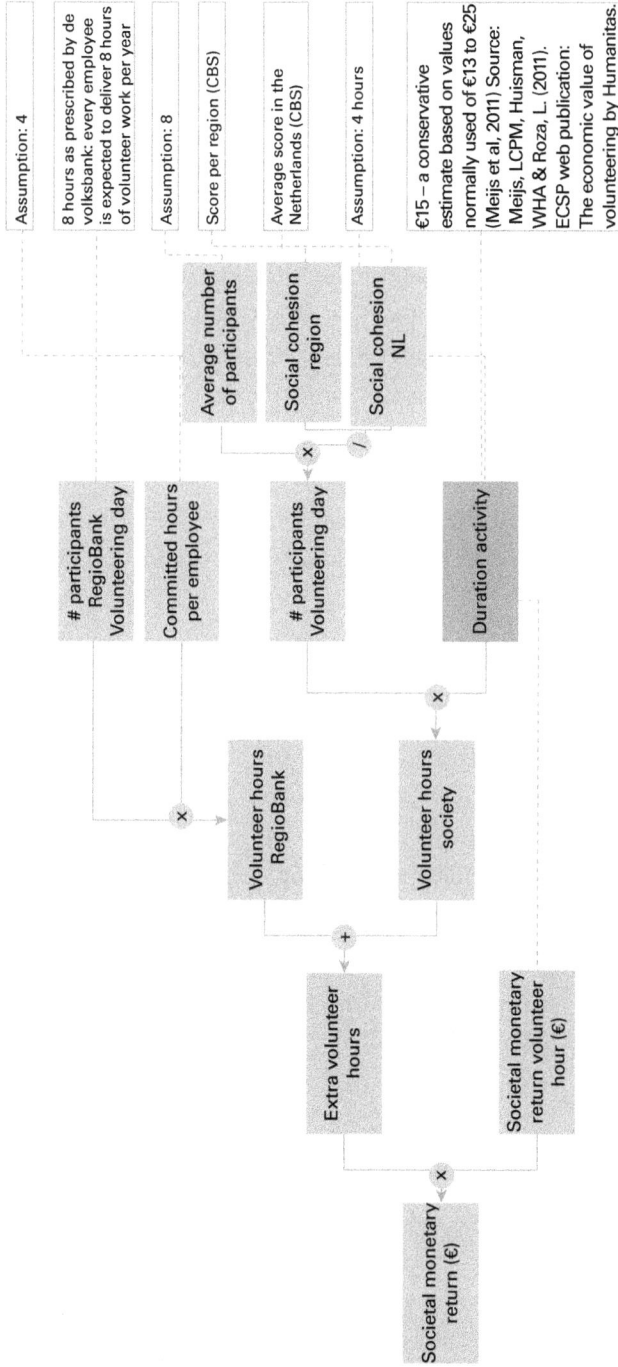

Assumption: 4

8 hours as prescribed by de volksbank: every employee is expected to deliver 8 hours of volunteer work per year

Assumption: 8

Score per region (CBS)

Average score in the Netherlands (CBS)

Assumption: 4 hours

€15 – a conservative estimate based on values normally used of €13 to €25 (Meijs et al, 2011) Source: Meijs, LCPM, Huisman, WHA & Roza, L. (2011). ECSP web publication: The economic value of volunteering by Humanitas.

Average number of participants

Social cohesion region

Social cohesion NL

participants RegioBank Volunteering day

Committed hours per employee

participants Volunteering day

Duration activity

Volunteer hours RegioBank

Volunteer hours society

Extra volunteer hours

Societal monetary return volunteer hour (€)

Societal monetary return (€)

consider student debts in a mortgage application has on affordability is more complex and is still a work in progress.

Evaluating options by assessing strategic priorities

For all three brands discussed in this case, a major part of assessing strategic priorities comes down to identifying which services impact the various key outputs and to what extent. Here, the benefit of data at a regionally granular level comes into play, since the impact of a service depends on regional circumstances. For example, when 40 per cent of citizens are already members of an association, there is not much more to gain by investing in services that – among others – focus on stimulating people to become members of an association. Typically, franchisees and financial advisors have too limited a capacity to deliver the full set of services. Using the Responsible Business Simulator they are enabled to compile a package of services that fits their capacity, that takes into account the current regional liveability, and that reflects their preferences for which key output and/or sub-themes to focus on.

Another part of the assessment involves the calibration of the parameter settings in the new franchise compensation model for RegioBank. Every franchisee of RegioBank had access to the Responsible Business Simulator to simulate the future impact of the new compensation in their market area. Due to the confidentiality of these settings, we restrict ourselves to showing in Figure 10.7 the output of this step by means of a comparison of the impact of five potential packages of services across the key outputs for one selected market area of RegioBank when all key outputs are equal.

Evaluating options by assessing risk appetite

A large part of this case study is getting inspired about new services aimed at creating social value by estimating their effect as a basis to

Figure 10.7 Comparison of interventions across key outputs for RegioBank case

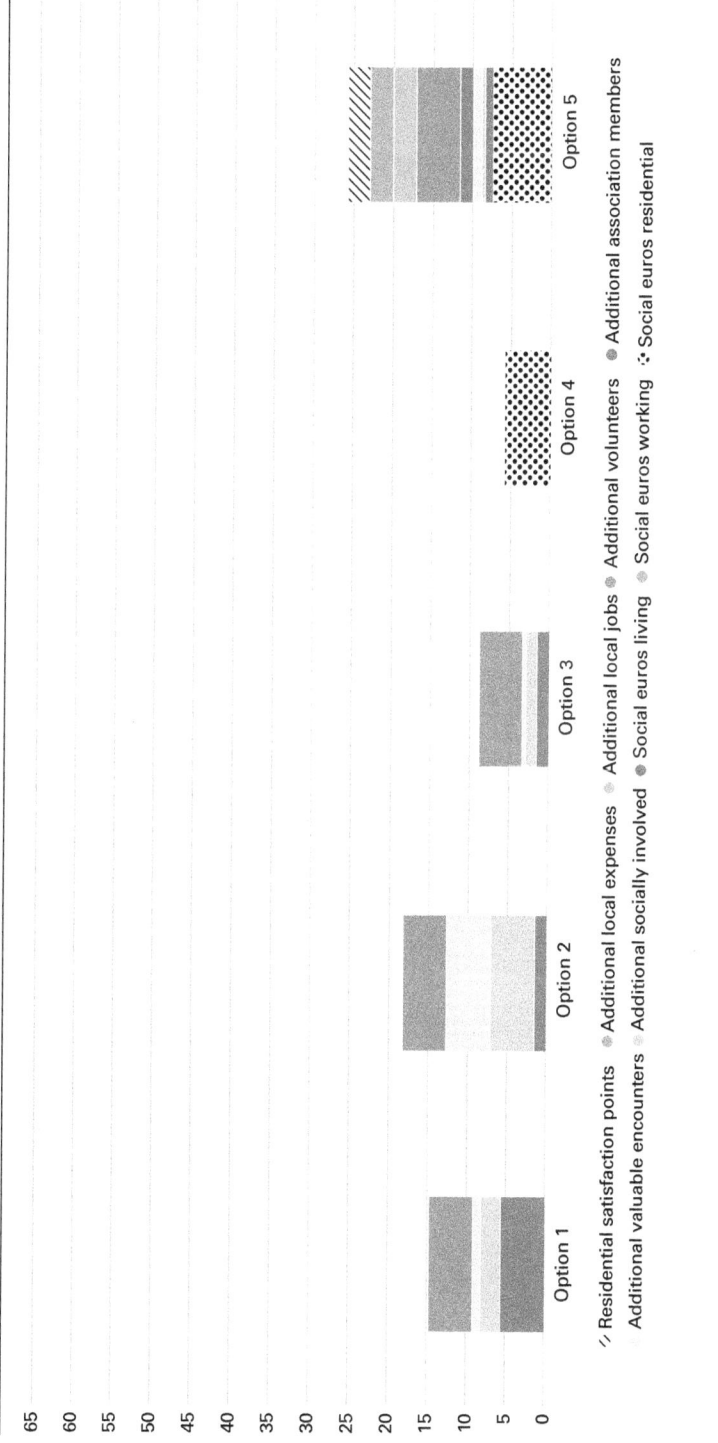

Residential satisfaction points • Additional local expenses • Additional local jobs • Additional volunteers • Additional association members
Additional valuable encounters • Additional socially involved • Social euros living • Social euros working • Social euros residential

decide on the launch of such services. This means that there is not one big decision at one point in time, but rather a series of smaller decisions on when to go live with a new service. Only the services that performed robustly enough had already been launched. Services whose simulated impact was not yet robust enough are redesigned or postponed until more research could give narrower confidence intervals for the expected effects. As such, the more pessimistic scenarios in Step 5 have rather been used as potential showstoppers for decision makers' options rather than as a true reflection of de Volksbank's risk appetite. This also means that the process of designing new services is still ongoing.

For the decision on the new franchise compensation models, Step 7 also took the form of looking at franchisees who would lose or gain the most because of the new model. On some occasions this analysis resulted in implementing so-called 'cushions' in the new model to provide a soft landing for franchisees who would suffer from too extreme effects. Similarly, on some occasions extreme effects in the opposite direction have been capped in the new compensation scheme before it was set in stone.

Reflections

De Volksbank has been a pioneer in quantifying their progress in generating societal impact next to shareholder value and incorporating societal impact in their decision making. In this chapter we have seen two examples of decision making in two of de Volksbank's brands that required the involvement of many stakeholders. These decisions are not set in stone forever: as more research and measurements become available, the underlying relations in generating social impact are updated and lead to new and better decisions. As such, the cases discussed in this chapter are still work in progress. As this will probably continue forever, the pitfall can be to also wait forever before disclosing and using the results of this work in progress.

The one reflection that stands out from all the other ones in this case is the involvement of franchisees in deciding on a new franchise compensation model. Designing this type of model is often perceived as a series of tough negotiations between franchisees and the franchisor about how to divide up the pie. Money either lands in the wallet of a franchisee or in that of de Volksbank. Give or take. However, when franchisees and franchisor sit together to explore other ways of compensation with full transparency of the simulated impact for each of these approaches, the discussion is changed from one of dividing up the existing pie to increasing the size of the whole pie.

It turned out to be crucial that all stakeholders gained confidence in the underlying simulation model. This was achieved in two ways:

- being able to reproduce every penny paid out according to the previous model with the same simulation model, and
- giving full transparency about all details of every step in the seven-step framework including the simulation model by granting each stakeholder full access to this case in the Responsible Business Simulator

The second point does not imply that the simulation model is a crystal ball that always predicts the future in an accurate way. On the contrary, the inherent challenge of making a strategic decision is that the decision makers cannot wait until they know how the future will unfold. Making decisions under conditions of uncertainty lies at the heart of the matter, especially in the context of systems change. The Responsible Business Simulator is not able to get rid of this phenomenon. But it is documenting all the assumptions against a range of possible events, and how decision makers' options would behave under these assumptions in a structured and easy to understand way.

References

BLG Wonen (nd) www.blgwonen.nl/over-ons/woontoegankelijkheidsmonitor/kansen-woningmarkt-in-beeld.html (archived at https://perma.cc/2NVD-5ZFS)

CBS (2022) Regional key figures for the Netherlands, Centraal Bureau voor de Statistiek, www.cbs.nl/nl-nl/cijfers/detail/70072ned (archived at https://perma.cc/B8E8-LUTB)

CBS (2023a) Key figures by postal code, www.cbs.nl/nl-nl/dossier/nederland-regionaal/geografische-data/gegevens-per-postcode (archived at https://perma.cc/XUE8-S4WU)

CBS (2023b) Safety monitor, www.cbs.nl/nl-nl/maatschappij/veiligheid-en-recht/veiligheidsmonitor (archived at https://perma.cc/7SDD-DN2R)

Consumentenbond (2022) Banking monitor: the best bank according to consumers, www.consumentenbond.nl/betaalrekening/bankenmonitor (archived at https://perma.cc/5RSE-QAQ5)

De Volksbank (2018) Salient Risk Analysis, www.devolksbank.nl/assets/files/de-Volksbank-N.V.-Annual-Report-2021.pdf (archived at https://perma.cc/7TYH-A3ZR)

De Volksbank (2021) Strategy 2021-2025, www.devolksbank.nl (archived at https://perma.cc/E4EH-KJV5)

De Volksbank (2023) Integrated Annual Report 2022, www.devolksbank.nl (archived at https://perma.cc/28BC-WJSF)

EFRAG (nd) ESRS Exposure Drafts, www.efrag.org (archived at https://perma.cc/GYU9-XZ3J)

FBD Bankmensen (2018) www.fbd.nl (archived at https://perma.cc/6YS8-LSXE)

Meijs, LCPM, Huisman, WHA and Roza, L (2011) *The Economic Value of Volunteering by Humanitas*, ECSP

NOCNSF (2022) Zo sport Nederland NOCNSF sports research 2021, nocnsf.nl/wat-doet-nocnsf/sport-in-nederland/sportonderzoek/zo-sport-nederland (archived at https://perma.cc/T2GQ-NTWN)

NVM (2023) Market information for owner-occupied homes, www.nvm.nl/wonen/marktinformatie/ (archived at https://perma.cc/XN2Y-SXFL)

OECD (2011) How's Life? Measuring wellbeing, OECD Publishing, dx.doi.org/10.1787/9789264121164-en (archived at https://perma.cc/PUQ5-ZUAD)

Pichère, P and Cadiat, A-C (2015) *Maslow's Hierarchy Of Needs*, Lemaitre

Romein, J (1935) De dialectiek van de vooruitgang: Bijdrage tot het ontwikkelingsbegrip in de geschiedenis, *Forum* (4-2), 732–77

Verwey-Jonker Instituut (2020) NTD Eindrapport

WoON (2023) Housing Survey Netherlands, www.woononderzoek.nl (archived at https://perma.cc/A7DD-UUZU)

Waarstaatjegemeente (2023) Sport and Culture, www.waarstaatjegemeente.nl/dashboard/dashboard/sport-en-cultuur/ (archived at https://perma.cc/XSF4-VF9E)

Creating a healthy and productive working environment

11

Creating a working environment that stimulates healthy living is key to attracting talent, retaining employees who deliver better quality, and preventing sick leave. Particularly in organizations with a high stress factor, such as healthcare, it is a challenge to shape conditions for a sustainable workplace. The IZZ Foundation (IZZ) is dedicated to the strategic goal of creating a better working environment and reducing the costs of health- and stress-related absenteeism. This chapter illustrates the application of strategic decision making at the IZZ Foundation.

IZZ had been investing in healthy employees for years, but never knew what the impact and effects of these investments were. Using the Responsible Business Simulator (tRBS) we were able to indicate very precisely where to invest and what the impact would be. The unique thing about the IZZ Foundation is that they embedded the strategic decision-making process in all their conversations with the boardroom members of health institutions. We will start by introducing the Foundation and its background in the context of making strategic decisions to benefit People, Planet and Profit.

About IZZ

The IZZ Foundation is a non-profit organization in the Netherlands that has been promoting the interests of healthcare professionals (in hospitals, nursing and care homes, home care, handicapped care, mental health and youth care) since its establishment in 1977. On the basis of its focus on people and wide knowledge of and commitment to the healthcare sector, IZZ provides healthcare insurance on a non-profit basis for almost half a million Dutch healthcare employees and their families. That insurance is tailored to the needs of this special group and takes full account of the specific health risks involved in working in the sector. IZZ is the market leader in the healthcare sector, and what makes it unique is the input and influence that employers and employees in the healthcare sector together have on improving health and employability for healthcare professionals. On the one hand there is the collective IZZ insurance, which is an important employee benefit and is therefore incorporated into many collective labour agreements, and on the other hand is the extensive programme for improving healthy working conditions and the organizational climate. The Responsible Business Simulator is part of this programme.

Empowering employees

Halfway through 2020 more than 1.5 million people were working in the healthcare sector in the Netherlands (CBS, 2020). For the last few years, the inflow of healthcare personnel in the Netherlands has been higher than the outflow (Arbeidsmarkt Zorg en Welzijn, 2021). Nevertheless, the sector faces some major challenges: an increasing population that is in need of healthcare, high work pressures experienced by the employees, and increasing absenteeism as well as high turnover for employers to cope with (ten Arve, 2022).

The frequency of absenteeism in this sector is higher than in any other sector (CBS, 2021) and in the first quarter of 2022 was at its highest level ever (NOS, 2022). The number of long-term sickness absences has increased as well, from 92 to 720 days (Vernet, 2021).

The probability that someone will change jobs in the healthcare sector is linked to employee satisfaction. The Dutch National Healthcare Monitor, Zorgbarometer, showed that in 2011 no less than 54 per cent of the employees in the healthcare sector had considered looking for another job outside the sector (ADV Market Research, 2011). For 93 per cent of this group, the most important reason was poor employee benefits. Other reasons given were high levels of pressure, low salary and too much bureaucracy. Contact with clients was the single most positive aspect of a job in healthcare (according to 81 per cent), even though strict scheduling often means that staff don't have time for a chat with clients. To IZZ these developments were a call to action. Research among 5,000 healthcare professionals in the Netherlands in 2022 (Pensioenfonds Zorg en Welzijn, 2022) found that leadership (support), the content of the job and pressures of work were the main reasons for staff leaving. Financial reward is deemed to be a less important reason for leaving, partly because of several rounds of salary increases. The Dutch Central Bureau of Statistics (CBS Statline, 2022) reports that in 2022 the percentage of employees leaving the healthcare sector was 26 per cent higher compared to the year before.

Healthcare employers that apply a purely financial approach when managing their organization run the risk of becoming embroiled in a downward spiral. Costs must be reduced, which means it is no longer possible to invest in staff. This leads to a less committed workforce, which in turn leads to greater staff turnover and more absenteeism. The consequence is an increase in personnel costs, which necessitates further reductions. Once one downward step has been taken, it is very difficult for organizations to extricate themselves from the spiral.

In an integrated approach, the starting point is different and the spiral need never develop. Sustainable measures must be taken to ensure the deployability of personnel, so that future clients of healthcare institutions can be cared for at an acceptable price. Investing in staff leads to greater employee commitment and satisfaction, as a result of which staff turnover and absenteeism decrease. The knock-on effect is an overall reduction of costs. Both the profit and the people objectives are achieved if this eventual cost reduction is greater than the investment made in the staff.

This knowledge, along with innovation and renewal, plays an important role in IZZ's strategy to maintain optimal deployability for employees in the sector. Some examples of their approach are programmes to reduce absenteeism among care-sector employees and to improve their productivity and employability. Such programmes could prove invaluable, given the current shortages in the healthcare labour market. IZZ's specific knowledge of and involvement in this market puts it in a unique position to create added value for healthcare institutions. As part of its strategy for innovation and renewal, IZZ applied the concept of strategic decision making using the Responsible Business Simulator.

The aim of the strategic decision making at IZZ is to satisfy the need to empower employees in the healthcare sector by quantifying the effects of various interventions. In other words, translate 'gut feelings' into statistics, so that a healthcare institution can take well-founded actions.

The strategic decision-making process

The strategic decision-making process at IZZ takes place in the form of multiple workshops with the Executive Board and in close collaboration with content experts from IZZ and several healthcare institutions. When describing the process we will follow the steps as set out in Chapter 5.

Describing the strategic challenge that requires a decision

IZZ's rationale is that if the image of the healthcare sector is to be improved and the severe staff shortages are to be resolved, it is important that sustainable ways are found to make the profession more attractive. This will not only help the people who work in the sector, but will also help the patients and ultimately society as a whole.

As the introduction to this chapter makes clear, there is a serious need for measures that will help achieve a balance between supply and demand in the healthcare sector while taking the welfare of personnel into account. This means that it will need to be determined, from the perspective of a healthcare institution, what measures will help make healthcare a more pleasant, efficient and attractive working environment.

The hypothesis is that by investing in people aspects, positive effects will also occur on the profit side. The strategic objective of using tRBS has been formulated as follows: 'to enable the IZZ Foundation to offer healthcare institutions objective insight into what – for them – is the optimal decision regarding the sustainability and empowerment of their employees'.

Defining key outputs involving stakeholders

The objective for IZZ in this case is to contribute to the people and profit aspects by supporting healthcare institutions with their decision making. Goals that fall within this remit are: healthy, committed and motivated healthcare professionals; sustainable deployment and empowerment of personnel in the healthcare sector; access to top-quality care; keeping sector-specific health problems at manageable levels; low staff turnover costs; low costs of absenteeism; and conditions of employment that have a specific added value for the healthcare sector.

The key outputs are those by which the organization seeks to achieve its goal. With the above-mentioned goals in mind, the key outputs are defined not only from the perspective of the decision maker within the healthcare organization, but also from the perspective of its employees and customers. This decision maker can be a Board member in the organization, but can also be an HR officer. In order to give insight to the decision maker as to whether it pays to invest in employees, key outputs addressing people aspects are formulated next to key outputs addressing profit aspects. The process of defining and refining the key outputs initially took place in close collaboration with the Board and content experts from IZZ. Next, in an explorative dialogue, stakeholders and experts occupying various functions within several healthcare institutions were asked for their feedback on the first drafts of sets of key outputs. This resulted in Table 11.1, which lists all the key outputs, to which theme they relate, and their description.

Note that the key outputs are all expressed in terms of changes to current levels. To determine these changes, we calculate the difference in value between the original situation and the final situation after the interventions have been applied. As such, the key output 'Total Investment' also relates to a change in investments in employees compared to current levels of investments.

Table 11.1   Key output definitions for IZZ case

Key output	Theme	Description
Decrease in staff turnover costs	Profit	Reflects the decrease in staff turnover costs caused by the internal variable inputs that affect staff turnover costs
Decrease in absenteeism costs	Profit	Reflects the decrease in absenteeism costs caused by the internal variable inputs that affect absenteeism costs
Decrease in wage costs	Profit	Reflects the decrease in wage costs caused by the internal variable inputs that affect wage costs An 'effect on wage costs' can only occur in the simulation model if productivity changes; the effect that absenteeism and staff turnover have on wage costs is therefore not included in this key output
Increase in production capacity	Profit	If productivity increases, more production capacity becomes available
Total investment	Profit	Sum of all types of investment in all employees

(continued)

Table 11.1 (Continued)

Key output	Theme	Description
Decrease in staff turnover %	People	Reflects the decrease in turnover percentage caused by the internal variable inputs that affect turnover percentage
Decrease in absenteeism %	People	Reflects the decrease in absenteeism percentage caused by the internal variable inputs that affect absenteeism percentage
Increase in employee satisfaction	People	Reflects the increase in employee satisfaction caused by the internal variable inputs that affect employee satisfaction
Increase in customer satisfaction	People	Reflects the increase in customer satisfaction caused by an increase in employee satisfaction

It should be realized that the simulation model primarily assumes that the production volume remains constant. This implies that when productivity increases, the same work can be performed by fewer people and wage costs decrease. However, one could also conclude that increased productivity releases capacity that can be deployed elsewhere. Wage costs would then remain constant but more revenues could be generated. Since we want to refrain from modelling the revenue side as well, for the financial business case we focus on the decrease in wage costs. However, the increase in production capacity is also reported as a key output. In Step 6 of the decision-making process (evaluating options by assessing strategic priorities), we will see that we make a choice between focusing on reducing costs or increasing capacity by weighting either decrease in wage costs or increase in production capacity.

Determining decision maker's options

This stage in the process concerns the defining of the internal variable inputs – the inputs which can be controlled by the decision maker. In this case, these take the form of several types of investments (also referred to as measures or interventions) in employees of healthcare institutions aimed at improving their working conditions. Measures suggested by nurses and care workers that would make the health-care profession more attractive are (Maurits et al, 2014):

- better opportunities for personal growth and development
- measures to reduce the pressure of work
- involvement in policy and decision making
- appreciation from co-workers
- independence to carry out their work
- a more socio-emotional style of leadership (as opposed to a more instrumental style)

Further research has shown that healthcare professionals feel that there is room for improvement in the conditions under which they work. Almost half of the healthcare professionals' absenteeism is caused by physical stress and strain (Ministerie van Sociale Zaken en Werkgelegenheid, 2012) and almost half (47 per cent) of them feel they have to work under pressure (CBS, 2020). Around a quarter find it difficult to achieve a good work–life balance (Eurofound, 2014) and more than a quarter (26 per cent) feel that there are insufficient opportunities for training and/or development (Maurits et al, 2014). Finally, over half (65 per cent) are dissatisfied with their salaries (ADV Market Research, 2011).

On the basis of this research and IZZ's own experience, nine internal variable inputs were chosen. These have an impact on the working conditions of staff in the care sector and thus have an impact on the key outputs. We divided the nine internal variable inputs into the categories of psychological, physical and other, as seen in Table 11.2. These internal variable inputs were inserted into the simulation model in terms of 'euros per employee' and refer to a collective term

Table 11.2 Internal variable input definitions for IZZ case

Internal variable input	Category	Description
Psycho-social stress reduction	Psychological	Investments to counter or prevent pressure of work, aggression and violence on the work floor: the relief of psycho-social stress has a positive effect on staff turnover, absenteeism and productivity
Work–life balance	Psychological	Investments to improve the balance between the individual, his or her private life and the working environment: an improved work–life balance has a positive effect on staff turnover and employee satisfaction
Physical strain reduction	Physical	Investments to counter or prevent physical strain caused by work and job-related movements: reducing physical strain has a positive effect on staff turnover, absenteeism and employee satisfaction
Physical exercise	Physical	Investments to encourage physical activity that has no relationship to the employee's tasks: getting enough physical exercise has a positive effect on productivity and absenteeism
Smoking reduction	Physical	Investments to reduce or avoid the time that people spend smoking: prevention of smoking has a positive effect on productivity and absenteeism
Healthy eating	Physical	Investments to encourage employees to eat more healthily: consuming sufficient nutritious food has a positive effect on absenteeism

(continued)

Table 11.2   (Continued)

Internal variable input	Category	Description
Training and development	Other	Investments to empower employees by improving their individual skills: opportunities for training and personal development have a positive effect on staff turnover and employee satisfaction
Salary increase	Other	Investments in the gross salary of an employee: a good salary has a positive effect on staff turnover and employee satisfaction (as long as this is combined with other appropriate investments)
Leadership development	Other	Investments to improve the management qualities and empowerment of employees and the relationships between employees: good leadership has a positive effect on staff turnover and employee satisfaction

for the type of investment indicated by the name of the internal variable input. The exact details of the type of investments were deemed to be less important. The idea behind this is that, given the strategic priorities of a healthcare institution, there will be many parties that have the expertise needed to put the budget available for each type of investment to optimum use. For example, in determining the investment for training and education, the simulation model makes no recommendations for specific courses; this could be looked at as a follow-up with the aid of a specialized training agency.

Now that the internal variable inputs have been determined, it is time to attach numbers to these inputs, thus specifying the decision maker's options. For reasons of confidentiality, we will do so on the basis of an imaginary geriatric care home named 'Golden Years'. In the remainder of this chapter, we illustrate the application of the simulation model to Golden Years. However, values shown here are representative of those used by many health institutions that followed this decision-making process.

Golden Years is aware that its employees work under great pressure and are struggling to maintain a good work–life balance. It considered three options for the decision maker, each with an investment price tag of €100 per employee but with different focus areas:

- *Physical*: An investment of €35 in physiotherapy sessions, €20 in a company fitness scheme, €20 in an anti-smoking programme and €25 to make nutritious food available in the workplace.

- *Social*: An investment of €35 in a session with a psychologist, €25 in a programme to improve work–life balance, €25 in competence training, €5 in increased salaries and €10 in a leadership course for the line managers.

- *Mix*: An investment of €11 in each of the interventions, with €1 extra for psycho-social stress.

Drawing up scenarios

Now that the decision maker's options are defined, we arrive at the stage of the strategic decision-making process in which we define the external variable inputs, i.e. exogenous factors related to the business environment in which the organization operates.

We distinguish between direct and indirect effects: the direct effects indicate a change in intermediates or key outputs that are directly affected by a change in the internal variable inputs; the indirect effects indicate a change in intermediates or key outputs due to changes in other intermediates and key outputs as a result of direct effects. These two types of effects form the basis for the scenarios. This way, tRBS allows us to investigate how sensitive key outputs and intermediates are to any change in internal variable input. Here, we defined six external variable inputs for these effects (see Table 11.3).

Additionally, we decided on a pessimistic, a neutral and an optimistic scenario. For example, let's say, in the pessimistic scenario, that the value of the external variable input that relates to the effect of employee satisfaction on productivity is 0.9. The effect of employee

Table 11.3 Specification of scenarios for IZZ case

	Scenarios		
External variable input	**Pessimistic**	**Neutral**	**Optimistic**
Direct effect on productivity	0.9	1	1.1
Indirect effect on productivity	0.5	1	1.3
Direct effect on absenteeism %	0.9	1	1.1
Direct effect on staff turnover %	0.9	1	1.1
Direct effect on employee satisfaction	0.5	1	1.1
Indirect effect on customer satisfaction	0.7	1	1.3

satisfaction on productivity that was initially estimated on the basis of secondary research sources and/or expert opinions is multiplied by 90 per cent.

Table 11.3 displays the external variable inputs and the value with which they will be multiplied. The values, depending on the scenario, have been determined with the consultation of experts in the health-care sector and are often kept the same when applied to different institutions.

Constructing the simulation model

Up until now all information has been collected during the explorative dialogues with stakeholders and experts. However, for tRBS to provide clear insights to the decision maker, additional information is required. Outside of the boardroom, but in collaboration with the stakeholders, desk and field research was carried out to complete the model. This section discusses this additional information and its origins. Subsequently, the information specific to the health organization under review, additional characteristics of the nine types of investments in employees, and types of dependencies between the outputs and inputs, are discussed. Finally, the conversion from input to output is described.

Input related to health organization

Table 11.4 specifies some characteristics of Golden Years, inputs which are used to calculate the key outputs.

Table 11.4 Specification of fixed inputs for imaginary Golden Years elderly care home for IZZ case

Fixed input	Value	Description
Current number of employees	1,200	Current headcount
Average number of workable days per year per employee	175	Number of days in the year minus weekends, holiday leave and compulsory training days, multiplied by the average part-time factor
Average wage cost per employee per annum, excluding absenteeism	€40,000	Total annual wage cost divided by the total number of employees
Current productivity level	70%	Average percentage of the workable day that an employee is engaged in carrying out his or her assigned tasks, excluding absenteeism
Average cost of a day lost through absenteeism	€500	Average wage cost per day multiplied by the loss of productivity around the days of absenteeism (Burdorf and Elders, 2010)
Current absenteeism %	6.4%	Total number of days of absenteeism in the past year divided by the current total number of employees, multiplied by the number of workable days per year

(continued)

Table 11.4   (Continued)

Fixed input	Value	Description
Average cost of staff turnover	€3,000	All costs that are incurred when an employee leaves and is replaced by a new employee, e.g. the costs of the interview and recruitment procedure, and the cost of training up a new employee
Current turnover %	8.6%	Relative number of employees that have left the organization in the past year as a percentage of the total number of employees
Current employee satisfaction	6.0	Average of the scores that employees gave their employer during the most recent employee satisfaction survey on a scale of 1 to 10
Current customer satisfaction	6.5	Average of the scores that customers gave the organization during the most recent customer satisfaction survey on a scale of 1 to 10

Input related to impact of investments

Table 11.5 displays four characteristics of the investments that are taken into account when modelling the impact of the investments on the key outputs.

The first three inputs in Table 11.5 only relate to the type of investment. Their values and – if available – references to their sources are listed in Table 11.6. The probability of success and the saturation points were mostly determined by experts.

The maximum possible effects do not only depend on the type of investment, but also on what is affected: absenteeism, staff turnover, employee satisfaction or productivity. Their values are listed in Table 11.7, again including – if applicable – their reference. In case a cell contains no value, it means that no relevant secondary research or expert opinion could be found and we assume, implicitly, that there is no correlation.

Table 11.5 Fixed inputs definitions for direct effect calculations for IZZ case

Fixed input	Description
Accessible population	Percentage of the population on which the investment will have an effect: statistics based primarily on desk research
Probability of success	Likelihood that the investment will prove successful: statistics based on expert knowledge
Saturation point	Maximum effective investment, or the ceiling above which further investment has no further effect on productivity, absenteeism, staff turnover and employee satisfaction: statistics based on expert knowledge
Maximum possible effect	Maximum proportion of lost productivity, absenteeism, staff turnover and lack of employee satisfaction that can be eliminated with an optimal intervention: statistics based primarily on desk research

Table 11.6 Specification of fixed inputs for IZZ case

Type of investment	Accessible population	Probability of success	Saturation point
Psycho-social stress reduction	71% (ADV Market Research, 2011)	20%	€180
Work–life balance	24% (Eurofound, 2014)	40%	€270
Physical strain reduction	19% (CBS Statline, 2013)	50%	€200

(*continued*)

Table 11.6   (Continued)

Type of investment	Accessible population	Probability of success	Saturation point
Physical exercise	50% (van der Lucht and Polder, 2010)	25%	€125
Smoking reduction	23.2% (CBS Statline, 2016)	13.7% (Halpern et al, 2015)	€390
Healthy eating	92% (van der Lucht and Polder, 2010)	80%	€100
Training and development	57% (Maurits et al, 2014)	80%	€2,000
Salary increase	65% (ADV Market Research, 2011)	70%	€3,600
Leadership development	73% (Maurits et al, 2014)	70%	€1,500

Table 11.7   Specification of maximum effects for IZZ case

Type of investment	Absenteeism	Staff turnover	Employee satisfaction	Productivity
Psycho-social stress reduction	36.5% (ArboNed, 2019)	31% (Pensioenfonds Zorg en Welzijn, 2022)	–	7% (van Wormer et al, 2011)
Work–life balance	38% (Antai et al, 2015)	95.8% (Saeed et al, 2013)	64% (Mercer, 2011)	–

(*continued*)

Table 11.7 (Continued)

Type of investment	Absenteeism	Staff turnover	Employee satisfaction	Productivity
Physical strain reduction	30% (AZW, 2015)	50% (Veer et al, 2007)	57% (Mercer, 2011)	–
Physical exercise	4% (van der Lucht and Polder, 2010)	–	–	10% (Robroek et al, 2011)
Smoking reduction	31% (Troelstra et al 2020)	–	–	25% (Robroek et al, 2011)
Healthy eating	36% (Fitzgerald et al, 2016)	–	–	–
Training and development	–	19% (Anis et al, 2011)	52% (Robert Walters, 2017)	–
Salary increase	–	22% (Pensioenfonds Zorg en Welzijn, 2022)	10% (Glassdoor, 2015)	–
Leadership development		36% (Pensioenfonds Zorg en Welzijn, 2022)	22% (Saleem, 2015)	–

Previous research (Sellgren, 2007; Long et al, 2012), that surprisingly showed the zero maximum effect of leadership development on staff turnover, became obsolete when more recent research found that leadership or management is one of the main reasons staff leave an organization (Pensioenfonds Zorg en Welzijn, 2022) . By default, we use the most recent research results, but of course, in dialogues a stakeholder may argue that a certain leadership development programme or some other intervention may have a different effect on staff turnover at their organization. If so, this stakeholder is asked to what extent they think this may cut down staff turnover and the resulting value is imported into the model as expert opinion. The added value of using tRBS lies in the ease of assessing the sensitivity of the key outputs for changes in this expert opinion. Depending on this sensitivity one may decide to put further effort into investigating the effectiveness of leadership development for staff turnover reduction.

Combining the information from Tables 11.6 and 11.7 with the investment amounts, the direct effect of each investment can be calculated. The direct effect of an investment i on j, where j is either absenteeism, staff turnover, employee satisfaction or productivity, is calculated by means of the following formula:

$$\text{Direct effect}_{ij} = \text{Accessible population}_i * \text{Probability of success}_i$$
$$* \frac{min(\text{Investment amount}_i, \text{Saturation Point}_i)}{\text{Saturation Point}_i}$$
$$* \text{Maximum possible effect}_{ij}$$

In this formula, we assume that the effect of the investment increases in a linear fashion up to the saturation point and that investments larger than this saturation point do not result in any additional effect. This holds for all investments, except for the investment in salary. For an investment in salary, we also take into account the so-called extinction effect: if increases in salary are not accompanied by a sufficient volume of other investments, the effect of the salary increase will be short-lived. This is reflected in the model by assuming the saturation point for salary decreases to zero when the investment in salary amounts to more than half of the total investments.

On the side of caution, we assume that no investment will have any further effect after one year. In reality, an employee can experience a positive effect from an internal variable input for a far longer period; take, for example, a training course for helping to deal with stress in the workplace. But limiting the shelf life of internal variable input to just one year reduces the risk of overestimating the effective period.

By way of illustration, let us consider an investment to encourage healthy eating, specifically, providing two pieces of fruit for each employee every day. It is estimated that this is going to cost €100 per employee per annum. Let's suppose that we want to know what direct effect this investment has on absenteeism. From published research we know that 92 per cent of the Dutch population (i.e. the accessible population) eats too little fruit and that 36 per cent of absenteeism through illness (the maximum possible effect) is caused by not eating sufficient nutritious food with enough vitamins. Experts have determined that this intervention has an 80 per cent probability of success, and that those two pieces of fruit represent the saturation point. The direct effect of this investment in fruit on absenteeism is a reduction of absenteeism through illness of 92% × 36% × 80% = 26.5%. This means that the new level of absenteeism can be expected to be 100% − 26.5% = 73.5% of the current level, simply by providing the fruit.

Let's now assume that an institution is not willing or able to spend €100 per employee per year on the purchase of healthy nutrition, but only €75. The direct result is then 26.5% × (75/100) = 19.9%. The institution could therefore reduce absenteeism by 19.9 per cent by investing €75 per employee in the healthy eating option with more focus on offering nutritious food.

We also modelled two indirect effects, which are the effects of a change in employee satisfaction on customer satisfaction and productivity. Both are drawn straight from secondary research. Harter et al (2002) concluded that an increase in employee satisfaction automatically led to greater productivity. The measure of the relative productivity increase as a result of greater employee satisfaction proves to be approximately 23 per cent. A similar correlation has been proven to exist between customer satisfaction and employee satisfaction. Research carried out by the Corporate Leadership Council (2003) in fact showed that when employee satisfaction increases, customer satisfaction increases as well. For any given increase in employee satisfaction, customer satisfaction will rise by approximately 26 per cent of that increase. Just as the saturation point ensures that unrealistically large direct effects are pared down, a similar mechanism has been incorporated to achieve the same result for indirect effects. A comprehensive description of such technical details can be found in Chapter 7.

Conversion of inputs to outputs

The conversion of inputs to outputs is effected in four steps. First, we calculate the direct effects of the investments in terms of productivity, absenteeism and staff turnover, and employee satisfaction as illustrated above. Recall from Chapter 5 that in order to provide transparency, the results of sub-steps in the calculations that convert inputs to outputs are stored in intermediates. These, among others, concern the new number of employees, new productivity level, new cost of absenteeism, new turnover percentage and new level of employee satisfaction. As the effect on employee satisfaction has a knock-on effect on productivity and customer satisfaction, these indirect effects are calculated in the second step. In the third step we make use of the external variable inputs to quantify the key outputs' sensitivity to fluctuations in the estimations of effects. In the final step we express the effects on productivity, absenteeism and staff turnover in monetary terms as well as in percentages, so that we can appraise the people- and profit-related key outputs. At this stage we also incorporate extra management information in the form of additional outputs. In this case the additional outputs include both the absolute and relative return on investment as well as the new customer satisfaction.

By way of illustration, let us consider how the key output 'Decrease in absenteeism costs' comes about. First we calculate the current cost of absenteeism on the basis of organization-specific input:

Current cost of absenteeism =

Average cost of a day lost through absenteeism
  × Current absenteeism %
  × Average number of workable days per year employee
  × Current number of employees

The new cost of absenteeism is then calculated – by analogy – after the necessary adjustments have been made. The 'decrease in absenteeism cost' is then the difference between the new and the current cost of absenteeism.

Using all of the above, tRBS calculates all key outputs for all combinations of the decision maker's options and scenarios. This amounts to the calculation of 81 key output scores (9 key outputs × 3 decision maker's options × 3 scenarios).

Evaluating options by assessing strategic priorities

To be able to create the best possible mix of internal variable inputs, the key output scores will need to be weighted against each other. Before this can be done, the key outputs have to be made mutually comparable by means of appreciation functions. In this case, we rely on the simulation model's automatic calculation of these functions. For a comprehensive description of how these appreciation functions are calculated and applied, refer to Chapter 7.

Returning to our example and using the 'Mix' intervention and the neutral scenario as a basis, we illustrate how the key outputs can be interpreted. Table 11.8 sets out the relevant nine key output values for the Golden Years care home.

Table 11.8 Key output values calculated for 'Mix' intervention in neutral scenario for IZZ case

Key output	Value
Total investment	€120,000
Decrease in staff turnover costs	€4,947
Decrease in absenteeism costs	€313,416
Decrease in wage costs	€221,006
Increase in production capacity	777 days
Decrease in staff turnover %	0.01%
Decrease in absenteeism %	0.02%
Increase in employee satisfaction	4.6%
Increase in customer satisfaction	1.2%

We see that the 'Mix' intervention calls for an investment of €100 for each employee, leading indeed to a total of €120,000. Golden Years can easily recoup this investment, primarily through the positive effect on absenteeism costs and, in case the production capacity remains at the same level, wage costs. If we express the increase in productivity of employees in being able to perform more work with the same number of employees, we see that the investment leads to an extra production capacity amounting to approximately 778 days, or five employees.

Figure 11.1 illustrates how the different decision maker's options are evaluated when the key outputs are made mutually comparable via appreciation functions. To avoid information overload, the data has been aggregated to theme level (people or profit). When all key outputs are equally weighted, the 'Physical' option proves to be best. The natural question is whether the settings of this option, which were defined in Step 3, can be improved. More precisely, is there a better way to divide the €100 per employee between the various investment types than the way defined by the 'Physical' option, given that all key outputs are deemed equally important? To answer this question, we employ the optimization algorithm within tRBS. The

Figure 11.1 Comparison of decision maker's options when all key outputs have equal weights in neutral scenario for IZZ case

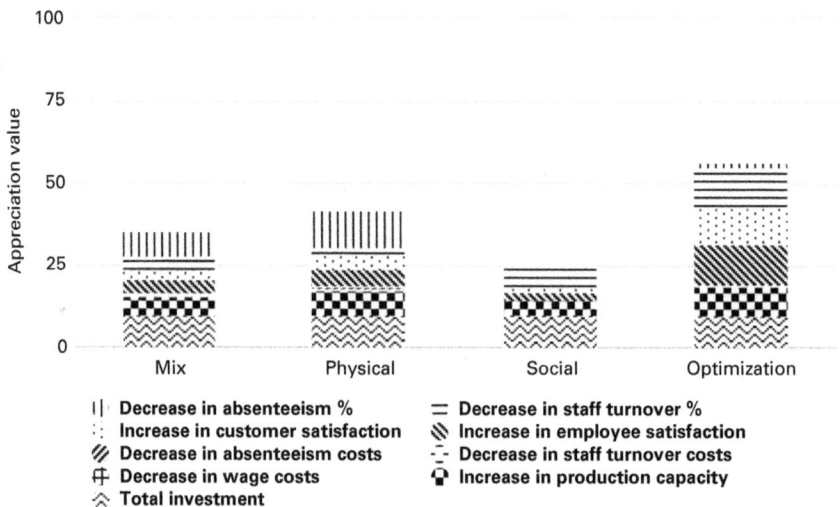

results are also shown in Figure 11.1, from which it is clear that the 'Physical' option can be 'beaten'. The optimal decision turns out to be to invest in a mix of one physical and one social intervention, highly skewed to the physical intervention: €90 per employee should be spent on physical strain reduction and €10 on psycho-social stress reduction. Of course, this decision is only optimal if the exogenous factors behave as described in the neutral scenario, if all key outputs are deemed to be equally important, if all organization-specific data has been put in correctly, and – last but not least – if one is willing to accept all expert opinions and all results and assumptions in the secondary research employed in this case.

To illustrate the effect of adjustments in strategic priorities, let's now look at which decision maker's option scores best if we focus less on employees: we only put – equal – weight on all key outputs but absenteeism reduction and customer satisfaction. Figure 11.2 illustrates that for this setting of strategic priorities, the 'Social' option now scores better than the 'Physical' option. Again, the 'Optimization' engine results in even better outcomes, in which case the advice is to spend €20 on nutritious food, €50 on physical strain reduction, €15 on training and development and €15 on leadership development.

Figure 11.2 Comparison of decision maker's options when equal weights are assigned to absenteeism and staff turnover only in neutral scenario for IZZ case

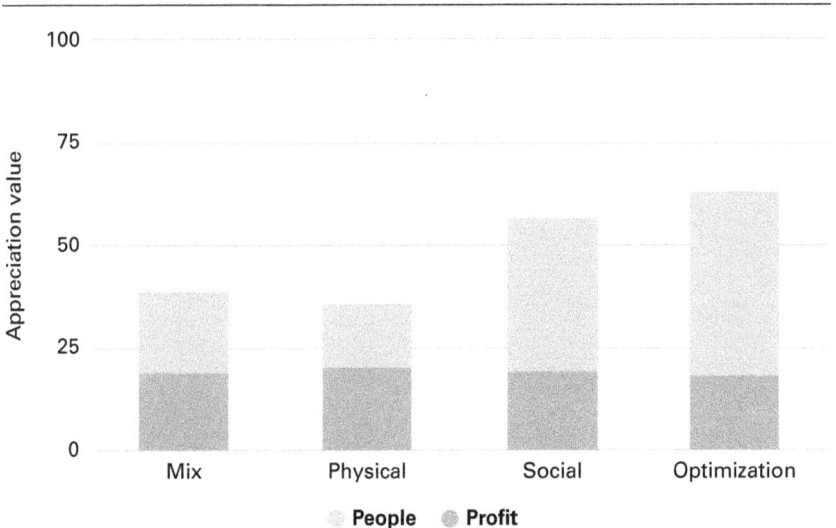

Evaluating options by assessing risk appetite

In the last step of the seven-step decision-making process, we investigate the impact risk appetite has on decisions. For this case, it turns out that the aforementioned optimal decisions are robust in the sense that they outperform the other options in optimistic, neutral and pessimistic scenarios. However, this is not always the case. Let's suppose that the decision maker could only choose between investing €100 per employee in physical strain reduction and investing €100 per employee in psycho-social stress reduction. For this situation, Figure 11.3 shows that the investment in physical strain reduction outperforms the investment in psycho-social stress reduction in the neutral and optimistic scenarios. In the pessimistic scenario, it is the other way around. If all three scenarios are weighted equally, then the decision maker should choose physical strain reduction, because the positive differences in the optimistic and neutral scenarios outweigh the negative difference in the pessimistic scenario. If the decision maker has a very low risk appetite, more weight could be assigned to the pessimistic scenario and the investment in psycho-social stress reduction

Figure 11.3 Score per scenario for two specific decision maker's options when all key outputs have equal weights for IZZ case

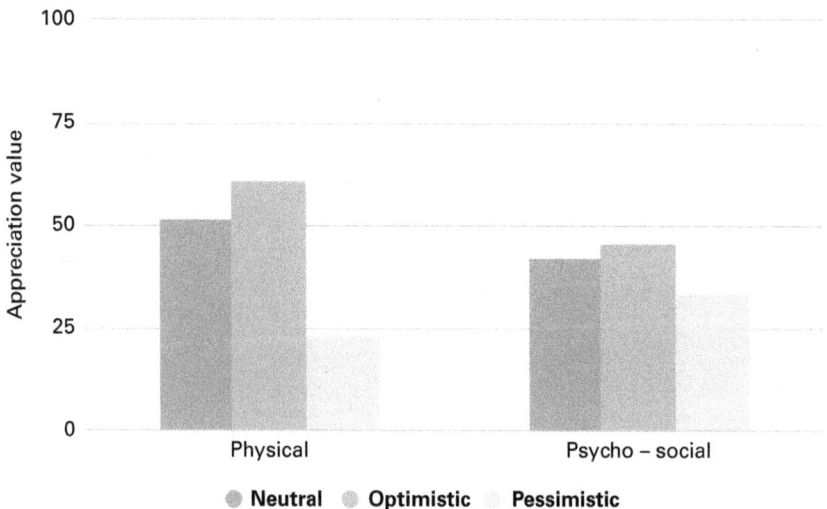

would eventually win. It turns out that this happens as soon as the weight of the pessimistic scenario is at least 3.5 times higher than the (equal) weights of the other two scenarios. Figure 11.3 also shows that when comparing scenarios, physical strain reduction behaves in a more volatile way than psycho-social stress reduction. So if the decision maker prefers certainty about the outcome over the attractiveness of the outcome, then psycho-social stress reduction is also the option of choice. This illustrates how this last step can facilitate a dialogue on risk appetite.

Reflections

The IZZ Foundation played an important role – from the very beginning – by helping to ensure that the decision-making model really reflected the world in which a healthcare institution operates. Modelling has been an interactive process, involving various participants from the IZZ Foundation as well as decision makers from other healthcare institutions. A number of sessions were held which were not only aimed at ensuring that the simulation model worked as it should, but also that it accurately reflected the decision-making process. In determining the interventions, constant attention was paid to the issues and the occupational hazards inherent in the healthcare sector. The IZZ Foundation was able to incorporate its firsthand knowledge of the sector into the model and provide relevant support literature.

Steps 6 and 7 of the decision-making process confirmed once more that the best strategy for any healthcare institution depends on both its strategic priorities (the weighting of the key outputs) and its risk appetite (the weighting of the scenarios). Irrespective of how advanced the construction of the simulation model is, it will not provide these weights; they can only be provided through strategic dialogue.

In this case, tRBS comprises organization-specific input, literature research and expert opinions, and as a result it can be used to determine what the best intervention would be for any particular healthcare institution. This application of strategic decision making actually evolved into a ready-to-use application known as 'Simulatie-model Gezond werken in de zorg' (Simulation model for sustainable healthcare work). This model is being made available to healthcare institutions so that they – with assistance from IZZ – have an instrument with which to guide their own strategic healthcare policies.

From the beginning of this exercise, the perspective of the healthcare institution has taken centre stage in the decision-making process surrounding the decision maker's options and scenarios, the pivotal question being: in which way (with which options) can a healthcare institution improve itself in the people domain?

Getting a healthcare institution involved right from the beginning of the decision-making process has distinct advantages. Besides the actual modelling, it provokes further and new discussions that lead to further improvement and possible adaptations or adjustments for the future. According to Anouk ten Arve, manager at the IZZ Foundation, there are four essential themes for establishing a safe and healthy working environment (ten Arve, 2022):

1 Healthcare landscape and health condition of the healthcare professional: how to anticipate the increasing demand for care and the changing working climate?

2 HR and organization strategy: how to create a win–win situation for employer and employee with clear allocation of responsibilities?

3 Organization structure and climate: how to increase health, work pleasure and the quality of care?

4 (Self) Leadership: how to empower employees?

One question that the model provoked was: how do you go about putting investments into practice? The trend towards more flexible working in terms of both hours and location (known as 'the new way of working') has found its way into the healthcare sector. Giving employees the opportunity to determine their own working schedules, more flexibility in working times, greater individual employee responsibility and less supervision are all matters that are central to this new way of working and that could also be introduced into healthcare. FNV Zorgbarometer (2022) research with over 4,500 healthcare professionals confirms that a lot of healthcare professionals are switching or have switched to become employed as flexi-workers or independent contractors. The main arguments for this switch are: more flexibility in or control over working times (62 per cent), a better work–life balance (50 per cent), and improved salary (36 per cent).

Another possibility is the use of social media and e-health (ten Arve, 2012), whereby healthcare professional and client have remote (i.e. non-physical) contact with each other. This makes it easier for the healthcare professional to decide where their help is most urgently needed, without first needing to make the usual rounds. That would be beneficial to the client and to the employee as well. Ten Arve, programme manager for sustainable healthcare at IZZ, stresses the importance of a working climate that makes dialogue part of the daily routine and the facilitating role the HR department can play.

For the client it is reassuring to know that a healthcare professional is available whenever it suits the client best. For the healthcare professional it means better oversight, more autonomy and a less monotonous routine. It would be interesting to see what benefits a relatively small investment in a course on the effective use of social media would ultimately have for the employee (in terms of self-development, sense of wellbeing) and for the client (in terms of customer satisfaction).

The simulation model is a dynamic instrument for strategic decision making which can be adapted at any time in the future to reflect the changing needs of healthcare institutions. The issue of flexible working could be incorporated, for example, as could other issues such as 'inspiration' and 'presenteeism' (mental absenteeism). All these are subjects which, because of its modular design, could be added to the Responsible Business Simulator.

References

ADV Market Research (2011) Zorgbarometer, www.werknemersindezorg.nl/overzicht-inhoud/arbeidsomstandigheden/zorgbarometer

Anis, A, Jaz-Ur-Rehman, Nasir, A and Safwan, N (2011) Employee retention relationship to training and development: a compensation perspective, *African Journal of Business Management*, 5 (7), 2679–685

Antai, D, Oke, A, Braithwaite, P and Anthony, DS (2015) A 'balanced' life: work–life balance and sickness absence in four Nordic countries, *International Journal of Occupational & Environmental Medicine*, 6 (4), 205–22

Arbeidsmarkt Zorg en Welzijn (2021) dashboards.cbs.nl/v3/AZWDashboard/ (archived at https://perma.cc/CP8P-9UAX)

ArboNed (2019) Ziektespecifiek verzuim, www.volksgezondheidenzorg.info/onderwerp/ziekteverzuim (archived at https://perma.cc/U4RH-8N3J)

AZW (2015) *Arbeid in Zorg en Welzijn 2014 Integrerend jaarrapport*, www.vgn.nl/documenten/arbeid-zorg-en-welzijn (archived at https://perma.cc/SR3A-6FJD)

Burdorf, L and Elders, L (2010) *Werkvermogen en Productiviteit: Feiten en fabels*, Erasmus Medisch Centrum, Rotterdam

CBS Statline (2013) Arbeidsomstandigheden werknemers; geslacht en leeftijd 2005–2013, statline.cbs.nl/StatWeb/publication/default.aspx?VW=T&DM=SLNL&PA=71204NED&D1=a&D2=1-2&D3=0&D4=a&HD=110413-1433&HDR=G2%2cG1%2cG3&STB=T (archived at https://perma.cc/XJC9-WXYN)

CBS Statline (2016) Leefstijl, preventief onderzoek; persoonskenmerken; 2010–2013, statline.cbs.nl/StatWeb/publication/?VW=T&DM=SLNL&PA=81177NED&D1=0-1%2c4-5%2c8-12&D2=0-2%2c5-13%2c34-38&D3=0&D4=l&HD=110905-0957&HDR=G3%2cG2%2cT&STB=G1 (archived at https://perma.cc/DY7A-QE35)

CBS Statline (2022) Mobiliteit van werknemers; AZW (breed), instroom, uitstroom, saldo, regio, azwstatline.cbs.nl/#/AZW/nl/dataset/24050NED/table?ts=1591279185724 and dashboards.cbs.nl/v3/AZWDashboard/ (archived at https://perma.cc/U6H9-886A)

CBS (2020) Arbeidsmarktprofiel van zorg en welzijn, www.cbs.nl/nl-nl/longread/statistische-trends/2020/arbeidsmarktprofiel-van-zorg-en-welzijn?onepage=true (archived at https://perma.cc/C7ZR-QSAT)

CBS (2021) Ziekteverzuim zorg en welzijn blijft op hoogste niveau sinds 2003, www.cbs.nl/nl-nl/nieuws/2021/37/ziekteverzuim-zorg-en-welzijn-blijft-op-hoogste-niveau-sinds-2003 (archived at https://perma.cc/MYK3-FTCN)

Corporate Leadership Council (2003) Linking employee satisfaction with productivity, performance, and customer satisfaction, Corporate Executive Board, Arlington County, VA

Eurofound (2014) Human health sector: working conditions and job quality, www.eurofound.europa.eu/publications/information-sheet/2014/working-conditions/human-health-sector-working-conditions-and-job-quality (archived at https://perma.cc/48VT-B8FW)

Fitzgerald, S, Kirby, A, Murphy, A and Geaney, F (2016) Obesity, diet quality and absenteeism in a working population, *Public Health Nutrition*, **19** (18), 3287–295

FNV Zorgbarometer (2022) Meerderheid jonge zorgmedewerkers overweegt vaste baan in te ruilen voor flexbaan, www.fnv.nl/ nieuwsbericht/sectornieuws/zorg-welzijn/2022/09/meerderheid-jonge-zorgmedewerkers-overweegt-vaste (archived at https://perma.cc/ NHU7-UM43)

Glassdoor (2015) Does money buy happiness? The link between salary and employee satisfaction, www.glassdoor.com/research/does-money-buy-happiness-the-link-between-salary-and-employee-satisfaction/ (archived at https://perma.cc/U8YN-DHF7)

Halpern, SD, French, B, Small, DS, Saulsgiver, K, Harhay, MO, Audrain-McGovern, J, Loewenstein, G, Brennan, TA, Asch, DA and Volpp, KG (2015) Randomized trial of four financial-incentive programs for smoking cessation, *The New England Journal of Medicine*, **372**, 2108–117

Harter, JK, Schmidt, FL and Hayes, TL (2002) Business unit-level relationship between employee satisfaction, employee engagement, and business outcomes: a meta-analysis, *Journal of Applied Psychology*, **87** (2), 268–79

Long, CS, Thean, LY, Ismail, WKW and Josoh, A (2012) Leadership styles and employees' turnover intention, *World Applied Sciences Journal*, **19** (4), 575–81

Maurits, EEM, Veer, AJE de, Spreeuwenberg, P and Francke, AL (2014) *De Aantrekkelijkheid van Werken in de Zorg 2013*, Nivel, Utrecht

Mercer (2011) What's working, www.mercer.nl/press-releases/minderheid_nederlanders_tevreden_over_salaris (archived at https://perma.cc/ WFP7-J842)

Ministerie van Sociale Zaken en Werkgelegenheid (2012) *De Juiste Hulpmiddelen Verlichten het Werk en Verminderen de Arbeidsrisico's*, Rijksoverheid, Den Haag

NOS (2022) Ziekteverzuim recordhoog, maar 'persoonlijke aandacht maakt wel verschil', nos.nl/l/2432113 (archived at https://perma. cc/666U-8C8D)

Pensioenfonds Zorg en Welzijn (2022) Meer mensen zeggen zelf hun baan op in zorg en welzijn, www.pfzw.nl/over-pfzw/actueel/archief/nieuw-pfzw-onderzoek-naar-uitstroom.html (archived at https://perma. cc/23ZW-6QSJ)

Robert Walters (2017) Attracting and retaining millennial professionals, www.robertwalters.co.uk/content/dam/robert-walters/country/united-kingdom/files/whitepapers/robert-walters-whitepaper-millennials.pdf (archived at https://perma.cc/UHF8-MYHM)

Robroek, SJW, van den Berg, TIJ, Plat, JF and Burdorf, A (2011) The role of obesity and lifestyle behaviours in a productive workforce, *Journal of Occupational & Environmental Medicine*, **68** (10), 134–39

Saeed, R, Lodhi, RN, Ahmed, K, Afzal, N, Mahmood, Z and Ahmed, M (2013) Work–life balance and stress with the turnover rate of the employees, *World Applied Sciences Journal*, **26** (6), 834–39

Saleem, H (2015) The impact of leadership styles on job satisfaction and mediating role of perceived organizational politics, *Procedia: Social and Behavioral Sciences*, **172**, 563–69

Sellgren, SF (2007) *Leadership and Staff Turnover*, Karolinska Institutet, Stockholm

ten Arve, A (2012) *Sustainable Business Modelling*, 12 April, interview with Jacques de Swart

ten Arve, A (2022) Zuurstof voor zorgprofessionals: Zorg voor het hart van je organisatie en behoud medewerkers, Auteurscollege, Gieten, Netherlands, www.managementboek.nl/boek/9789490969363/zuurstof-voor-zorgprofessionals-anouk-ten-arve (archived at https://perma.cc/M593-GB2H)

Troelstra, SA, Coenen, P, Boot, CR, Harting, J, Kunst, AE and van der Beek, AJ (2020) Smoking and sickness absence: a systematic review and meta-analysis, *Scandinavian Journal of Work, Environment & Health*, **46** (1), 5–18

van der Lucht, F and Polder, JJ (2010) *Towards Better Health: Main report on the public health status and forecasts 2010*, National Institute for Public Health, Bilthoven

van Wormer, JJ, Fyfe-Johnson, AL, Boucher, JL and Johnson, PJ (2011) Stress and workplace productivity loss in the Heart of New Ulm project, *Journal of Occupational and Environmental Medicine*, **53** (10), 1106–109

Veer, AJE, Poortvliet, EP, Vogel, B and Francke, AL (2007) *De Aantrekkelijkheid van het Beroep: Een peiling onder het panel verpleegkundigen en verzorgenden*, Nivel, Utrecht

Vernet (2021) Vernet verdieping: verzuim in 2021, www.vernet.nl/2022/01/26/vernet-verdieping-verzuim-in-2021/ (archived at https://perma.cc/VQ5M-4QA7)

Reducing greenhouse gas emissions

12

This chapter illustrates the application of the Responsible Business Simulator in the case of Koninklijke DSM NV or Royal DSM (DSM). Climate change is driven by many things, among them greenhouse gas emissions from fossil fuel combustion, resulting in calls for the decarbonization of DSM's energy systems. DSM, a global frontrunner in sustainability, takes a leading role in climate action. Since some of DSM's production processes are energy intensive, it is important for DSM to improve its energy efficiency, while increasing the percentage of energy purchased from renewable sources, and making strategic choices in the area of renewable energy. The two main options for DSM are generating renewable energy as an activity of DSM or sourcing renewable energy from an external supplier. However, the decision-making process is not as simple as it seems, since the decision should also take into account the country from which the CO_2 certificates originate, and whether or not an internal carbon price should be applied. The Responsible Business Simulator (tRBS) was able to process all required inputs and helped to give the decision makers the relevant scenarios to make a sustainable decision on energy sourcing and the use of an internal carbon price.

We will start by introducing this global science-based company in the context of making strategic decisions to benefit People, the Planet and Profit. The current situation at DSM can be found on their website (DSM, 2016a).

It should be noted that the work done at DSM with the Responsible Business Simulator was conducted some years ago, and the case was reported in the first edition of this book. The information, facts and figures as outlined in this chapter reflect the position in the business at that time, but as they are still entirely relevant to the simulation model and the process involved, they have not been updated.

About DSM

Royal DSM (DSM) is a global science-based company active in health, nutrition and materials. DSM operates in global markets such as food and dietary supplements, personal care, animal feed, automotive, electronics, alternative energy and bio-based materials (DSM, 2016b).

Sustainability is both a core value and a sustainable growth driver. By connecting its unique competences in life sciences and materials sciences, DSM strives to create economic, social and environmental value. The organization has been named among the worldwide leaders in the materials industry group in the Dow Jones Sustainability World Index, holding the No 1 position seven times since 2004 (DSM, 2016c), including most recently in 2015. *Fortune* magazine recently included DSM in its 2016 'Change the World' list of 50 companies worldwide that are making an important social or environmental impact through their profit-making strategy and operations (*Fortune*, 2016). By 2020, DSM aims for 65 per cent of its sales to be 'Brighter Living Solutions', products and services that, when considered over their whole life cycle, offer better social and/or environmental impacts, compared to the mainstream competing solutions.

With their aspiration to remain a frontrunner, DSM wants to continuously improve its sustainability performance simultaneously on the themes of people, planet and profit.

This chapter details the specific case where DSM wants to reduce its greenhouse gas emissions, first of all by becoming more energy efficient, and secondly by sourcing renewable energy. The strategic challenge, therefore, has been formulated as: 'how to balance various criteria used when deciding upon the sourcing of (renewable) energy', including those criteria that are hard to compare. In this chapter the focus will be on the strategic dialogue facilitated by tRBS regarding renewable energy sourcing and how this dialogue supported the introduction of using an internal carbon price.

Since the context of the strategic challenge DSM faces around energy sourcing is quite complex, some additional background information is provided on carbon footprint, greenhouse gas emissions, renewable energy, Guarantees of Origin and the internal carbon price.

About energy sourcing

During the entire decision-making process, energy sourcing terminology such as greenhouse gas emissions, renewable energy and carbon footprint, plays a key role. Since there are multiple definitions and interpretations of these concepts , this section explains how terminology is applied in the context of this study.

Carbon footprint

The definition of 'carbon footprint' is complicated. Historically, it has been defined as the total set of greenhouse gas (GHG) emissions caused by an organization, event, product or individual, but since GHG can also be produced by natural occurrences, Wright et al (2011) have proposed a more refined, though technical definition. Here, for simplicity, we will express carbon footprint in kilotons of carbon dioxide, or its equivalent of other GHGs, emitted (CO_2e).

Sustainability Reporting Guidelines (Global Reporting Initiative, 2013) divide energy use and emissions into three separate scope levels:

- Scope 1: direct GHG emissions are emissions from sources that are owned or controlled by the reporting entity.

- Scope 2: indirect GHG emissions are emissions that are a consequence of the activities of the reporting entity, but occur at sources owned or controlled by another entity.

- Scope 3: other indirect GHG emissions such as the extraction and production of purchased materials and fuels, transport-related activities in vehicles not owned or controlled by the reporting entity, outsourced activities, waste disposal, etc.

In this case, only Scopes 1 and 2 CO_2e emissions are taken into account. In the remainder of this article, they will be referred to as GHG emissions or carbon footprint. The type of energy focused on in this case is electricity.

Before we define carbon footprint, we first introduce the notions of renewable energy, Guarantees of Origin and Renewable Energy Certificates, since its definition depends on these concepts.

Renewable energy

Renewable energy means: 'Energy from renewable non-fossil sources: wind, solar, aerothermal, geothermal, hydrothermal and ocean energy, hydropower, biomass, landfill gas, sewage treatment plant gas and biogases' (European Parliament, 2009). Sometimes renewable energy is loosely referred to as 'green energy' and non-renewable energy as 'grey energy'.

Renewable energy consumption for DSM consists of two components: direct use via its own energy production, and indirect use by using energy purchased from the grid or another external supplier. For the organization's own production, it is clear how renewable electricity is produced and how much GHG emission is involved. As for the electricity from the grid, this is not as straightforward since it is impossible to distinguish renewable from fossil fuel-based electricity as an end consumer (an electron is an electron).

Guarantees of Origin (GoOs) or Renewable Energy Certificates (RECs)

Since energy from a renewable source cannot physically be differentiated from electricity from fossil fuel-based power plants when supplied through the grid, an administrative solution is used, named Guarantees of Origin (GoOs) (Dutch Ministry of Economic Affairs, 2010). GoOs are sometimes referred to as RECs (Renewable Energy Certificates). Several governments have introduced a system of GoOs or certificates to distinguish energy that is generated in an environmentally friendly way from conventionally generated energy. One

GoO is equivalent to one MWh of energy. The GoO system provides insight into how the power was produced: by using fossil fuels, nuclear or renewable power plants. In the Netherlands, certificates for renewable electricity are the only official proof that a retailer delivers 'green electricity' to the end user.

Certificates can be used for international trade. Installations receiving certificates are wind turbines, biomass power plants, solar power systems and hydropower plants. Since 2007, it has also been possible to obtain certificates for electricity from highly efficient combined heat and power (CHP) plants.

As an example, RECs in the Netherlands are issued and managed by CertiQ, a subsidiary of TenneT, the Dutch electricity transmission system provider, in accordance with the Electricity Act of 1998 and a number of government regulations. Dutch distribution system operators (DSOs) such as Liander, Stedin and Enexis, validate whether the electricity generated in an installation can be defined as renewable energy (or energy from CHP) and whether the volumes of electricity can be clearly measured. Subsequently, the DSO sends the information to CertiQ, which converts the measured data into certificates. Many countries have a similar set-up for dealing with certificates.

It is important to realize that energy is only named 'renewable' when it originates from a non-fossil or renewable source and is accompanied by a certificate.

DSM's focus is on realizing power purchase agreements with third parties whereby long-term commitment is given to source renewable power from, for example, a wind or solar park. One such example is Windpark Krammer, announced in October 2016, where Philips, AkzoNobel, Google and DSM teamed up with a citizens' initiative for a wind park in the Netherlands (Edelman, 2016). Ninety-five per cent of the power generated from this park will be purchased by these four companies. DSM's share is 90 GWh and will cover 50 per cent of the electricity needs in the Netherlands as of 2019, when the park will be operational. In the meantime, as a transitional measure to support more renewable electricity projects, DSM is considering buying a limited number of RECs from recently initiated projects, thus stimulating the addition of more renewable power to the grid (so-called 'additionality').

Using the above definition of GoOs, there are three methods for calculating carbon footprint when buying energy from a third party or the grid:

- *Uncorrected country factor* (location-based method): a country factor corrected for combined heat and power plants is used (Brander et al, 2011). This is an easy calculation, but the offtake does not take into account the allocation of GoOs, which increases the risk of double counting with parties that have claimed them. The impact of increasing the share of renewables is low since benefits are also harvested by other users of power from the grid.

- *Corrected country factor* (location-based method): a country factor is used for the residual mix, which is the amount of electricity that has not been claimed via tracking systems such as GoOs. Using this factor, the share of renewable energy is determined (Reliable Disclosure Systems, 2015). Since claimed GoOs are subtracted, the threat of double counting is mitigated. Offtake depends on contractual agreements, so using a country average will provide a deviation from an organization's actual renewable energy (RE) percentages and GHG emissions. The risk of double counting in case RE is produced but not claimed through a GoO is expected to be small.

- *Supplier contract* (market-based method): an offtake contract for electricity provides, at least in the Netherlands, information about percentages of RE and GHG emissions per kWh. The information is backed up by GoOs. This approach avoids double counting since the supplier is obliged to report the percentage renewables and GHG emissions according to the GoOs used.

Country of origin, availability of data and time are all reasons for organizations to make different choices from the options listed above.

Internal carbon price

Organizations that acknowledge the process of ongoing climate change as a key relevant business factor for which they wish to be prepared often implement an internal carbon price. Addressing climate change will be both a business cost and a possible business opportunity, regardless of the regulatory environment (Carbon Disclosure Project, 2013).

An internal carbon price is a price on each unit of reported CO_2e emission. This 'penalty' for CO_2e emission can actually be collected or used when evaluating business cases. DSM uses the latter approach, a so-called 'shadow carbon price' in business case evaluations. The idea of evaluating business cases with the incorporation of an internal carbon price is 'forward-looking' as pricing of carbon pollution will eventually be part of day-to-day business.

The number of organizations that incorporate an internal carbon price for their decision making almost tripled from 150 in 2014 to 435 in 2015. This number grew to 1,249 in 2016 (Carbon Disclosure Project, 2016) and is expected to keep growing (Carbon Disclosure Project, 2015). Organizations such as Shell, BP, ExxonMobil, General Electric and Microsoft are well-known users of an internal carbon price. Globally, the internal carbon price varies from \$0.97 to \$357.37 for every ton of CO_2e emission (Carbon Disclosure Project, 2015).

The strategic decision-making process

At DSM, we collaborated with a team that represented various fields of expertise from a range of departments (operations, energy, sourcing, life cycle assessment, finance) as well as the Sustainability Department. The team members' knowledge of this wide range of parts of the organization facilitated the data collection process and resulted in a meaningful strategic dialogue. The successive outcomes of the simulation model were compared and analysed carefully. As a result, key outputs were refined and new ones were added, and factual data could be input in a meaningful way. We now provide more detail on each of the seven steps in the decision-making process. For the purpose of this book we have used – where necessary – fictitious data to illustrate the decision-making process so as not to disclose competitively sensitive information.

Describing the strategic challenge that requires a decision

A brainstorming session between decision makers and experts resulted in the following formulation of the strategic challenge: 'how to source renewable energy, meeting 3P criteria'. In particular, an existing business case was selected as a case study, with the intention that any similar type of decision regarding energy sourcing in the future could be treated in the same manner. The existing business case had been drawn up internally for the sourcing of a US-based production facility by building a power plant consisting of solar panels. Relevant internal stakeholders were listed and approached. External stakeholders were represented via the Global Brand and Communications department. With this business case in mind, the next six steps were followed.

Defining key outputs involving stakeholders

Table 12.1 gives an overview of the key outputs, to which theme they relate and their definition.

The first three key outputs clearly address the planet aspects of this business case. The key outputs that directly link to profit are energy cost and CAPEX, which are expressed in dollars (since the production facility is US-based). These financial, profit-related key outputs were also present in the existing business case. The people-related outputs can be seen as indirect effects that the type of energy sourcing may have. As such, this business case generalizes the existing financial business case to a triple bottom line (3P) business case. Productivity, financial results and revenues are not listed among the key outputs, even though desk research indicates that the planet and people aspects in Table 12.1 indirectly boost productivity (Lyubomirsky et al, 2005), financial results (Gallup, 2013) and revenue (Kossovsky et al, 2012). These three financial effects were discussed and selected for the long-list of outputs. However, in order to make the decision-making process easier to manage, and because their effects could be mimicked by the employee engagement score and brand value anyway, they did not make it to the shortlist.

Table 12.1 Key output definitions for DSM case

Key output	Theme	Definition
RE %	Planet	Percentage of renewable electricity use of total energy usage of DSM at a specific power plant. Here, renewable electricity means that the electricity originates from non-fossil sources (renewable sources) and is accompanied by a Renewable Energy Certificate (REC).
Carbon footprint reduction	Planet	Reduction of emission of carbon dioxide, or its equivalent of other GHGs, for reporting purposes. Here, carbon footprint reduction may only be reported as such if the electricity originates from non-fossil sources and is accompanied by Renewable Energy Certificates (RECs).
Actual carbon emission	Planet	Actual emission of carbon dioxide, or its equivalent of other GHGs (tons). Here, actual means that this emission is measured regardless of whether it is accompanied by Renewable Energy Certificates (RECs).
Energy cost	Profit	Costs are expressed as energy usage (MWh) times cost of energy ($/MWh).
CAPEX	Profit	Capital Expenditure ($) for the construction of a power plant that produces RE.
Increase in employee engagement score	People	Increase in employee engagement as measured by yearly employee engagement surveys (%).
Increase in employee recommendation rate	People	Increase in the rate at which employees recommend DSM as an employer in a favourable way (%) due to an increase in employee engagement as measured by yearly employee engagement surveys.
Increase in Net Promotor Score	People	Increase in customer satisfaction as measured by the yearly Net Promotor Score (%).
Increase in brand value	People	Increase in brand value ($) due to carbon footprint reduction.

Determining decision maker's options

Recall from Chapter 5 that in order to determine the decision maker's options, internal variable inputs must first be formulated. These inputs refer to the six choices that have to be made when sourcing energy:

1 *Make or buy?* The first decision awaiting the decision maker is a classical make-or-buy decision. If the decision maker produces energy, it is assumed that a solar plant is financed, set up and run by DSM, and the RECs issued are kept by DSM in order to be able to declare the produced energy as being RE.

2 *Where to buy energy?* If energy is bought instead of produced, it can be bought either from a partner or from the market. If a partner is involved, it is assumed that a partner will be sought to finance, set up and run the solar panel plant instead of DSM. This implies that the energy from a partner comes from a renewable source (RS).

3 *What type of energy to buy from the market?* In the case of energy being bought from the market, the decision maker has the option to buy energy from an RS or to buy it from a non-renewable source (NRS). Energy from an NRS will be referred to as 'grey energy' or GE.

4 *How many RECs to buy?* The number of RECs to buy is limited to the number of RECs available. The decision maker may want to buy a number of RECs that does not correspond to the volume of energy from their RS.

5 *Where to buy RECs?* If the decision maker decides to buy RECs, the next question is where to buy them. The supplier could either be the partner or the market. We also included the option to optimize, i.e. choose the cheapest supplier. It should be noted that in practice RECs can only be bought from a partner if energy is bought from the partner as well.

6 *What internal carbon price to use?* Finally, the decision maker can decide upon using an internal carbon price, which represents the internal charge for CO_2e emission.

This leads to seven internal variable inputs, which – together with their units – are listed in the first two columns of Table 12.2. Here, the unit % refers to the percentage of the total energy requirement of the production plant. The reference to the number of each choice is included as well. In the fifth choice, deciding where to buy RECs, there are three alternatives to choose from. This leads to two internal variable inputs, % REC partner and % REC market. The percentage of RECs that is bought according to the optimization strategy is then modelled as % REC – % REC Partner – % REC Market. By varying the settings of these internal variable inputs, we formulated six decision maker's options. The settings per option are listed in the remaining six columns of Table 12.2.

Note that initially we set the internal carbon price to 0. The decision tree in Figure 12.1 displays the six choices graphically.

Table 12.2 Specification of decision maker's options for DSM case

Internal variable input	Unit	No RE	No RS with REC	RS partner without REC	Market RE	Partner RE	Make RE
				Decision maker's options			
1. % RE make	%	0	0	0	0	0	50
2. % RS partner	%	0	0	50	0	50	0
3. % RS market	%	0	0	0	50	0	0
4. % REC	%	0	50	0	50	50	0
5a. % REC partner	%	0	0	0	0	50	0
5b. % RECs market	%	0	0	0	0	0	0
6. Internal Carbon Price	$	0	0	0	0	0	0

Figure 12.1 Decision tree for energy sourcing in DSM case

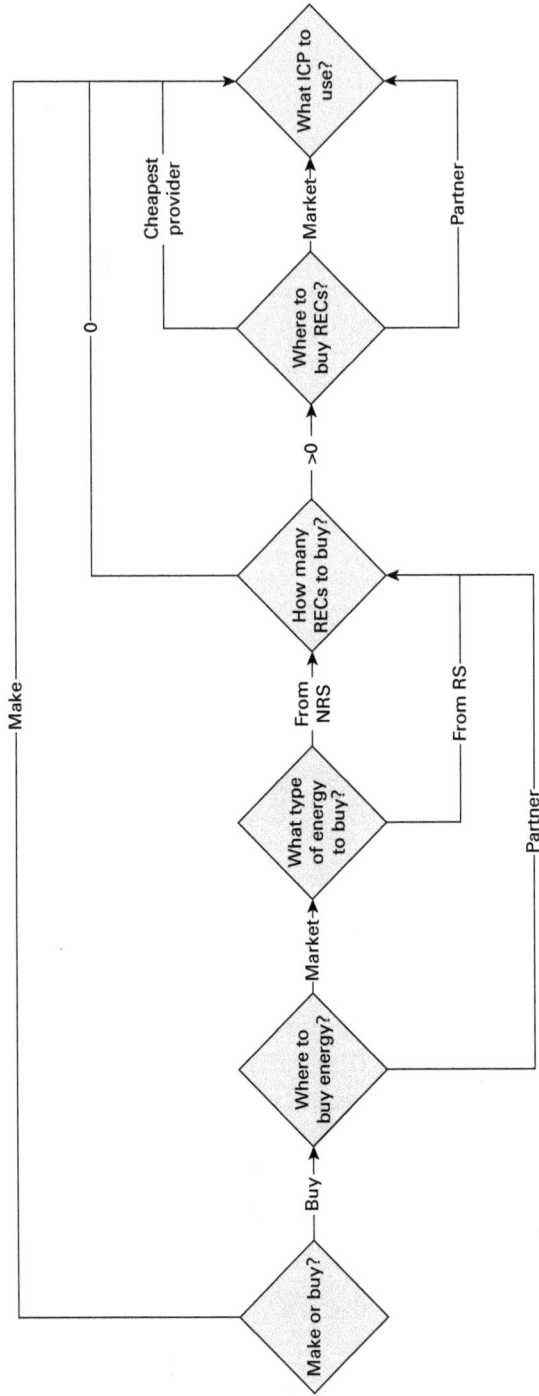

Drawing up scenarios

Historical prices of energy and certificates have been quite volatile. Therefore, the uncertainty in predicting these prices should be taken into account. In some territories CAPEX for RE production is incentivized by governments via subsidy and tax discount rates. These rates may vary as well. Just like energy prices, subsidies and tax discounts cannot be controlled by the decision maker. Therefore, these inputs were formulated as external variable inputs in order to account for the possible uncertainties in the outcomes of the decision.

Thus eight uncertainties were considered and their influence on key outputs monitored:

- the price of grey energy
- the price of energy from renewable sources (RS) from the partner
- the price of energy from renewable sources (RS) from the market
- REC prices from the partner
- REC prices from the market
- the RE subsidy rate as a percentage of CAPEX
- the RE tax discount rate as percentage of CAPEX
- the reduction factor that applies for a non-visual way of sourcing green energy

The prices are based on historical power purchase agreements with producers or suppliers.

The uncertainties enabled us to draw up three scenarios. We have chosen the views 'pessimistic' and 'optimistic' from the perspective of a decision maker that tends to use RE. All scenarios and corresponding values of the external variable inputs per scenario are displayed in Table 12.3.

Constructing the simulation model

The information collected so far was inserted into the Responsible Business Simulator. However, for the simulation model to provide

Table 12.3 Specification of scenarios for DSM case

| External variable input | Unit | Scenarios | | |
		RE pessimistic	Neutral	RE optimistic
Price NRS market	$/MWh	108	108	108
Price RS partner	$/MWh	60	51	40
Price RS market	$/MWh	130	115	90
Price REC partner	$/MWh	140	130	120
Price REC market	$/MWh	320	270	220
RE CAPEX subsidy rate	%	0	30	60
RE CAPEX tax discount rate	%	25	30	35
No visual observation reduction factor	%	70	80	90

clear insights for the decision maker, additional information was required. In collaboration with the stakeholders, additional information in the form of fixed inputs, intermediates and dependencies was collected from several sources in order to complete the model.

Fixed inputs are inputs that typically remain constant during the decision-making process. Here, we distinguish internal fixed inputs from external fixed inputs depending on whether the decision maker will be able to choose values for these inputs or not, respectively. Internal fixed inputs refer to the investment costs, the total energy demand and the capacity of the plant. An overview of these fixed inputs and their values, which are fictitious because of their competitively sensitive nature, are displayed in Table 12.4.

The external fixed inputs, their values and (public) sources are listed in Table 12.5.

The process of calculating key outputs from different types of inputs involved several steps. Intermediates store the results of these steps; they are used to make calculations easy and transparent and are based on inputs and/or other intermediates. Examples of intermediates are the number of certificates, the new employee engagement score and the percentage of grey energy per decision maker's option.

Table 12.4   Specification of (internal) fixed inputs for DSM case

Internal fixed input	Value	Unit	Source
Energy demand	30,000	MWh/year	(DO&RC, 2015) Note that data has been made fictitious for publication purposes.
Capacity RE make	15,000	MWh/year	(DO&RC, 2015) Note that data has been made fictitious for publication purposes.
Investment cost RE make	40,000,000	$	(DO&RC, 2015) Note that data has been made fictitious for publication purposes.
Capacity RS partner	15,000	MWh/year	(DO&RC, 2015) Note that data has been made fictitious for publication purposes.

Table 12.5   Specification of (external) fixed inputs for DSM case

External fixed input	Value	Unit	Source
CO_2 emission per MWh (uncorrected US emission factor)	0.676	tCO_2/MWh	(US Energy Information Administration, 2007)
Effect of maximum carbon footprint reduction on employee engagement	1.73	%/tCO_2	(Vinerean, Cetina and Dumitrescu, 2013)
Effect of carbon footprint reduction on brand value	212	$/$tCO_2$	(Matsumura, Prakash and Vera-Muñoz, 2014)
Effect of using an internal carbon price on employee engagement	1.73	%	(Vinerean, Cetina and Dumitrescu, 2013)
Engaged employee recommendation rate	78	%	(KPMG, 2011)
Disengaged employee recommendation rate	13	%	(KPMG, 2011)
Effect of employee engagement on customer satisfaction	10	%	(Gallup, 2013)
Current employee engagement score	70	%	(DSM, 2014)
Current Net Promotor Score	36	%	(DSM, 2014)

To illustrate a small part of the calculations, let us take a closer look at the percentage of renewable energy stored in the key output RE%. This percentage is calculated as follows:

RE% = %RE make + min (%RS partner + %RS market, %REC)

This formula adds the percentage of the total energy demand that is sourced by DSM's own solar panel plant to the sourcing from the market and the partner. The minimum operator in the formula ensures that only energy from renewable sources accompanied by certificates is counted as renewable energy.

Evaluating options by assessing strategic priorities

Having inserted all required inputs, outputs and information from desk and field research into tRBS, the decision maker can easily evaluate which option is the 'best' by assigning strategic priorities. Here, we assume the neutral scenario. Strategic priorities are expressed by assigning weights to key outputs. From the various settings considered, we will highlight three.

First, we considered a decision maker who only assigns (equal) weights to the key outputs 'cost of energy' and 'CAPEX' and does not apply an internal carbon price. The decision maker's option 'RS partner without REC', which corresponds to buying energy from a renewable source via a partner without buying any of the associated certificates, is the best-performing option. Intuitively, one might expect that 'No RE' would be the best strategy in this case since grey energy is normally cheaper than energy from a renewable source. However, from Table 12.3 we know that the price of grey energy is higher than that of energy from the partner. The reason for this is the agreement between DSM and the partner: land is made available by DSM for the partner. Also, DSM's fixed energy demand is guaranteed to the partner. This results in a low energy price from the partner for DSM. However, when applying DSM's principles of not buying energy from renewable sources without buying the accompanying certificates, the 'No RE' option would be the best strategy from a pure cost aspect; the costs of buying RECs from the partner as well makes this option more expensive than the option to buy grey energy from the grid.

Second, we considered the situation in which there is still a focus on profit-related key outputs only, but a non-zero internal carbon price is added to the equation. In the neutral scenario it turns out that the option to source energy via the partner including RECs is beating the 'No RE' option as soon as the internal carbon price exceeds $108.

Finally, we assumed that the decision maker considers all key outputs equally important, meaning that they account for people and planet next to the usual profit aspects. Even without taking into account any internal carbon price, buying renewable energy including the certificates from a partner is the recommended strategy. This can be deduced from Figure 12.2, where the second-best strategy is buying RE from the market, followed by making RE. This should be no surprise as these are the three options that account for more than just profit aspects.

The evaluation of the three situations as described above implies that when all aspects are evaluated in a decision-making process, the decision maker is supported in making a balanced decision, weighing

Figure 12.2 Comparison of decision maker's options when all key outputs have equal weights in the neutral scenario for DSM case

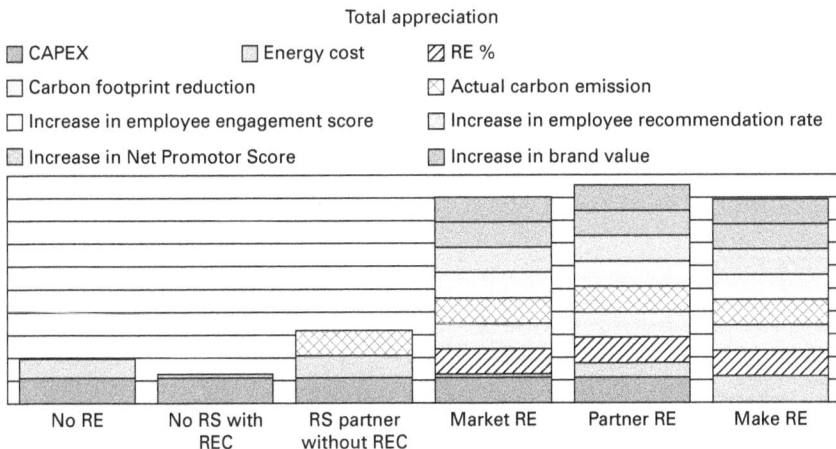

people, planet and profit dimensions. If there is only a profit-oriented business case available and time does not permit a full evaluation, then including an internal carbon price in the business case already enables the decision maker to account for more than profit-only aspects in an efficient way.

Evaluating options by assessing risk appetite

Risk appetite is indicated by assigning weights to scenarios. Figure 12.3 displays for each scenario a comparison of the decision maker's options where all key outputs are weighed equally. It can be deduced that the more weight is attributed to the RE optimistic scenario, the more attractive the 'Make RE' option becomes. However, if all scenarios are weighted equally, representing the search for a robust strategy, the option to partner is still the preferred option.

When focusing on profit-related key outputs only, but investigating the effect of internal carbon price, it turned out that in the RE pessimistic scenario, the option to buy grey energy from the grid was the recommended strategy until the internal carbon price exceeded $137. In the RE optimistic scenario, grey energy from the grid was

Figure 12.3   Comparison of decision maker's options when all key outputs have equal weights for all scenarios for DSM case

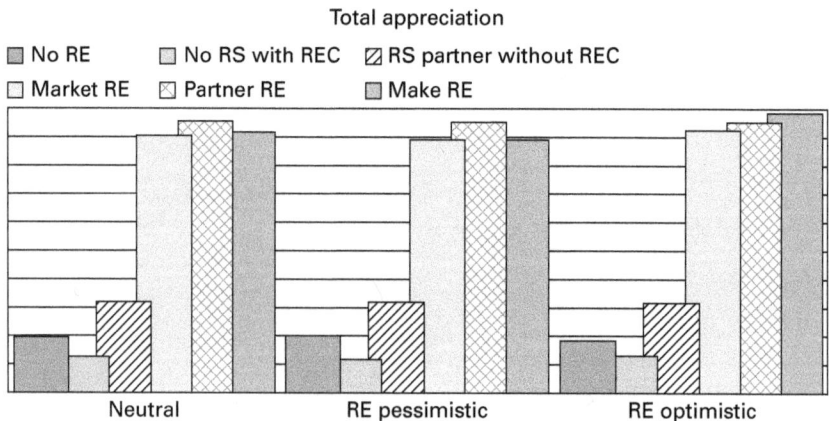

Total appreciation

the recommended strategy until the price exceeded $78. Thus the minimum value of the internal carbon price to favour a more sustainable decision declined as the decision maker becomes less risk-averse towards a declining trend in prices of renewable energy. This implies that when a decision maker is RE pessimistic they expect grey energy to be relatively cheaper than renewable energy. In that case there is a higher fine needed to compensate for the difference between the prices of grey and renewable energy.

Reflections

The importance of integrating sustainability into the corporate strategy has been recognized by DSM for a long time. The outcomes of the United Nations Climate Change Conference in Paris (United Nations, 2015) as well as the large amount of research and publications confirm their rationale that doing business in a sustainable way is a prerequisite for business continuity (McKinsey, 2011; Nidumolu et al, 2015).

The execution, however, requires a mind-shift for many multinational companies. Even for companies that already deal with more aspects than just profit, like DSM, eye-openers can still be created via the Responsible Business Simulator. For the case using fictitious data described here, an internal carbon price turns out to be necessary to favour energy from renewable sources over non-renewable sources for an organization that only focuses on profit-related aspects. The fact that the internal carbon price needs to exceed values ranging from $78 to $137, depending on the risk appetite, before a more sustainable decision is made, illustrates the great difference in price between grey and renewable energy.

Since the described strategic decision-making process at DSM was a multi-competency collaboration within the organization, previously described processes supported the already ongoing discussion of using an internal carbon price to evolve to a balanced and fact-based dialogue, which finally resulted in the introduction of an internal carbon price at DSM.

DSM considers the use of an internal carbon price as a step forward in the process of accounting for externalities in their decision-making process.

References

Brander, M, Sood, A, Wylie, C, Haughton, A and Lovell, J (2011) Electricity-specific emission factors for grid electricity, *Ecometrica*, ecometrica.com/assets/Electricity-specific-emission-factors-for-grid-electricity.pdf (archived at https://perma.cc/DAN3-RRDG)

Carbon Disclosure Project (2013) *Use of Internal Carbon Price by Companies as Incentive and Strategic Planning Tool*, CDP North America

Carbon Disclosure Project (2015) *Putting a Price on Risk: Carbon pricing in the corporate world*, CDP North America

Carbon Disclosure Project (2016) *Embedding a Carbon Price Into Business Strategy*, CDP North America

DO&RC (2015) Internal documentation, DSM Operations and Responsible Care, Heerlen

DSM (2014) Royal DSM Integrated Annual Report 2014, www.dsm.com/content/dam/dsm/corporate/en_US/documents/dsm-integrated-annual-report-2014.pdf (archived at https://perma.cc/5AHQ-2UP2)

DSM (2016a) Sustainability at DSM, www.dsm.com/corporate/sustainability.html (archived at https://perma.cc/97SZ-5ZUN)

DSM (2016b) Markets, www.dsm.com/corporate/markets-products/markets.html (archived at https://perma.cc/7Q2N-JGS3)

DSM (2016c) DSM named leader in Dow Jones Sustainability World Index, Press Release, www.dsm.com/corporate/media/informationcenter-news/2016/09/37-16-dsm-named-leader-in-dow-jones-sustainability-world-index.html (archived at https://perma.cc/U858-F2ZN)

Dutch Ministry of Economic Affairs (2010) Protocol monitoring hernieuwbare energie update 2010, www.rvo.nl/sites/default/files/Protocol%20Monitoring%20HE%20Interactief%20V3.pdf (archived at https://perma.cc/8SXS-BH9R)

Edelman (2016) AkzoNobel, DSM, Google en Philips werken samen aan lange termijn duurzame energiedoelstellingen, *Persberichten*, www.persberichten.com/persbericht/87109/AkzoNobel-DSM-Google-en-Philips-werken-samen-aan-lange-termijn-duurzame-energiedoelstellingen (archived at https://perma.cc/XJ5X-277H)

European Parliament (2009) Directive 2009/28/EC of the European
Parliament and of the Council of 23 April 2009 on the promotion of the
use of energy from renewable sources and amending and subsequently
repealing Directives 2001/77/EC and 2003/30/EC, *Official Journal of
the European Union*, **140**, Article 2

Fortune (2016) The Fortune 2016 Change the World list, fortune.com/
ranking/change-the-world/2016/ (archived at https://perma.cc/YU9U-
GHZZ)

Gallup (2013) *State of the Global Workplace*, Gallup, Washington, DC

Global Reporting Initiative (2013) *Sustainability Reporting Guidelines*,
Global Reporting Initiative, Amsterdam

Kossovsky, N, Greenberg, M and Brandegee, R (2012) *Reputation, Stock
Price, and You: Why the market rewards some companies and punishes
others*, Apress, New York

KPMG (2011) The real value of engaged employees, www.kpmg.com/US/
en/home/insights.html (archived at https://perma.cc/9LM3-34FZ)

Lyubomirsky, S, King, L and Diener, E (2005) The benefits of frequent
positive affect: does happiness lead to success? *Psychological Bulletin*,
131 (6), 803–55

McKinsey (2011) The business of sustainability: McKinsey Global Survey
results, www.mckinsey.com/business-functions/sustainability-and-
resource-productivity/our-insights/the-business-of-sustainability-
mckinsey-global-survey-results (archived at https://perma.cc/3V2Q-
K2UD)

Matsumura, E, Prakash, R and Vera-Muñoz, S (2014) Firm-value effects of
carbon emissions and carbon disclosures, *The Accounting Review*,
89 (2), 695–724

Nidumolu, R, Simmons, P and Yosie, T (2015) *Sustainability and the CEO:
Challenges, opportunities and next practices*, www.corporateecoforum.
com/wp-content/uploads/2015/04/CFO_and_Sustainability_Apr-2015.
pdf (archived at https://perma.cc/5482-ZQYG)

Reliable Disclosure Systems (2015) Improving significantly the reliability
and accuracy of the information given to consumers of electricity in
Europe, www.reliable-disclosure.org/Energie%20Update%202010%20
DEN.pdfnotfound (archived at https://perma.cc/W3RG-XMW5)

United Nations (2015) *Paris Agreement*, unfccc.int/files/meetings/paris_
nov_2015/application/pdf/paris_agreement_english_.pdf (archived at
https://perma.cc/2KWK-3RCJ)

US Energy Information Administration (2007) Voluntary Reporting of Greenhouse Gases, www.eia.gov/environment/pdfpages/0608s(2009) index.php (archived at https://perma.cc/EG2M-F68C)

Vinerean, S, Cetina, I and Dumitrescu, L (2013) Modeling employee satisfaction in relation to CSR practices and attraction and retention of top talent, *Expert Journal of Business and Management*, 4–14

Wright, L, Kemp, S and Williams, I (2011) 'Carbon footprinting': towards a universally accepted definition, *Carbon Management*, 2 (1), 61–72

Sustainable procurement decisions for waste collection systems

Sustainable procurement decisions for waste collection systems 13

Government procurement can be an important leverage when buying sustainable products from producers whose business model follows the principles of People, Planet and Profit. This is particularly the case if the customers are national government purchasing departments, who can raise the bar in terms of quality, sustainability, innovation and working environment. The same can be said for procurement departments at local government level. Municipalities are major buyers with substantial budgets. They buy vast amounts of goods and services for public infrastructure such as municipal gardens, administrative offices and maintenance of public buildings.

In this chapter we turn the spotlight onto decision making in public procurement and its impact on Rimetaal, a Dutch metalworking company with a good reputation of 'ticking the boxes' for delivering sustainable waste systems and working in a socially inclusive way. First we will introduce the company in the context of making strategic decisions to benefit people, planet and profit. We will then show how 'doing good' and having a sustainable business model does not necessarily result in a successful business output in terms of making a profit. Government institutions often say they are following the principles of sustainability in their procurement, but in practice the cheapest suppliers win the tenders, while the most sustainable proposals often come in second – which means no business. 'Doing good' sometimes has a high price for frontrunners in sustainable and socially inclusive business.

About Rimetaal (now part of Kliko)

Rimetaal BV was, until the end of 2014, a private limited company incorporated under Dutch law. At the end of 2014 it was taken over by Kliko, the No 1 specialist in waste systems and logistics in the Netherlands, but who also operate internationally, where it maintains a special position as a leader in sustainable, high-end technology for smart waste systems. Kliko decided to file Rimetaal for bankruptcy in 2016 and integrate the outstanding Rimetaal underground waste collection activities into Kliko's operations.

Rimetaal started life as a family firm and has specialized in the development, production, sale and maintenance of high-quality metal products since 1994. Its range includes underground waste collection systems and sound-insulating generator housings. The theme of 'sustainability' is a continuous thread throughout the company's policies, which are aimed at sustainable products, sustainable production methods as well as social inclusiveness. Hence, incorporating circular principles and taking social responsibility runs in the blood of the organization, its management and its employees. Rimetaal was one of the first partners in De Groene Zaak (Green Business), an entrepreneurial employers' organization established in 2010 and known as a collective of leaders in sustainability. The company's annual turnover at the time we did the research in 2011 was approximately €5 million, and it had around 35 employees. The following information, facts and figures therefore all relate to that period.

Sourcing waste collection systems

The market for waste collection systems consists primarily of local and regional government bodies. Rimetaal has made major investments in sustainable and socially responsible production methods, and product development is a proactive response to the social demands for sustainability. In order to continue to be able to compete on price, Rimetaal has also made investments designed to cut costs, such as reducing the throughput time of the production processes, lean working, more focus on pre- and post-costing, better collaboration between internal departments, training, a higher level of mechanization of the production machinery, and stock reduction. All in all, this has led to a reduction of the production cycle from 6 to 3.5 weeks.

In producing its waste collection systems, the company already embraces people and planet aspects in various ways. The people aspect is considered from the perspective of both employees and customers. For the employees, welding robots reduce accidents during the welding process. By providing a learning environment for students from technical colleges, and employment for rehabilitated 'problem' youngsters and people at a distance from the labour market, the company is helping specific groups gain access to meaningful work. For customers, robust hooks for the waste systems prevent accidents during emptying. The planet aspect becomes evident in the relatively long life cycle of the reinforced product and in low CO_2 emissions during the production process. This has been achieved thanks to the involvement of a research consultancy to help clean up the production process. The biggest challenge facing Rimetaal is to let potential customers, such as government procurement agencies, experience for themselves how their purchasing practices, sustainable or not, are affecting their strategic policies.

Some of the company's principal customers, local and national governments, aspire to be frontrunners in the field of sustainable procurement. Various targets have been set requiring 100 per cent sustainable procurement to be achieved by 2015. In that year, the European Commission published new EU guidelines on public procurement. It gave governments the chance to sharpen existing legislation around sustainable procurement and gave buyers at local level the chance to make use of the existing possibilities for sustainable product choices (TCO, 2016). RVO, the Dutch government agency for stimulating entrepreneurship in the Netherlands, has drawn up a set of criteria, but they are not very stringent. On top of that, in practice, it is all too often the case that suppliers are selected more on the basis of price (i.e. lowest) than on the basis of sustainability. Despite the fact that 'sustainability' is cited as an essential selection criterion, and that suppliers can certainly supply sustainable products that work out cheaper than non-sustainable products over the entire life cycle, tenders are still being published with highly detailed technical specifications, sometimes even with photographs of the desired products and their suppliers. Consequently, manifestly more sustainable products seem to be excluded. On paper the government of the Netherlands has criteria for sustainable public procurement (SPP – MVI in the Netherlands) to achieve greater sustainability and avoid any negative environmental and social impact. The website Dutch Public Procurement Expertise Centre gives an overview of criteria and tools to use (Government of the Netherlands, RVO, 2022).

This phenomenon is not exclusive to the Netherlands. TCO Certified, a Swedish company operating worldwide to certify sustainable IT products, together with leading sustainability organizations, published a study on sustainable public procurement in Sweden with similar examples. The report discusses the favourable rhetoric and the myths circulating about the level of sustainable procurement by government agencies, but in reality the picture is a lot less positive (TCO, 2016). More stringent legislation is needed to comply with the guidelines and certifications, but also changes in the behaviour of government buyers. Public procurement officers need to take more responsibility in delivering sustainable impact. Although this sounds reasonable, the rationale behind public procurement is often determined more by the yearly budget and how much is available to spend in a year, than by a longer-term view on sustainable use and maintenance of products, which could save public money and stimulate more sustainable producers.

The strategic decision-making process

For the research with the Responsible Business Simulator (tRBS) we used the data and dialogue approach in an action research setting. The focus was on how to develop a corporate decision-making process that would improve the success rate in the tendering processes of local and regional public procurement for underground waste systems. The decision-making process at Rimetaal was conducted in the form of multiple workshops with the executive Board and content experts. When describing the process we will follow the steps as set out in Chapter 5.

Determining scope of the decision

The company has been making a loss over recent years because competitors from low-wage countries are offering comparable products, even though there are manifest quality differences, such as weaker materials and less attention given to social aspects during the production process. It has been found that potential customers – despite giving sustainability high strategic priority – ultimately choose the lowest purchase price; municipal procurement officers clearly water down the sustainability criteria when it comes to the crunch.

Therefore, in an interactive setting, we formulated the objective for the strategic decision-making process at Rimetaal as follows: 'to offer the local government procurement officers insight into what – for them – would be the best procurement decision'.

Defining key outputs involving stakeholders

The key outputs have been defined from the perspective of the local government officer who needs to decide what waste systems their municipality should purchase. It is this procurement officer who actually holds the key to acquiring a sustainable product, but he or she must be able to compare alternative waste systems on the basis of the key outputs that should be important to their decision.

In order to support the procurement officer in reaching the prescribed goal, we defined, along with the stakeholders, the key outputs in such a way that they provided relevant insights. While defining these outputs, it turned out that when making a decision about the sourcing of waste collection systems, it was important for the procurement officer to get insight into the pricing structure of a product as well as into how procurement contributes to making the organization sustainable. To get insight into this pricing structure, it had to be recognized that the costs are more than just the purchase price (i.e. the invoiced price), as they also involve administration and operational costs (i.e. process costs). The concept of total cost of ownership (TCO), otherwise known as the life cycle concept, includes all these costs and was therefore a suitable key output.

Given that more and more purchasing is being put out to tender, procurement is the key to success in terms of making an organization sustainable. Products or services that fail to fulfil measurable and appraisable sustainability criteria will not be purchased: a 'knock-out' criterion. Determining these criteria calls for commercial, entrepreneurial and procurement competences. If the purchasing department applies the criteria in full, it will be able to make the contribution to sustainability visible. Basically, there is a need to express the effect of a decision in the same quantities or terms as those that the organization uses in its reporting. These could, for instance, be the same key outputs as are used to report on sustainability in annual reports.

Table 13.1 shows the chosen key outputs for the 3Ps. The outputs were suggested by Agentschap NL on behalf of government (Rijksdienst voor Ondernemend Nederland, 2016) and by De Groene Zaak, an organization working to accelerate 'sustainabilization' through sustainable purchasing (De Groene Zaak, 2016). The key outputs were further refined and made specific for Rimetaal in consultation with Rimetaal's Executive Board.

Table 13.1 Key output definitions for Rimetaal case

Key output	Theme	Meaning
CAPEX	Profit	Capital expenditure: the one-off investment in waste systems in the event of purchase (as opposed to lease)

(continued)

Table 13.1   (Continued)

Key output	Theme	Meaning
Total cost of ownership (TCO)	Profit	Total cost of ownership (TCO) of the waste systems. Two minor adjustments have been made to the standard definition of TCO in order to make it possible to compare the costs of leasing and buying waste systems with varying lengths of useful life: 1 In the case of outright purchase, the loss of interest is accounted as an expense; capital to the value of the purchase price is tied up in the waste systems and therefore no longer available for investment. This capital burden declines in a linear fashion to zero, because it can be assumed that the waste systems will be fully depreciated and will have no residual value at the end of their useful life 2 The TCO is here expressed as average cost per annum during the useful life of the waste systems. Future cash flows are therefore not converted into cash terms on the basis of a discount rate
CO_2 reduction	Planet	The reduction of CO_2 emissions during the production of Rimetaal's waste systems compared with the reduction of CO_2 emissions during the production of traditional waste systems
Rehabilitation	People	Number of jobs that can be created for the rehabilitation of problem youngsters if waste systems are ordered from Rimetaal. It is assumed that Rimetaal's competitors offer no such opportunities
Study tracks	People	Number of work experience placements for students that are created as a result of ordering waste systems from Rimetaal. It is assumed that Rimetaal's competitors offer no such placements
Health and safety incidents	People	Number of safety incidents that occur during the production of the waste systems ordered and the number of incidents that occur during actual use by the end user

Determining decision maker's options

As mentioned in Chapter 5, the internal variable inputs need to be defined for the decision maker to be able to formulate their options. From the perspective of the local government procurement officer, they can opt for a waste system from Rimetaal or from one of Rimetaal's competitors. If they opt for Rimetaal, they can then consider leasing the waste system instead of purchasing it outright. They can also opt to take out an all-inclusive maintenance contract. Such a contract would mean that Rimetaal would bear the risk of the maintenance needed, for example, because of vandalism. Note that Rimetaal uses the access-over-ownership model by offering the option to lease. The internal variable outputs and their meaning as formulated for the purchasing officer are summarized in Table 13.2.

Based on these inputs, we have formulated five options available to the decision maker. 'Traditional' describes the traditional type of decision based on price: purchase waste systems which, while cheap to buy, will be less durable. 'TradLease' describes the purchase of the same traditional systems, but within the framework of a lease construction. The options 'Rimetaal', 'RimLease' and 'RimServLease' all describe the purchase of Rimetaal systems, varying from outright purchase to lease to lease-plus-service.

Table 13.2   Internal variable input definitions for Rimetaal case

Internal variable input	Meaning
Share Rimetaal systems	Percentage of inhabitants that would be served by Rimetaal's waste systems: 0% if no system is ordered from Rimetaal, 100% if only Rimetaal systems are ordered
Lease instead of buy	1 if the municipality leases the waste systems; 0 if the municipality buys the waste systems
Service included	1 if a service contract is taken out with Rimetaal; 0 if not (a service contract can only be taken out in combination with a lease contract)

Table 13.3 Specification of decision maker's options for Rimetaal case

Internal variable input	Traditional	TradLease	Rimetaal	RimLease	RimServLease
Share Rimetaal systems	0	0	1	1	1
Lease instead of buy	0	1	0	1	1
Service included	0	0	0	0	1

Table 13.3 displays how this would work in practice within tRBS, showing how the internal variable input relates to the different options available to the decision maker.

Drawing up scenarios

External variable inputs are those inputs which the decision maker cannot control, but which play a role in the decision-making process. The occurrence of breakdowns, the variability in the length of the useful life of waste collection systems, and the interest rate for calculating the capital charges are all seen as the principal uncertainties from the operational environment that impact the outcome of the procurement decision. Table 13.4 describes the practical effects of these three uncertainties in the form of external input.

Additionally, three scenarios have been formulated: a pessimistic, an optimistic and a base-case or neutral scenario. This enables us to account for uncertainty regarding the external variable inputs. The values will be entered outside the boardroom, making use of simulation.

The number of breakdowns, the number of safety incidents and the length of the useful life of the waste systems have been determined on

Table 13.4 External variable input definitions for Rimetaal case

External variable input	Meaning
Breakdowns	Expected number of breakdowns per waste system per year. Breakdowns can be caused by vandalism, unexpected wear or by injudicious use
Life span variability	Spread in the useful life of a waste system due to wear and tear
Interest rate	Interest rate for calculating the capital charges for the purchase option; in the case of lease, a margin, payable by the user (lessee), is added to this interest rate in favour of the owner (lessor)

the basis of Monte Carlo simulation techniques. As explained in more detail in Chapter 7, this technique uses random numbers to generate multiple potential values for each of these parameters. The simulation model then computes the result for each of these values. In this way, we effectively create extra uncertainty about the input within any scenario. This makes the simulation model a stochastic model. Probability distributions suggest the likelihood of the possible values. The probability distribution for the occurrence of breakdowns is the Poisson distribution based on the number of waste systems multiplied by the external variable input 'Breakdowns'. The Poisson distribution has also been chosen for the number of safety incidents, with the number of waste systems to be produced multiplied by the expected number of safety incidents per system now as parameter. A triangular distribution has been chosen for the useful life of the waste systems, with the average useful life at the apex (this depends on the type of waste system) and with the external variable Life Span Variability as standard deviation. The resulting uncertainties are displayed in Table 13.5.

Table 13.5   Specification of scenarios for Rimetaal case

	Scenarios		
External variable input	**Pessimistic**	**Base case**	**Optimistic**
Breakdowns	0.12	0.08	0.04
Life span variability	4	3	2
Interest rate	0.09	0.08	0.07

Constructing the simulation model

Up until now all information collected in the group process has been completed and inserted into the simulation model. However, for the model to provide clear insights to the decision maker, some additional information is required. Separate from the stakeholder dialogue in Steps 1–4, but in consultation with the stakeholders, we collected this information from several sources to complete the model. The information takes the form of values of fixed inputs, definitions of intermediates, and dependencies that specify how outputs are calculated from intermediates and fixed and variable inputs.

Fixed inputs

In addition to the internal and external variable inputs, fixed inputs are inserted into the simulation model. Fixed inputs are inputs whose values are kept constant during the decision-making process. The Rimetaal case required a relatively large number of extra fixed inputs to be able to complete the calculation of the key outputs from the internal and external variable inputs. These extra fixed inputs were not promoted to variable inputs because possible variations were not deemed to be interesting enough to study in great detail. These inputs are both controllable (i.e. the decision maker can determine or set their value) and non-controllable (the decision maker has no control over them). The fixed inputs that we identified for Rimetaal are listed in Table 13.6.

Table 13.6   Specification of fixed inputs for Rimetaal case

Fixed input	Value	Meaning
Number of citizens	80,000	Number of inhabitants needed in the suburb where a new waste system is being considered
Number of citizens per Rimetaal system	500	Number of inhabitants that can make use of a single Rimetaal waste system
Number of citizens per traditional system	500	Number of inhabitants that can make use of a single traditional waste system
Number of Rimetaal systems per worker	32	Number of systems that a Rimetaal employee produces per year
Share rehabilitations in workforce	15%	Percentage of employees in Rimetaal's workforce that are part of the reintegration programme
Share study tracks in workforce	25%	Percentage of work experience placements in Rimetaal's workforce
Price per Rimetaal system	€4,000	Purchase price of a single Rimetaal waste system
Interest rate leasing surcharge	1%	Margin on the interest rate for the lease company
Service surcharge	2.5%	Margin added to the expected damage through vandalism to buy off the risk that the actual damage is greater than expected
Number of runs	50,000	Number of times that the future situation is simulated

(continued)

Table 13.6 (Continued)

Fixed input	Value	Meaning
Confidence level	95%	Used for aggregating the frequency distributions calculated by Monte Carlo simulation into key outputs
CO_2 reduction per Rimetaal system	500 kg	CO_2 reduction during production of a Rimetaal waste system in comparison with a traditional system
Average life span Rimetaal system	15 years	Average useful life of a Rimetaal waste system
Average life span traditional system	13 years	Average useful life of a traditional waste system
A priori probability breakdowns	5%	A priori probability that a waste system will be affected by vandalism (per year per system)
Cost per vandalization Rimetaal system	€1,000	Average cost of a vandalism incident to a Rimetaal waste system
Cost per vandalization traditional system	€2,000	Average cost of a vandalism incident to a traditional waste system
Health and safety incidents production Rimetaal system	1%	Expected percentage of safety incidents per Rimetaal waste system
Health and safety incidents production traditional system	2%	Expected percentage of safety incidents per traditional waste system
Relative surcharge Rimetaal	40%	Percentage difference between the prices of a Rimetaal and a traditional waste system

The values given for CO_2 production were based on a report that Rimetaal commissioned from Tüv Nord in order to ascertain the sustainability of its production methods (Tüv Nord, 2010) and on the certificate issued by the Climate Neutral Group (Climate Neutral Group, 2010). Other data was drawn from Rimetaal's internal HR documentation (especially the parameters needed to calculate the people-related key outputs) and from Rimetaal's own analysis of its competitive position.

Intermediates

As set out in Chapter 7, intermediates store the results of sub-steps in the calculations that convert inputs to the simulation model into outputs. Intermediates are used to make calculations easy and transparent, and are based on inputs and/or other intermediates.

Table 13.7 shows which intermediates had to be calculated first to keep the formulae simple and to be able to display the breakdown of calculations in small steps to the user.

Table 13.7 Definitions of intermediates for Rimetaal case

Intermediate	Unit	Meaning
Number of systems	#	Number of waste systems needed in the suburb for which new waste systems are considered
Price per system	€	Price per waste system. This corresponds to Price Rimetaal system if the Rimetaal system is chosen. If a traditional system is chosen, this price should be divided by 1+relative surcharge Rimetaal
Life span of system	year	The useful life of each waste system according to the Monte Carlo simulation
Number of breakdowns	#	The total number of vandalism incidents per year, calculated on the basis of Monte Carlo simulation

(continued)

Table 13.7   (Continued)

Intermediate	Unit	Meaning
Costs of breakdowns	€	Total costs of vandalism per simulation round per year
Service costs	€	Service costs per year if a service contract is taken out, taking account of the margin added for transferring the risk of breakdown to Rimetaal
Annuity	€	Debt servicing charges per simulation round per year if systems are purchased outright. The CAPEX is seen as a loan to be repaid by instalments over the useful life of the system (by conservative estimate): annual depreciation is such that repayment plus interest remains constant each year
Interest rate leasing	%	Interest rate, taking the lease company's margin into account
Lease payment	€	Lease payments per year. These are calculated as follows: the purchase price is furnished as a loan to be repaid in instalments over the useful life of the systems: instalments are such that repayment plus interest remains constant each year
Cash flow	€	Cash flow for the municipality per year

Dependencies

When constructing a simulation model, the user specifies via dependencies how key outputs are calculated from intermediates and fixed
and variable inputs. Most of these specifications are straightforward
since they follow directly from elementary business logic in combination with the names of the key outputs, intermediates and various
inputs. Therefore, these are not specified here. However, it is worthwhile spending a few words on how breakdowns and the system

lifespan have been modelled, since these are of stochastic nature. This makes the cash flow stochastic, and hence also the profit-related key outputs as well as the health and safety incidents. It is only when Rimetaal systems are chosen and procured by means of a lease-plus-service contract that the cash flows can be regarded as deterministic. The number of safety incidents remains stochastic in all cases. All stochastic outputs are calculated once for each of 50,000 simulation rounds. In each simulation round a random number generator is used to draw from a statistical distribution. To finally achieve a single score per key output per decision maker's option and per scenario, these 50,000 values are condensed into the percentile defined by the fixed input 'confidence level'. The setting of 95 per cent refers to the rather conservative case that the key outputs return the values for which the model expects that there is a 5 per cent risk that in reality the key output will score worse.

Evaluating options by assessing strategic priorities

For the decision maker it is crucial to account for the strategic priority ranking of the theme 'sustainability' in relation to other policy priorities. Experience and research alike corroborate that sustainability is cited as essential in nearly all policy documents. Without wishing to detract from the more successful examples, it is often quite a different matter to put sustainability into practice. If sustainability is to be given any priority, that priority must be thoroughly entrenched at executive, management and operational levels. Directors and managers must also continuously monitor the actual substance of the agreed sustainability objectives. In short, tRBS must be able to quantify the degree to which non-financial objectives will be achieved and take those values into consideration.

Now that all information for Rimetaal had been inserted into the simulation model, the decision maker could indicate their strategic priorities: to what key outputs do they assign the most weight?

First the situation that only capital expenditure (CAPEX) is important to the decision maker was considered. The outcome was hardly surprising: the traditional system won because it was cheaper to buy. All the various lease options scored even better, of course, simply because there was no CAPEX. Post-purchase maintenance costs do not fall under CAPEX and can therefore be disregarded on the basis of 'let tomorrow take care of itself'. Nonetheless, this simplistic reasoning was often the reason that Rimetaal failed to be selected as the best option in public tender skirmishes. As soon as the total cost of ownership is considered, instead of only the cost of purchase, the picture changed significantly, as can be seen in Figure 13.1.

The 'traditional' choice had to give way to the strategy to lease Rimetaal systems with a service contract.

It must be borne in mind, however, that all these considerations were based on the 'profit only' selection criterion. That just goes to show that, in this case, sustainable decision making was aided by looking further ahead than the one-off purchase cost and considering the expenses over a longer period.

If the outputs that address the people and planet aspects were also weighted, as in Figure 13.2, it was clear that the traditional systems soon lost ground to the more durable systems produced by Rimetaal. The question of whether it is better to lease or buy the Rimetaal systems, with or without a service contract, depends on the local authority's risk appetite, which will be discussed in the last step of the decision-making process.

Figure 13.1 Comparison of decision maker's options when weight is assigned only to key output 'TCO' in the base-case scenario for Rimetaal case

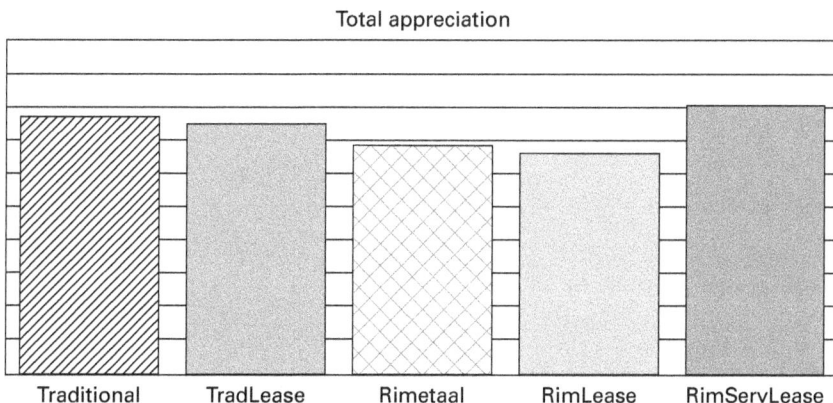

Total appreciation

Traditional   TradLease   Rimetaal   RimLease   RimServLease

Figure 13.2   Comparison of decision maker's options when all key outputs have equal weights in the base-case scenario for Rimetaal case

Total appreciation

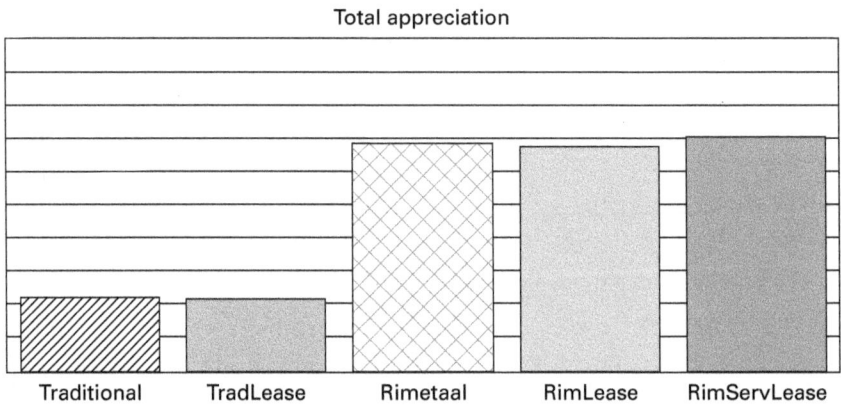

| Traditional | TradLease | Rimetaal | RimLease | RimServLease |

Evaluating options by assessing risk appetite

The decision maker's risk appetite reflects how they perceive the balance of its performance in terms of risk aversion. Just like assigning weights to the key outputs, weights can be assigned to the different scenarios. In Figure 13.3 we see that the risk appetite determined which of the three options related to choosing Rimetaal systems was the preferred one. In the pessimistic case, the purchasing officer expected more breakdowns and a shorter lifetime of the system than in the base-case and optimistic scenarios. In this pessimistic view, it was better to transfer the risk of breakdowns and shorter lifetimes to Rimetaal by choosing the lease option including service. If he or she were more optimistic, it becomes favourable not to pay the premium price for de-ownership and service.

If we take a step back and again focus on TCO only, then Figure 13.4 shows that – unlike in Figure 13.3 – in the optimistic case the outright purchase of a traditional system was the preferred option. It was only in the optimistic scenario that the traditional systems won because that scenario was based on optimistic estimates of useful life and costs due to vandalism. As soon as those estimates are toned down to the level of the base-case scenario, the traditional choice had to give way to the

Figure 13.3 Comparison of decision maker's options when all key outputs have equal weights for all scenarios for Rimetaal case

Total appreciation

☐ Traditional ☐ TradLease ☒ Rimetaal ☐ RimLease ☐ RimServLease

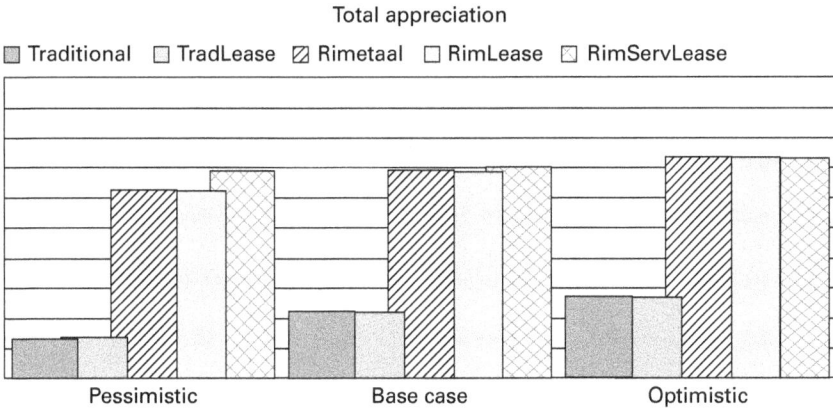

Pessimistic   Base case   Optimistic

Figure 13.4 Comparison of decision maker's options when weight is assigned only to key output 'TCO' for all scenarios for Rimetaal case

Total appreciation

☐ Traditional ☐ TradLease ☒ Rimetaal ☐ RimLease ☐ RimServLease

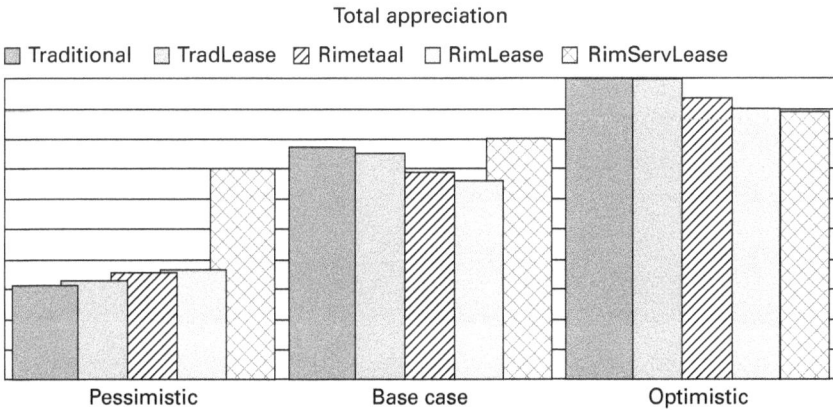

Pessimistic   Base case   Optimistic

strategy to lease Rimetaal systems with a service contract. Furthermore, we see that the more pessimistic the view and the lower the risk appetite, the sooner thoughts turned to leasing and a service contract, because then the interest rate risk and the risks of breakdowns and shortfalls in useful life are borne by third parties. If the scenarios are compressed by giving equal weight to each scenario, leasing the Rimetaal systems in combination with a service contract will be the first preference, followed by the purchase of traditional systems.

Reflections

If tender specifications are already full of details and descriptions of what is required, this can prohibit suggestions from suppliers for innovative solutions. Detailed specifications of this nature are usually based on historic insight, knowledge and experience of products, and do not therefore stimulate innovation. Within the criteria for procurement there must be some leeway to encourage innovation. Suppliers must be able to distinguish themselves by virtue of their inventiveness, but bureaucracy stifles innovation. Experience has shown that this is precisely where the tension lies: government organizations and local authorities want to maintain control over the quotation and procurement process and, because of their anxiety to avoid legal or liability problems, do not want to be surprised by issues that have not been part of their calculations from the offset.

Innovation, on the other hand, is precisely a matter of managing uncertain and unknown quantities, with a view to finding a timely solution to the problem. This perspective is far from new, even in government circles, as Rijkswaterstaat (the Dutch Department of Transport, Public Works and Water Management) has been promoting innovative tendering (Ministerie van Verkeer en Waterstaat, 2007) since 1992. In short, there is no need to produce specifications for the waste system itself, but it must be clear how the procurement of such a system contributes to the objectives of the organization that purchases it.

Since Rimetaal wants to let potential customers experience for themselves how their purchasing practices, sustainable or not, are affecting their strategic policies, it is crucial to provide insight into the uncertainty of outcomes. The procurement of waste collection systems is a long-term decision and it is impossible to accurately and reliably forecast the effect that the decision will have. The simulation model therefore needs to provide insight into the reliability of the forecasts of those effects. This is accounted for when completing the simulation model.

Setting the strategic priorities and assessing the risk appetite makes it possible to select the best strategy for the municipal procurement officer. This selection depends on the weights that have been allocated to the key outputs and to the scenarios.

Recall from the previous section of this chapter that a comparison of the computation on the basis of CAPEX alone with the computation on the basis of TCO alone produces a very interesting observation. Only the profit aspects were taken into account. Since the TCO evaluation would automatically lead to a sustainable choice, and this choice is not being made, there are clearly other factors to be taken into account that persuade the decision maker to give less credence to TCO.

We organized a round-table meeting and invited senior procurement officers from various municipalities to take part. We outlined the problem and explained our strategic decision-making approach. We discovered that the principle of procurement on the basis of TCO had not yet taken root in the public sector. Even though there had been reports on this subject, and there was a verbal commitment to sustainable purchasing from those in charge, the policies were not yet being put into practice. With the exception of the two largest cities, Amsterdam and Rotterdam, it seemed that procurement policies were based primarily on price. Three main reasons were pinpointed: the short time horizon of municipal appointees (four-year tenure and the need to be seen to realize objectives within that period); the separation of responsibility between investment (purchasing) and operations; and the fact that finances were often segregated by district within cities. Another reason proved to be the vast number of policy targets and the lack of any clearly communicated priority ranking.

On the basis of the decision-making process, we concluded that it is difficult, in practice, to persuade procurement officers to allocate sufficient weight to the non-financial key outputs during their selection of suppliers. The added value of the research into this decision-making process lies in the fact that it has resulted in three actions required for an improvement of the procurement process:

- The selection process to be conducted using the principles of circularity with the aid of tRBS, including the allocation of minimum weights to people- and planet-related key outputs.

- A sustainable product must fulfil a number of explicitly defined knock-out criteria in terms of sustainability. Subsequently, the cheapest tender from the range of suppliers that fulfil these criteria must be selected. In terms of the simulation model, this means that the key output scores on people, planet and profit aspects are not aggregated when scoring the purchasing options, but are each scored separately.

- A lease construction to be chosen, so as to spread the cost over time. This will compel municipal authorities to consider TCO, because it will automatically exclude CAPEX-based reasoning. The sustainable option would then be likely to come out on top, even without allocating any explicit weights to people and planet aspects, because we noted that some people- and planet-related key outputs are already incorporated into the TCO concept.

Rimetaal went bankrupt in 2014. The company paid the price for being a frontrunner in terms of dedication to high-technology, long-lasting materials and sustainable working practices. However, the metal industry was keen to keep Rimetaal precisely for these qualities, and it was not difficult to find a buyer for the company. For the current owner, Kliko, it proved very important for them, as a waste systems company at the lower end of the technological spectrum, to take over Rimetaal and totally integrate its knowledge and production system, which has now given them a high-end asset. Kliko is now up to speed in the production of advanced, sustainable waste systems, and is able to deliver much more advanced services to local municipalities and companies.

An important impetus has been given by the EU. The EU taxonomy (EU, 2022), a classification system which defines which economic activities can be considered environmentally sustainable, will be used across entire production and supply chains. With the increased need now to comply with EU guidelines on sustainability by local, regional and national governments, the climate for buying waste systems that score more highly on people, planet and profit aspects has improved. Kliko has made substantial investments in cleaning systems for waste bins underground, in digital technology, dashboards for measuring content and undertaking predictive maintenance, and lease contracts have also been developed. In that sense the integration of Rimetaal's leading-edge expertise in sustainable practices into the much larger organization has allowed Kliko to expand its operations globally (Kliko, 2022).

References

Climate Neutral Group (2010) *Certificaat Rimetaal*, Climate Neutral Group

De Groene Zaak (2016) Creëert de economie van morgen vandaag, degroenezaak.com/ (archived at https://perma.cc/RKD8-Y3Z9)

EU (2022) finance.ec.europa.eu/sustainable-finance/tools-and-standards/eu-taxonomy-sustainable-activities_en (archived at https://perma.cc/LYV8-85HD)

Government of the Netherlands (2022) About MVI criteria (sustainable public procurement), www.mvicriteria.nl/en/How%20this%20tool%20works (archived at https://perma.cc/HL3Z-2GNF)

Kliko (2022) kliko.nl (archived at https://perma.cc/H7PM-ZCQ4)

Ministerie van Verkeer en Waterstaat (2007) *Handreiking Systeemgerichte Contractbeheersing*, Rijkswaterstaat, Den Haag

Rijksdienst voor Ondernemend Nederland (2016) Rijksdienst voor Ondernemend Nederland, www.rvo.nl/ (archived at https://perma.cc/L4FE-TGGU)

TCO (2016) Sustainable public procurement: from rhetoric to practice: Dispelling myths and exploring effective solutions. A case study from Sweden, tcocertified.com/nl/news/sustainability-lacking-public-purchasing/ (archived at https://perma.cc/44QW-HUTS)

Tüv Nord (2010) *Rimetaal Green Check*, Tüv Nord, Hanover

Putting roof renovation in a strategic context

This chapter illustrates the application of strategic decision making in the case of the NEMO Science Museum in Amsterdam, the Netherlands. We will start by introducing this science museum in the context of making strategic decisions to benefit People, Planet and Profit.

About NEMO

The NEMO Science Museum (NEMO for short) aspires to be the biggest and most entertaining science centre in the Netherlands. Figures for the year 2019 show that NEMO is fifth in the top 15 museums in the Netherlands in terms of visitor numbers, attracting 664,979 visitors. Moreover, after the Covid-19 lockdowns, the number of visitors is still very high (NEMO, 2022). With five floors of interactive, interesting things to do and discover, for many people it is the place to go to be introduced to science and technology in a playful manner. For the education sector, NEMO is the biggest interactive non-school-like informal learning environment and forms part of many science and engineering educational programmes. In 2019 more than 91,000 students visited NEMO for educational programmes. NEMO also organizes training programmes for teachers and has intensive exchange programmes with an international network of science centres. About 40 per cent of its visitors come from abroad.

The museum is housed in a prominent building above the entrance to the IJ lake tunnel, one of the main roads into the centre of the city of Amsterdam. The building was designed by the famous Italian architect Renzo Piano. He considered Amsterdam to be a 'flat city', in contrast to many other capital cities, since it lacked high and prominent viewpoints. He designed the building to look like a ship rising from the IJsselmeer (IJ lake), with the roof of the museum representing the ship's deck. The roof acts as a public square, is freely accessible to the public, and provides Amsterdam with a high viewpoint. It is the highest elevated square in Europe and very popular among people of all ages.

NEMO aims to be a sustainable cultural enterprise and is doing pioneering work to draw attention to technology and innovation in the field of sustainability. 'Walking the talk' makes NEMO eminently suitable for showcasing to the public how it is applying technology in innovative ways to make its own operations more sustainable and to work towards a circular economy. This consists of both energy-saving measures and the decision-making process in which the measures are decided upon.

Renovating NEMO's roof

Ever since the NEMO building was finished in 1997, there have been problems with the roof. As such, NEMO's roof plays a key part in this case study. Recurring leaks have required complicated and expensive repairs and the roof also falls short of current insulation standards for this type of public building. Therefore, in 2013, the Board of Directors and the Supervisory Board decided to build up an additional contingency fund to enable a structural solution to be found for the problems that beset the roof. Sufficient funds were set aside and the various options for repairs were investigated.

During this investigation, in which NEMO's own maintenance staff were assisted by external experts from an engineering consultancy firm, the question arose whether or not it would be desirable to re-evaluate the function of the roof. The roof already housed the Splashing Water Wonder playground, and people could enjoy the view of the city. The Board was considering the possibility of letting the roof play a prominent part in the NEMO GREEN programme. This programme is dedicated to doing everything technically, organizationally and financially possible, and in accordance with the triple bottom line, to make NEMO the most progressive, sustainable cultural enterprise in Amsterdam.

A plan was devised not only to recoat and reinsulate NEMO's roof, but also to have it house an experimental roof garden and a power-generating system. The roof garden would have a good insulating effect; in addition, it would clean the air and rainwater and put visitors in contact with nature. In its capacity as a power generator, the roof would offer the opportunity for companies to demonstrate new developments, for visitors to learn about alternative sources of energy and, on top of that, the chance to supply the building itself with energy.

As is usual with such proposals, a business case was drawn up to see whether the required investment would yield sufficient returns. The report, which was drawn up with the help of external consultants (Hommersen and Kasteel, 2010), compared the costs required for realization and operation with the estimated savings on energy. The comparison concluded with the following remark:

> Moreover, additional revenue can be generated by attracting more visitors. The business case refrains from making any statements on this matter as it cannot be quantified.

Because of this rider, it is possible that an important aspect of the decision-making process has been ignored. This leads to the question of whether or not traditional, financially driven methods for evaluating business cases are still applicable in a world which demands more and more accountability in the domains of people and planet next to profit.

The purpose of strategic decision making, and the application of the Responsible Business Simulator in particular, is precisely to quantify the people and planet aspects and make them comparable to the profit aspects. It is of particular importance for NEMO, where profit maximization is not a primary goal, to be able to evaluate complex scenarios and compare financial and non-financial indicators with each other. The primary goal of the application of tRBS was to advise the Board of Directors and the Supervisory Board as to which choice for repairing and arranging the roof would best satisfy all of NEMO's stakeholders' wishes. In other words, to give a well-founded answer to the question of 'how to renovate a roof'. The secondary goal was to gain experience in bringing more transparency to this form of sustainable decision making, so that it can eventually be shared with NEMO's visitors.

The strategic decision-making process

For the development of the strategic decision-making process at NEMO, we worked with a team that represented a cross-section of the personnel. With their own individual areas of expertise, they took an active part in setting out the strategy and providing material for the simulation model. Their knowledge of the various parts of the organization, in combination with the active support of the directors, not only resulted in a meaningful strategic dialogue but also gathered a large quantity of useful data. The input of NEMO's team proved to be a good example of the ideal way to work. The successive outcomes of the simulation model were compared and analysed carefully. Because of this, key outputs could be refined, new ones could be entered, and factual data could be brought into the strategic dialogue in a meaningful way. By working in this way, the NEMO team was surprised at how far they could go in making the roof more sustainable. The plans might have started tentatively, but they eventually ended in a completely new design from architect Renzo Piano for an advanced climate-neutral roof with an even more pronounced public function, including an overview of sustainable energy-generating methods, a sustainable stairwell that provides its own power and light, a restaurant, and a new layout for the roof's upper section. The combination of action research and strategic decision making worked out well for NEMO and resulted in a good strategic plan. At the time of writing, most parts of this plan have been realized or are in the process of being implemented.

Table 14.1 Key output definitions for NEMO case

Key output	Unit	Theme	Stakeholders
Increase in customer satisfaction, where customer satisfaction is measured as report mark on a scale 0–10	.	People	Customers, media and the Dutch Ministry of Education, Culture & Science
Increase in landmark value, where landmark value is measured as report mark on a scale 0–10	.	People	Local residents, the city of Amsterdam and the media; primarily involves the People aspect
Energy savings measured in kilowatt-hours per year	kWh / year	Planet	Media and suppliers
Energy savings measured in € per year	€ / year	Profit (Other)	Management
Additional revenues from admission tickets, measured in € per year	€ / year	Profit (Other)	Employees and management (in order to guarantee continuity)
Additional restaurant revenues	€ / year	Profit (Other)	Employees and management (in order to guarantee continuity)
Capital expenditure (CAPEX)	€ / year	Profit (CAPEX)	Management
Operational expenditure (OPEX)	€ / year	Profit (Other)	Management

Describing the strategic challenge that requires a decision

As mentioned in the introduction, NEMO's Board of Directors and the Supervisory Board built up a contingency fund to enable a structural solution for the problems that beset the roof to be found. At the same time they considered the possibility of giving the roof a prominent role in the NEMO GREEN programme with the aim of doing everything that is technically, organizationally and financially possible to make NEMO the most progressive, sustainable cultural enterprise in Amsterdam. The hypothesis is that by investing in the people and planet aspects, positive effects will occur as a bonus on the profit side. The objective of using strategic decision making was formulated as follows: 'to empower NEMO to obtain insight into the optimal decisions regarding a sustainable repair of their roof and sharing this insight with its stakeholders.'

Defining key outputs involving stakeholders

Even though NEMO's Board made the final decision on how to repair the roof, the multiple stakeholders of this cultural enterprise were key in the decision-making process. With the objective of a sustainable repair of the roof in mind, in collaboration with NEMO's staff we started by listing NEMO's stakeholders and their qualitative interests. We then operationalized the extent to which those interests could be served: in other words, we made them quantitatively measurable. This resulted in a list of over 30 outputs, which was subsequently reduced to a shortlist of just eight key outputs.

Table 14.1 gives an overview of the key outputs, which theme they relate to, and the stakeholders involved. Here, we have broken down the profit theme into capital expenditure (CAPEX) and other.

Determining decision maker's options

Recall from Chapter 5 that in order to formulate the decision maker's options, internal variable inputs must first be formulated. We therefore looked at the different sub-decisions awaiting the decision maker. We divided the choices for the new layout of the roof into three types of decision:

1 whether or not to repair the current roof

2 whether to further insulate the roof

3 make a decision about the layout of the roof

For the last decision, we split the roof into three sections: the lower roof (2,800 m^2), the upper roof (1,200 m^2), and the roof of the existing restaurant ('bar roof', 250 m^2). Figure 14.1 shows an image of the roof.

The visitors' terrace originally took up most of the lower roof area. The precondition for this terrace is that its minimum area must be 1,800 m². Because of the building's support structure, such a terrace can only be located on the lower roof. In accordance with the engineers' report, this left three possible arrangements for the roof: wind turbines (which can only be placed on the upper roof due to the wind), a garden and solar panels. In addition to two types of wind turbine from the manufacturers Skystream and Montana, we considered the PowerPlane from the manufacturer Ampyx Power. We also considered the option of making a visitors' walkway on the upper roof, so that visitors could see the wind turbines, the PowerPlanes, the garden and the solar panels at close quarters. We assumed that the garden would provide additional insulation and also offer greater recreational value.

Based on these choices, we defined 13 internal variable inputs, two of which indicated whether or not the lower and upper roofs should be repaired. Two further internal variable inputs determined whether or not these sections of the roof should receive additional insulation. A separate internal variable input determined whether or not there would be a visitors' walkway. Up until this point all internal variable inputs

Figure 14.1   NEMO's roof: the upper roof is the higher, rounded section

could be categorized as binary, implying that the decision maker has a choice between intervening or not. Two additional internal variable inputs represented the surface area (in square metres) to be laid out as gardens on the lower and upper roofs. Three more internal variable inputs indicated the number of square metres of solar panels for each roof section. The final three internal variable inputs indicated the number of wind turbines from Skystream (Xzeres, 2016), Montana (National Centre for Appropriate Technology, 2016) and/or Ampyx (Ampyx Power, 2016).

At a later stage, six more internal variable inputs were added to the simulation model. These inputs did not originate from the engineers' report, but were based on Renzo Piano's ideas; he became more and more involved in the decision-making process as time went by. The first two inputs were binary and concerned new accommodation for the restaurant facilities based on his own innovative tent-shaped design called the Piano Tent, and a separate elevator for direct access to the roof. The third and fourth variables concerned the extent to which the lower and upper roofs could be covered in a step-like planting pattern with seating for visitors. The fifth additional input represented the presence of solar panels that could also be used as benches, and the sixth concerned the instalment of Renzo Piano's innovative wind turbine design called the Piano Mill. All in all, this resulted in a total of 19 internal variable inputs.

Making use of the different internal variable inputs, it was decided to work out the implications of six decision maker's options. The first option was simply to do nothing. The second was to repair only the roof. The third, fourth and fifth options consisted of repairing and insulating the roof along with a new layout focused on the garden, on wind and solar energy, and on a combination of both in accordance with the options described in the engineers' report. The sixth option was the relatively capital intensive option of implementing Renzo Piano's ideas. For each non-trivial option, the number of square metres for each zone of the roof was input into tRBS. Table 14.2 shows an overview of the internal variable inputs mapped onto the six decision maker's options.

Table 14.2 Specification of decision maker's options for NEMO case

Internal variable input	Decision maker's options					
	Do nothing	Just repair	Gardening	Energy	Mix	Renzo Piano
Piano tent						1 @ bar roof
Gardening			1,150 m² @ upper roof 1,000 m² @ lower roof		505 m² @ upper roof 500 m² @ lower roof	
Planter steps						1,130 m² @ upper roof 600 m² @ lower roof
Visitor path			Yes	Yes	Yes	
PV field (solar panel)				1,110 m² @ upper roof 300 m² @ bar roof 1,000 m² @ lower roof	505 m² @ upper roof 300 m² @ bar roof 500 m² @ lower roof	
PV steps						1,670 m² @ lower roof

(*continued*)

Table 14.2   (Continued)

Internal variable input	Decision maker's options					
	Do nothing	Just repair	Gardening	Energy	Mix	Renzo Piano
Montana windmills				2 @ upper roof	2 @ upper roof	
SkyStream windmills				2 @ upper roof	2 @ upper roof	
Ampyx power planes					1 @ upper roof	
Piano Mills						2 @ upper roof
Roof repair		1 @ upper roof 1 @ lower roof	1 @ upper roof 1 @ lower roof	1 @ upper roof 1 @ lower roof	1 @ upper roof 1 @ lower roof	1 @ upper roof 1 @ lower roof
Extra insulation			1 @ upper roof 1 @ lower roof	1 @ upper roof 1 @ lower roof	1 @ upper roof 1 @ lower roof	1 @ upper roof 1 @ lower roof
External elevator						1 @ bar roof

Drawing up scenarios

Next to inputs that can be controlled by the decision maker, external variable inputs were formulated to account for exogenous uncertainties. This enabled us to draw up scenarios. We initially considered four sources of uncertainty that we wanted to monitor for their influence on the key outputs:

- The first external variable input was the energy price, which was used to translate the value of energy generated by the solar panels and wind turbines, and the energy saved by additional insulation, into monetary terms.

- The second was the factor translating the increase in customer satisfaction into additional visitors.

- The third was the equivalent of the second, but in terms of an increase in landmark value.

- The final uncertainty was the extent to which the suppliers of the wind turbines, solar panels and PowerPlanes might be willing to sponsor the purchase, considering that the placement of these systems would be an advertisement for their products.

Later on, a fifth external variable input was added to determine the relative effect that the direct elevator up to the roof would have on restaurant revenues. This concerned a factor by which we could multiply our initial estimate of this effect in order to do justice to the inherent uncertainty that surrounds the revenues of such an unusual elevator-accessed restaurant. Another reason for this separate assessment was that this revenue is not connected to additional restaurant revenues from users paying to visit the science museum, since the elevator enables direct access to the restaurant without visiting the museum.

Besides a base-case scenario, an optimistic scenario and a pessimistic scenario were both defined. Table 14.3 illustrates how the uncertainty of the external variable inputs finds expression in wide variations in the figures across the scenarios.

Table 14.3 Specification of external variable inputs for NEMO case

		Scenarios		
External variable input	**Unit**	**Pessimistic**	**Base case**	**Optimistic**
Price	€/kWh	€0.05	€0.06	€0.07
Increase in annual number of visitors per unit increase in customer satisfaction measured on a scale 0–10	# / year	125	150	500
Increase in annual number of visitors per unit increase in landmark value measured on a scale 0–10	# / year	100	250	400
Share of CAPEX covered by sponsoring (only for innovative energy-saving investments)	.	60%	75%	100%
Influence of elevator on restaurant revenues	.	0%	20%	60%

Constructing the simulation model

The information collected so far was inserted into the simulation model. However, for the model to provide accurate and clear insights to the decision maker, a large amount of additional information was required. In collaboration with stakeholders, we collected this additional information via desk research from several sources and completed the model. We distinguished fixed inputs, intermediates and dependencies, which we will now consider.

Fixed inputs are inputs that – in principle – are not modified during the decision-making process. Most of these are straightforward and will not be mentioned here. However, to illustrate the use of fixed inputs, here are some examples:

- costs of repairing the roof sections and fitting extra insulation
- costs of purchase and maintenance for the three types of roof layouts

- footprint of the wind turbines, PowerPlanes and Piano Mills
- average restaurant revenue and admission revenue per additional visitor
- expected costs to remedy damage resulting from the roof not being repaired
- expected energy savings in kWh per type of investment
- effects of investments on customer satisfaction and landmark value

The first four fixed inputs can be determined relatively accurately as they are predictable and more or less in control. The fifth and sixth are beyond the direct control of management, but were not deemed influential enough to be promoted to external variable inputs.

Assessing the effects of the seventh input, effect of investments on customer satisfaction and landmark value, was a challenging task. We made these assessments by consulting NEMO on the variations in customer satisfaction as determined in surveys carried out during earlier exhibitions, and by thoroughly examining previous surveys on brand awareness. Instead of listing values of all fixed inputs, we only cited their sources. All technical data concerning repairs, insulation, purchase costs and maintenance costs of energy-saving measures – gardening, wind turbines and solar panels – was taken from the engineers' report. This report also gave expected energy savings for each wind turbine, each square metre of solar panels and each square metre of garden. For the layout of the garden, a distinction was made between extensive and intensive gardening. We simply assumed that when a part of the roof is used as a garden, 70 per cent of its area will be extensive gardening and 30 per cent intensive gardening. The costs and expected energy yield of the PowerPlanes and the footprint needed for the investment in wind energy were calculated from desk research sources. The expected costs to repair damage resulting from not repairing the roof and the average revenues per visitor were easily determined on the basis of historical data held by NEMO.

To keep the calculations of key outputs based on the internal variable inputs, external variable inputs and fixed inputs easy and transparent, these were broken down into several steps. Intermediates stored the results of these steps; they were based on inputs and potentially on other intermediates as well. Formulating intermediates helped to pinpoint the influence each investment had on CAPEX, OPEX (operational expenditure), customer satisfaction and landmark value, and how those influences in turn resulted in more visitors and more revenues. The intermediates formulated for NEMO depended on roof application, time, or both.

Next, the way in which inputs, intermediates and outputs were mutually dependent was defined. Most of these relationships were straightforward due to the breakdown of the calculations into small steps via the introduction of intermediates. These dependencies were fed into tRBS in the form of a matrix as described in Chapter 7. We will not discuss this whole process, but restrict ourselves to some examples. The expected incremental effects on customer satisfaction and landmark value for each unit of investment in wind turbines, PowerPlanes, Piano Mills, visitors' walkway, roof garden and solar panels were modelled as linear elasticity; for each additional unit of investment, the key outputs would increase to an extent dependent on the kind of investment and the current level of investment. Another part of the model consisted of a number of validation rules or safety measures to prevent assigning impossible combinations of values to internal variable inputs – for example, defining decision maker's options that would create a layout for the roof that would be too congested. The financial part of the simulation model closely resembled a traditional discounted cash flow model, with the time horizon set to 10 years and the discount rate set to 10 per cent.

After setting up these fixed inputs, intermediates and dependencies, the simulation model was ready to calculate the values of the key output per decision maker's option per scenario. This results in 8 × 6 × 3 (# key outputs × # decision maker's options × # scenarios) = 144 key output values, supplemented by values of intermediates. In order to validate the feasibility of these outcomes, we studied the graphs and tables containing various representations of this data set extensively. We also analysed the sensitivity of the outcomes for variations in the inputs, especially for those inputs that had no unequivocal source. This demonstrated that the decision maker's option to do nothing was burdened significantly by the increase in OPEX because of repairing water damage. This stage of interpretation also helped to formulate the five other options, as well as draw up the three scenarios shown in Table 14.3. These interpretations also showed that the visitors' walkway was not very profitable because of the relatively high costs associated with the additional constructional features required for the upper roof. The wind turbines were relatively unprofitable as well, due to the number of square metres required for safety margins in proportion to visitors' appreciation; moreover, the roof was not high enough for relatively small, cheap wind turbines to suffice. The model did, however, make a relatively high estimation for the additional restaurant revenues attributable to providing direct access to the roof. This estimation was further justified as it lowered the threshold for visiting the science museum after visiting the roof free of charge by means of a direct elevator to a spectacular restaurant. This analysis is an example of how the model was refined iteratively, because the correlation between elevator and restaurant revenues was originally not included in the set of external variable inputs.

Evaluating options by assessing strategic priorities

Having inserted all required inputs, outputs and information from desk and field research into tRBS, the decision maker could easily evaluate which option is the 'best' by assigning strategic priorities to the key outputs. As the key outputs were condensed into the people, planet and profit themes, NEMO's Board could decide upon a 'best strategy' by assigning strategic priority to the three different themes. Table 14.1 gives a clear overview of how the key outputs were mapped onto the themes.

Figure 14.2 shows the contribution of all themes to the total appreciation of the decision maker's option for the base-case scenario. Let us first look at the lower two parts of the bars, meaning that we only focus on profit aspects. When determining the best option we see that it is a close call between the option to do nothing and the option to just repair the roof. In the first option there is no CAPEX but there are periodic repair costs. The latter option has CAPEX but performs better on OPEX, due to lower periodic repair costs and a

Figure 14.2 Comparison of decision maker's options when all themes have equal weights in the base-case scenario for NEMO case

Total appreciation

□ Profit (Capex)   □ Profit (other)   ☑ Planet   □ People

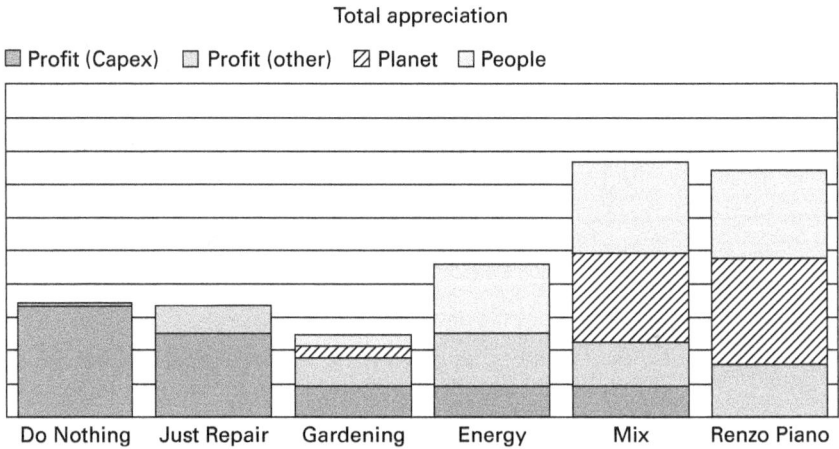

Do Nothing   Just Repair   Gardening   Energy   Mix   Renzo Piano

lower energy bill. The other options perform worse because they require even more CAPEX and also some additional OPEX to maintain the additional facilities built on top of the roof, which is apparently not yet compensated for by additional revenues from these facilities.

However, if we also take into account the upper parts of the bars in Figure 14.2, meaning that we give equal weight to all four themes, we then conclude that the 'Mix' option outperforms the other option, closely followed by the 'Renzo Piano' option. We also see that 'Gardening' is a cheaper option than 'Energy', 'Mix' and 'Renzo Piano', but also has less impact on people and planet.

Evaluating options by assessing risk appetite

Up until now we have not accounted for the uncertainties that go hand in hand with the modelling process. In order to include the uncertainties in our evaluation to determine which decision maker's option is the 'best', we need to indicate a risk appetite as well as assigning strategic priorities to the themes. For example, if only the profit themes are prioritized, the combination 'Mix' and the 'Renzo Piano' options

Figure 14.3 Comparison of decision maker's options when weight is assigned only to theme 'profit' for all scenarios for NEMO case

Total appreciation

☐ Do Nothing ☐ Just Repair ▨ Gardening ☐ Energy ☐ Mix ☐ Renzo Piano

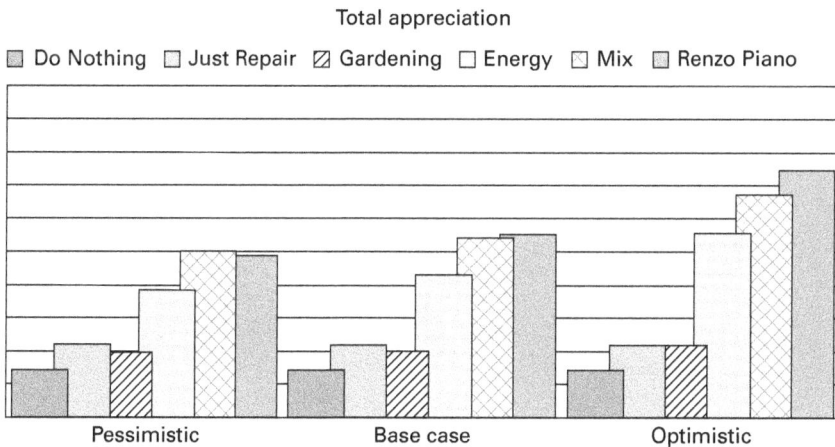

Pessimistic   Base case   Optimistic

outperform the other decision maker's options in the optimistic scenario, since in that scenario we have an optimistic view on additional revenues from both the restaurant and admission tickets by attracting more visitors.

Figure 14.3 illustrates the performance of the various decision maker's options for the pessimistic, base-case and optimistic scenarios when all profit-related key outputs are deemed equally important. We see that the 'mix' option is the preferred option in the pessimistic scenario. In the base-case and optimistic scenarios the 'Renzo Piano' option is not only the best option from a profit-only perspective but also from a triple bottom line perspective.

Therefore, it transpired that the formulated decision maker's options differed considerably in their contributions and that all these contributions were also heavily dependent on the risk appetite of the decision maker.

Based on these evaluations, NEMO decided to build a restaurant on the roof that can host 300 visitors, and which can be accessed by the elevator from the main hall without it being necessary to enter the science centre itself. Initially it was thought that a new elevator had to be built to make it possible to enter the restaurant without entering the science centre, but in fact it could be achieved by turning the elevator round 180 degrees. Since the opening of the restaurant, revenues per visitor from hospitality have tripled. Furthermore, green roofing (referred to as 'a garden') has been arranged in a way that keeps the restaurant cooler. Special roof insulation will soon be installed to further regulate temperatures inside the building. Beside these larger projects, small adjustments such as automatic light switches in the toilets also work towards substantial energy savings.

Reflections

As we facilitated a series of sessions on strategic decision making, we were able to observe the process closely. During the first session, when tRBS represented little more than a very high-level prototype simulation model, it was noticeable that participants were still really keen to start expanding on the model. Participants already knew that a great deal of data was available in the areas of finance, marketing and accommodation, and that this data had never been interlinked to support integrated decision making.

The longlist of key outputs from the initial examination proved to be very extensive indeed. This was mainly because NEMO is a socially committed organization, and there are many stakeholders whose perspectives all have to be taken into account. The first session involved a group of participants from a wide variety of disciplines, and this proved beneficial when appraising the interests of all those stakeholders. Unfortunately, the task of reducing the longlist to a shortlist and operationalizing the remaining key outputs could not be undertaken as a plenary process, but had to be split up into smaller working parties because the time allotted for the workshop simply flew by.

The range of disciplines represented at the first session unlocked a treasure trove of information in the form of reports, system printouts and personal experiences that were very useful when refining the prototype model into the first 'real' version. This did much to underpin the credibility of the figures presented during the second workshop with members of the Board. There was, admittedly, still some uncertainty about various crucial external variable inputs and fixed inputs, but the figures that were presented were thoroughly substantiated. The integrated approach of taking all 3P aspects together also forestalled any tendency to take a 'penny wise, pound foolish' approach. It was soon obvious that there was little added value to be gained from deliberating over the enormous pile of data about wind speeds at heights of 80 metres in Amsterdam to make an estimation of the power that could be generated if wind turbines were to be located on the roof, because – although a thorough study still had to be carried out – it was already clear that scenic value would probably have a greater positive effect on future visitor numbers.

The facilitator of the workshop set the conditions under which each participant could contribute, as long as they could be sure they knew which discipline that participant represented. For example, if a participant has expert knowledge on certain variables or values, it is easy for them to question the validity and accuracy of any estimates proposed for them within their area of expertise, and they are thereby encouraged to play a bigger role in the process.

It might then be possible to convert the sceptic who seems to have little faith in the approach by inviting them to add extra stress scenarios or by making them feel that they have influence over the decision-making process in another way. Last but not least, it proved to be easy to expand the simulation model when Renzo Piano suggested alternatives for the options that had been described in the engineers' report.

The added value of this new way of conducting the decision-making process does not lie solely in the fact that NEMO can now make a detailed calculation of the value of each key output score for each alternative strategy. More importantly, strategic decision making demonstrated that an issue that seemed to be the responsibility of the technical department – because it concerned a leaking roof – turned out to have far wider implications; it soon expanded to encompass the strategic decision-making process about a substantial expansion of the public function of the centre. In addition, it may also give rise to new revenue models, as the roof will be accessible and usable even outside NEMO's normal opening hours. A restaurant on the roof that can be accessed via an elevator was incorporated into the plans and, at the time of writing, had already been built.

It was not, of course, possible to carry out all of those plans straight away, but NEMO took the opportunity in the summer of 2013 to increase the green value of the roof and it is very clear that the ambitious suggestions for further 'greening' supplied by the infectiously enthusiastic Renzo Piano have excited the imagination. By 2016, almost all plans had been implemented and the public square with the outdoor exhibition has proven to be a great success. It is open to the public without the need to buy a museum ticket, and creates a new free space with a fantastic view for Amsterdam's citizens and visitors. To date, the restaurant on the green roof has created a substantial increase in revenue from hospitality. Interestingly, the NEMO team's proposal convinced both the Board of Directors and the Supervisory Board that investment in the roof would have an added value, and they gave approval for a further development of the architect's plans. In 2015 NEMO had 591,776 visitors and this increased in 2019 to 664,879 visitors. As it proved for many museums, Covid-19 lockdowns was a difficult time, but in 2022 more than 570,000 visitors were welcomed. These successes speak volumes. All in all, they demonstrate that it is certainly possible and worthwhile, in the interests of sustainable decision making, to quantify the impact that uncertain effects can have on combinations of the various aspects of people, planet and profit.

A new chapter in the success story of NEMO's sustainable roof will be revealed in 2023. Currently NEMO is investigating plans for the roof as a public square that goes even further in terms of sustainability. It is foreseen that in 2024 'NEMO: the outdoor experience' on the sustainable roof will be implemented.

References

Ampyx Power (2016) Energy of the future, www.ampyxpower.com/ (archived at https://perma.cc/QXN6-RN9P)

Hommersen, M and Kasteel, R (2010) Business case 'roof' [Business case dak], commissioned by the NEMO Green working party

National Centre for Appropriate Technology (2016) Wind power, www.montanagreenpower.com/wind/ (archived at https://perma.cc/5TSR-AZSF)

NEMO (2022) www.nemosciencemuseum.nl/en/about-nemo/organization/nemo/ (archived at https://perma.cc/D83N-CY7W)

Xzeres (2016) Skystream, www.windenergy.com/products/skystream (archived at https://perma.cc/P39M-TGZ7)

Conclusions   15

Facilitating decision making for systems change and sustainable practice

The world is in a state of transformation and there is no escape. The impact of geopolitics is far-reaching at all levels of society. Tensions in politics and international trade make the news headlines. Instability and volatility are conditions we have to live with.

Transformations are challenging, but also offer opportunities. One of the main long-term trends is sustainability. From the 1970s onwards, scientists, academics, the Club of Rome, NGOs and early-adopting companies have shown the way towards an economy that is more in balance with planet and people. We know it can be done, but more action is needed to support sustainable practices. The historic UN Paris agreement on climate change, adopted by 192 countries in December 2015, was a watershed, signalling the move from a neo-liberal policy dominated by the rules of finance and powerplay economics to an age of systems change that seeks to achieve a sustainable and inclusive economy. The widespread acceptance by companies of the Sustainable Development Goals (SDGs) to make the world a better place gave clear directions for purpose-driven business strategies. Through insight and understanding of the limitations of the dominant economic and financial paradigm, and with the help of new knowledge and disruptive technologies, we are witnessing the beginning of a long-term systems change.

A key element of this systems change is that sustainable practice must become the rule for all rather than the exception for a few early adoptors. A transformation means a rethinking of business models, including the reshaping of supply chains, use and reuse of materials, modes of transportation, as well as searching for balanced ways of working and healthier living. These combined efforts can lead to a better, more sustainable balance between People, Planet and Profit objectives in the corporate world and society at large. Where in the past businesses and authorities regarded sustainability as a cost, thanks to a larger group of frontrunners in business and government institutions, it is nowadays seen as the only way for new growth potential with a licence to operate. Creating shared value by investing in societal challenges is serious business, for here are the explorative fields for innovation, led by business and supported by governments with the Green Deal in Europe and the Inflation Reduction Act in the United States.

Contributing to systems change means making strategic choices and allocating investment. In this book we introduce the Responsible Business Simulator (tRBS) as a decision tool for decision makers, entrepreneurs, advisors, policymakers and those interested in sustainable business growth. The Responsible Business Simulator is the product of the qualitative strategic dialogue and the quantitative modelling software for simulation and visual clarification of the impact of potential decisions. Together these two elements create a powerful tool for helping decision makers reach profound decisions in the transition towards an economy based on a transparent balance between people, planet and profit.

In the past few years environmental, social and governance issues (ESGs) have become more important and will be embedded in reporting. SDGs are important guidelines for objectives and values in organizations, and tRBS is a valuable method for taking decisions based firmly on solid data and strategic dialogue. The strategic dialogue is based on action research and action learning and sets the interactive context in which management, employees, co-creators and stakeholders can formulate strategic goals, milestones and priorities. The strategic dialogue activates the participants in the search for facts, figures, reports, and formal and informal knowledge. The results of the strategic dialogue and fact-finding form the resource material for the quantitative modelling and simulation processes. The smart use of data science techniques and the complex computation modelling bring forward factual outcomes of clear potential choices based on strategic goals and priorities set in the strategic dialogue. The simulation model makes it possible to avoid vague discussions in the boardroom and eliminates prejudice and hobby horses. It facilitates the conversation with external stakeholders. It leads to transparency in the decision-making process by combining strategic goal-setting with the robust justification of data. Choices for less or more sustainable business decisions can be clarified and explained. With tRBS, decision makers can fine-tune their choices and adapt them over time, making it a dynamic learning tool on the way towards creating a sustainable economy integrating economic, social and environmental objectives.

Although sustainability is the dominant trend, this does not mean that it is easy to implement sustainable business practices. First, the fact that the world is changing at a rapid speed forces companies to respond by making strategic decisions with more uncertainty. Second, balancing people, planet and profit objectives, and similarly those for ESGs, instead of solely focusing on financial profits, only increases the problem of having highly diffuse strategic considerations. Third, in general the focus is often more on the short term to satisfy shareholders, whereas sustainable business development requires a medium- to long-term vision and a clear set of values embraced by management and employees.

The implementation of investments that change the system and its paradigm is already taking place in many industries. The shift towards e-mobility, as well as the climate goal-setting, means a tremendous shift in orientation. It is no longer a 'nice to have' but a 'necessity to survive'. Not all companies and organizations can convince their shareholders and stakeholders that a bold decision for sustainability and a circular economy will pay off in the short timeframes management is often confronted with. The large oil and gas industry is an example of consciously lagging behind and squeezing the existing business models for high profits, even with stranded assets, in the decades to come. Those companies and organizations that want to go forward towards a more balanced way are seeking ways of how to do it in practice. No matter whether you manufacture jeans, cars, domestic appliances or medical equipment, the imperative is that the supply line must be transparent and the end product sustainable. With the organizational tools and software techniques combined in tRBS we make life easier for top management when it comes to responsible business decision making to achieve strategic impact based on data and dialogue. In all the case studies presented in this book we were able to show that the strategic dialogue with employees, management and stakeholders leads to ambitions and the formulation of highly concrete key outputs to realize those ambitions. The data science techniques offer the possibility of making Big Data computations for the numerous relationships between the different key outputs, scientific data and the potential amount of investment.

Standard in the academic world is the knowledge that by realizing change within a system you forego the opportunity to acquire 'pure' academic insight; change and insight are to be separated. However, within the paradigm of systems change we cannot pause change in order to gain insight. In such a shift there is a need to realize change while gaining knowledge, which can be done using action research. By creating iterative cycles of intervention, investigation and reflection, action research has the potential to realize insights and learning dynamics within a changing environment while contributing to fine-tuning the impact of a decision or investment to be made. This kind of action research is not damaging the integrity of the knowledge obtained; it is making action research more relevant. This is where the toolbox of the corporate decision maker collides with the methodology of the action researcher. Hence action research was not only used in the development of tRBS; we applied it in the case studies, and based on the results we recommend it as an integral part of the simulation model.

Data analysis, AI and machine learning are powerful inputs for decision makers when used properly and checked for bias. The underlying data analysis of all the cases in this book has been updated with new data techniques. Technology is highly promising, but it will not in itself solve any problems. As with other technologies, data science brings its own pitfalls and can only be a powerful input when it is used correctly and effectively by professionals who know how to use and interpret the results. It is important that data science techniques are used to support decisions and decision makers, not dictate to them. Used correctly, data science techniques enable decision makers to utilize large amounts of data in a transparent, testable and flexible manner. Hence the simulation model was built to facilitate strategic dialogue and bring to the forefront facts and figures to make informed and justified decisions, and not replace the importance of face-to-face communication during the strategic dialogue.

In a rapidly changing environment, decision makers cannot afford to let opportunities go to waste. This is why we recommend that interactive sessions with management, employees and external stakeholders be incorporated into the strategic decision-making process. By bringing together true cross-sections of employees, management and stakeholders, it can be guaranteed that a diversity of knowledge, experience and latest insights will be available as inputs for the decision-making process to formulate goals. It also makes it possible to identify unsubstantiated assumptions, which can sometimes prove vital in altering the way the strategy is looked at.

By combining dialogue via action research with data science, the method becomes a collective exercise and not a 'black box', as would be the case when advisors are allowed to conjure statistics from Excel files like rabbits out of a hat. The combination of qualitative and quantitative approaches, of data and dialogue as applied in the case studies, is meaningful for decision makers, especially for those who look ahead and have to meet people, planet and profit objectives.

Overview of cases

The following is an overview of the companies and organizations that we have worked with and the resulting case studies in this book. It is worth mentioning that these are all companies and organizations that were already on the path towards incorporating sustainable practices and were anticipating the transition towards a circular economy and/or social inclusion. In the first case – concerning SDGs at PwC – people and planet aspects were evaluated; in the following three cases – Refugee integration, de Volksbank and IZZ Foundation – our research focused on empowerment, health and other people-related issues. The final three cases – DSM, Rimetaal and NEMO – have a greater focus on sustainability and planet issues, although the latter two cases address some health and inclusivity aspects as well. Within all of these cases, however, we have been able to do justice to all three people, planet and profit considerations. In order to guide the decision-making process with tRBS we had multiple iterative group sessions with all stakeholders involved. We obtained consent from all these stakeholders to present the cases in this book.

PwC

Company

PwC is an international professional services brand of firms, operating as partnerships under the PwC brand. The organization offers clients various professional business services, including accounting, tax and strategy or management consulting. PwC's objective is to build trust in society and solve important problems. PwC Netherlands (PwC NL) considers the SDGs in line with their objective as well as supportive of their ambition to become a purpose-led and values-driven organization. They link the SDGs to policies and activities.

Case

This case study addresses the main challenge for PwC: how to operationalize its objective to guide their actions. It illustrates how tRBS is used to gather insights into PwC's performance against the sustainable development goals (SDGs). We show how tRBS was applied to fit the objective of this case, and how data was maximized in order to create transparency and the insights necessary to steer.

Key insight

The SDGs are a powerful tool for transparent reporting and obtaining insights to enable strategic direction to be set. PwC has made a bold move to be transparent about their positive as well as their negative impact. It can now extend the impact measurement to its service delivery as well.

Key impacts

Measuring and reporting on impact is becoming increasingly important for organizations and will soon be (partially) required by law. The Responsible Business Simulator approach stimulated internal discussions within PwC on where to focus in both its short- and long-term strategy. This case also made clear that – given that most organizations are not transparently reporting yet – application of this way of thinking offers an easy way to make current reporting more transparent.

Refugees

Situation

The Russian invasion of Ukraine on 28 February 2022 (Reuters, 2022) caused many Ukrainians to leave their homes and find shelter elsewhere. UNHCR stated that around 7 million people had already crossed Ukraine's borders by 31 May 2022 (2022, ECB). In the Netherlands, nearly 75,000 Ukrainian refugees were registered in August that year.

At the same time, the Netherlands is still struggling to accommodate the refugees and economic migrants that entered the country in 2014–15.

Case

This case discussed how strategic decision making was used in the debate around the influx of Ukrainian refugees into the Netherlands and the distribution of budgets among the refugees over certain municipalities. Debate on this subject is sometimes based on emotion instead of on facts, or is reasoned from a silo perspective, so by giving all stakeholders a voice in the debate and translating these voices into quantified numbers, we facilitated policies in several municipalities based on facts and figures.

Key insight

The Responsible Business Simulator showed how the limited amount of money per Ukrainian refugee could best be allocated, accounting for the impact on both non-Ukrainian status-holders and local inhabitants. Instead of putting almost all the budget on learning the language, a mix of activities, sport and employment showed the best results in preparing refugees to integrate into the society.

Key impact

The model for Ukrainian refugees is currently being applied for discussions with local governments in the province of Utrecht. Showcasing the usefulness of integrated decision making with tRBS brought the model, developed originally for the refugee influx in 2014–15, to the attention of the European Commission, the Business Refugee Action Network (BRAN) and the Swedish and Italian governments.

De Volksbank

Company

De Volksbank is the fourth largest bank of the Netherlands. It has a history of being close to its customers via a unique local network of branches and financial advisors and, unlike its competitors that closed many branches over the past years, it maintains this network. This pays off in terms of customer satisfaction, as it is a top performer in a recent survey among customers of Dutch banks. Also, it explicitly focuses on creating societal value next to shareholder value. As a frontrunner in reporting and leading the way on non-financial value, the challenge for de Volksbank is to escape the handicap of being the first mover, now that all banks start to prepare for the Corporate Sustainability Reporting Directive (CSRD).

Case

This case study details the decision making at two of the four brands of de Volksbank. In the first of these two, tRBS was used to renew the franchise earnings model in a series of workshops. In between the workshops, new data was fed into the simulation model to give all stakeholders insights into the impact of new parameters to incentivize franchisees and the franchisor to have more interaction with local communities. For the second brand, the impact of innovative interventions to increase residential accessibility was modelled by collecting vast amounts of external data on the housing market and then complementing that data with their own internal data.

In the case study on neighbourhood quality of life, it is possible to prevent discussions on franchise earning models from focusing on 'dividing up the pie' between franchisees and franchisors. Instead, by simulating future impacts, discussions can be centred on increasing the size of the pie by focusing on creating impact in local communities. Creating full transparency by granting franchisees online access to the information and material in tRBS changed the atmosphere of the discussions. Because they could simulate the impact of potential new models on their own businesses and communities, they had a say in shaping the new franchise earning model. For the case study on residential accessibility, the key insight was that, in order to discover the real local differences in the root causes of lack of access to the housing market, it pays to collect data at a very granular, local level rather than use flawed data based on averages.

Key impacts

A truly interactive dialogue based on full transparency of all future impacts of potential decisions to all stakeholders at a detailed geographical level, without drowning them in the huge amounts of granular data needed to analyse those impacts, speeds up the decision-making process considerably and creates support for the final decision.

IZZ

Company

The IZZ Foundation (IZZ) is a non-profit organization in the Netherlands that has been promoting the interests of healthcare workers (in hospitals, nursing and care homes, home care, handicapped care, mental health and youth care) since its establishment in 1977. On the basis of its wide knowledge of and commitment to the care sector, IZZ provides healthcare insurance on a non-profit basis for almost half a million Dutch healthcare employees and their families. That insurance is tailored to the needs of this special group, and takes full account of the specific health risks involved in working in the sector. Being a market leader, what makes IZZ unique is the input and influence that employers and employees in the healthcare sector together have on the terms and conditions of their health insurance.

Case

This case study describes how IZZ offers healthcare institutions objective insights into what – for them – is the optimal strategy with regard to the people pillar, mainly focusing on the empowerment of their employees. There is a serious need for measures that will help achieve a balance between supply and demand in the healthcare sector but also account for the welfare of personnel. IZZ uses the strategic decision-making process to support many healthcare institutions in finding out what measures will help make healthcare a more pleasant, efficient, attractive and healthier working environment.

Key insight

If there is a higher risk appetite, an intervention focusing on the physical wellbeing of employees should be the preferred intervention, while with a lower risk appetite a psycho-social intervention is preferred. The Responsible Business Simulator showed what options work best under different circumstances and preferences.

Key impact

The first-hand knowledge and experience of the IZZ Foundation has become available in a model for the entire healthcare sector. Participation in the Responsible Business Simulator project led to the creation of a simulation model on healthy working in healthcare, a ready-to-use application for healthcare institutions to steer strategic decision making with assistance from IZZ.

DSM

Company

Royal DSM (DSM) is a global science-based company active in health, nutrition and materials. By connecting its unique competences in life sciences and material sciences, DSM is driving economic prosperity, environmental progress and social advances to create sustainable value for all stakeholders simultaneously. DSM operates in global markets such as food and dietary supplements, personal care, feed, medical devices, automotive, paints, electrical and electronics, life protection, alternative energy and bio-based materials.

Case

This case describes the decision making at DSM, who want to anticipate climate change by addressing their own environmental and carbon footprint by means of reducing greenhouse gas emissions and becoming more energy efficient. Their strategic challenge, therefore, has been formulated as 'how to source energy'. The strategic decision-making process at DSM was a multiple competency collaboration within the organization and triggered the already ongoing discussion of using an internal carbon price to evolve to a more strategic and fact-based dialogue.

Key insight

An internal carbon price is necessary in any organization that has a strong focus on profit-related objects, and favours energy from renewable sources over non-renewable sources.

Key impacts

There is a large price difference between grey and renewable energy, and tRBS showed that the internal carbon price needs to exceed the range of \$78–\$137, depending on risk appetite, before a decision for sustainable energy sourcing is made. The Responsible Business Simulator approach stimulated the existing internal discussion on the use of internal carbon price, but now encompassing a more strategic and fact-based dialogue. It contributed to the process of taking externalities into account in the decision-making process for energy sourcing, which finally led to the introduction of an internal carbon price.

Rimetaal

Company

Rimetaal is an innovative metal construction company that focuses on the development, production, sale and maintenance of high-quality metal products, for example (underground) garbage collection systems. Sustainability is key to Rimetaal's strategy, with a focus on sustainable products, sustainable production and social sustainability. The company proactively anticipates the societal necessity for sustainability, as well as considering government policy and competitive advantages. Furthermore, Rimetaal is a partner of De Groene Zaak, a Dutch employers' organization founded in 2010 and known as a protagonist for sustainability. Until the end of 2014 Rimetaal BV was a private limited company incorporated under Dutch law, but is now part of Kliko, the No 1 specialist in waste systems and logistics in the Netherlands. Kliko built further on the sustainable path designed by Rimetaal, and the innovative and robust products for waste management are part of the current Kliko portfolio.

Case

This case study explains how Rimetaal demonstrates that its principal customers, local authorities and national government, do not practise what they preach. The criteria set by RVO, the government agency for stimulating entrepreneurship in the Netherlands, are not stringent enough when it comes to the purchasing of sustainable products by government institutions. Rimetaal's track record showed that too often municipal authorities and other government organizations said they wanted to buy sustainable products, but in the end selected suppliers on the basis of price (i.e. lowest) rather than on the basis of sustainability. This occurred time and again, despite the fact that 'sustainability' is cited as an essential selection criterion in their purchasing processes.

Key insights

Suppliers can certainly supply sustainable products that work out cheaper over the entire life cycle than non-sustainable products. Rimetaal, as one of these sustainable suppliers, took action and used strategic decision making to show that investing in sustainable systems pays off in the long term. Another insight tRBS confirmed was the assumption that leasing a Rimetaal system in combination with a service contract for maintenance would be the best choice for customers and for the company. It would lead to sustainable solutions and contribute to a circular economy. Leasing takes into account the time factor, which is not the case with total cost of ownership.

Key impact

Purchasing officers from local government authorities realized that selecting the cheapest tender while asking for products that comply with strict sustainability criteria is not fair. They also saw that leasing contracts spread the costs over time. Sustainable solutions, which may cost more but last longer and need less maintenance, are more favourable from a circular economy point of view. However, it requires more collaboration between different parts of the (local) bureaucracy.

NEMO

Company

NEMO Science Museum (NEMO) in Amsterdam is the biggest and most interactive science museum in the Netherlands and Benelux countries. The iconic building with an impressive roof which acts as a city piazza was designed by Renzo Piano, and with five floors full of interactive, interesting things to do and discover, it is an exciting place, visited by more than 600,000 people every year who want to be introduced to science and technology in a playful manner. For the education sector, NEMO is the biggest interactive non-school-like informal learning environment and is part of many science and engineering educational programmes. NEMO also organizes training programmes for teachers and has intensive exchange programmes with an international network of science museums.

Case

This case addresses NEMO's decision-making process for solving its problems with the roof. Recurring leaks required complicated and expensive repairs and the roof also fell short of the insulation standards for this type of public building. The strategic decision-making process facilitated NEMO's expansion plans to do more than just repair a roof. In the process with tRBS, the importance of the public space on the roof and the iconic function of the building for the city of Amsterdam were both underlined. More intensive use of the roof would also lead to more visitors to NEMO. Multi-functionality turned out to be key in the decision-making process on the investment for the roof. In close collaboration with architect Renzo Piano, multiple uses and designs of the roof were discussed. The new roof opened in spring 2016 with a clear statement on sustainability: a green roof with plants producing energy and an outdoor exhibition on renewable wind energy. Today, the roof of the NEMO building is a meeting place; it has a large terrace and a restaurant, all with beautiful views of the city of Amsterdam. After the successful renovation of the roof the Board of NEMO will take a strategic decision in 2023 to take the next steps with the roof to embrace its public function and underline its sustainability goals.

Key insights

Interactivity and acknowledgement of the expertise of the participants engaged all of them in the decisions to be made. The integrated approach of taking all three aspects of people, planet and profit into account from the beginning also forestalled any tendency to take a short-term 'penny wise, pound foolish' decision. Expanding the simulation model at a later stage, as was done with Renzo Piano's alternative suggestions for the design of the roof, proved to be easy to do. It did not diminish the clarity of the model.

Key impact

The integration of data from the areas of finance, marketing and accommodation, which had never been linked before, unlocked a treasure trove of information. Another key impact came from a casual comment in a technical report about the possible effect of a sustainable roof on visitor numbers. The Responsible Business Simulator turned this information into quantified data. The simulation model also showed that a power-generating system on the roof would be less important in terms of financial income than the revenues from visitors enjoying the scenic view of the city of Amsterdam. The simulation also demonstrated the potential of new revenue models, specifically a restaurant on the roof.

Reflections – and looking forward

Combining the qualitative action research methodology in the strategic dialogue process with the data science techniques applied in the above-mentioned cases shows that there is added value in applying the Responsible Business Simulator in strategic decision-making processes to reach a balance between people, planet and profit objectives.

The case studies deal with very different types of companies and organizations. The reason for this was to test out tRBS in different contexts, from a profit-oriented international corporation to Dutch municipalities and a Dutch bank, and from a sustainability-conscious metals company to a human-centred healthcare insurance foundation and a science museum. This diversity was not a hindrance in applying tRBS. However, we did see that the more employees, managers and external stakeholders were actively involved in the process of dialogue, visioning and gathering of documentation, the better the formulation of the key outputs, and the more accurate the interpretation of the visualized facts and figures. The quality of the action research process with iterative cycles is critical for gaining access to data to justify and validate key outputs. Moreover, this process can guarantee a greater understanding within the group of the technical steps we take in the strategic decision-making process.

The complex computations made by advanced software and prepared by econometricians and data scientists are not easily understood. Elucidating the steps taken in the tRBS process helps participants to grasp how you can get from scattered information and data to objective facts and figures. Precisely the fact that the decision makers themselves can fine-tune the underlying objective data to a balanced point that fits the risk appetite of the company or organization means that the technical tooling is not just a black box but, on the contrary, it invites the participants to engage with the data. The two processes of strategic dialogue and data science are closely interlinked. These interdisciplinary qualitative and quantitative approaches are ideally also reflected in the team that advises and facilitates the decision-making process in companies and organizations. Purely data-driven advisors may overlook organizational matters, and dialogue-focused advisors or facilitators may overlook the substantiation of facts and figures justifying ambitions, key outputs and choices to be made.

Notwithstanding the fact that we are grateful for the diversity of cases to test out the Responsible Business Simulator, we see that more research is needed on a larger scale. The more companies and organizations that use the simulation model and make themselves acquainted with the (free) software package (see Contents page for how to access), the more experience decision makers will gain with the integrated approach. Since the first edition of this book we have explored many more cases, some of which are included in this edition.

At the beginning of the book we wrote that we are living in the age of transformation. Many innovations are now materializing that will have far-reaching impacts on business models, the way we work, the way we source energy, the way supply chains may look in the near future, and the way we invest for the continuity of companies and organizations. We may think of the mass application in the coming decade of artificial intelligence, sensors, smart logistics, connected healthcare, smart homes, connected cars and smart grids for renewable energy sources. No matter what kind of industry or service sector you are operating in, decision makers will have to make balanced decisions on investments to switch to new business models. With the Responsible Business Simulator we have shown that uncertainty can be reduced by clarifying and quantifying the financial and non-financial benefits of investments in sustainable business models that are beneficial for people, the planet and profit.

References

Reuters (2022) Timeline: The events leading up to Russia's invasion of Ukraine, www.reuters.com/world/europe/events-leading-up-russias-invasion-ukraine-2022-02-28/ (archived at https://perma.cc/34GR-TC9T)

European Central Bank (2022) The impact of the influx of Ukrainian refugees on the euro area labour force, *ECB Economic Bulletin*, Issue 4/2022, www.ecb.europa.eu/pub/economic-bulletin/focus/2022/html/ecb.ebbox202204_03~c9ddc08308.en.html (archived at https://perma.cc/6T3Q-7T2W)

GLOSSARY

access-over-ownership model Product strategy in which the customer does not buy a product, but only the access to it, so that the ownership stays with the producer.

action learning The exchange of knowledge in the course of several interactive sessions with stakeholders, while at the same time incremental decision making takes place about the principal key outputs that serve to achieve the enterprise's strategic objective.

action research A disciplined process in which, simultaneously, academic insight is acquired and change is realized in a real-life situation.

additional outputs Outputs that do not directly influence the decision making but are used as complementary information next to key outputs. When it turns out that there is an additional output that should be taken into account in the decision-making process, then this additional output should be promoted to key output.

appreciation function Functions which translate what a particular score on a key output means to the decision maker. An appreciation function can take on multiple shapes.

binary variable A binary variable can take on only two possible states; in this book these are the values 0 and 1.

circular economy An economy that is restorative and regenerative by intention and design, and which aims to keep products, components and materials at their highest utility and value at all times.

collective intelligence Group intelligence that emerges from the collaborative and collective efforts of multiple different individuals on a wide variety of cognitive tasks.

corporate social responsibility (CSR) Company activities that combine economic growth with limited impact on natural and social resources.

corporate sustainability reporting directive (CSRD) As entered into force on 5 January 2023, this new Directive modernizes and strengthens the rules about the social and environmental information that companies have to report.

decision maker The person whose point of view is used to design which inputs are internal and which are external. It is assumed that the decision maker has the power to choose values for all internal inputs.

decision maker's option A decision maker's option is defined by assigning a single value to all internal variable inputs. It assumes that every option within the scope of the decision can be completely described by one value per internal variable input. Since there typically is more than one internal variable input, a decision maker's option can be thought of as a package of potential sub-decisions, where each potential sub-decision is represented by choosing a single value for the corresponding internal variable input.

dependencies Relationships between internal inputs, external inputs, intermediates and outputs within the model. Dependencies consist of linear dependencies and non-linear dependencies.

environmental, social (and corporate) governance (ESG) Refers to a set of practices used to evaluate a company's operational performance as it relates to social and environmental impact.

external variable inputs The inputs that are not in the hands of the decision maker and hence are also known as exogenous variables or out-of-control inputs. The values of these external inputs are adjusted during the decision-making process. Every external variable input can be thought of as a single aspect of external uncertainty affecting the outcome of the decision in scope.

fixed inputs Inputs whose values are kept constant during the decision-making process. When it turns out that there is a fixed input for which it is useful to assess the effect of adjusting its value on the outcome of the decision, then this fixed input should be promoted to internal or external variable input, depending on the control the decision maker has on the input. In case of (partly) linear models, the constant first-order derivatives are not considered as fixed input but as a separate input category named 'linear dependencies'.

input Types of information for which data can be collected and fed into the simulation model in order to calculate outputs. Inputs may be variable and fixed inputs.

intermediate Intermediates store the results of sub-steps in the calculations that convert inputs of the simulation model to outputs of the simulation model. Intermediates are used to make calculations easy and transparent. Intermediates are based on inputs and/or other intermediates.

internal variable input Internal variable inputs are in the hands of the decision maker and hence also known as endogenous or in-control inputs. The values of these internal inputs are adjusted during the decision-making process. Every internal variable input can be thought of as a single aspect on which a sub-decision needs to be made.

Internet of Things (IoT) The network of physical devices, vehicles, buildings and other items, embedded with electronics, sensors, software and network connectivity that enable these objects to collect and exchange data.

key output Outputs on which the decision will be based. These outputs can be thought of as the basis for the decision criteria. Key outputs are often referred to as key performance indicators (KPIs).

linear dependencies Linear relations between variable inputs, fixed inputs, intermediates and outputs. Linear dependencies can be fed into the Responsible Business Simulator as matrix cells. The row of the cell represents the driver (i.e. the input or intermediate affecting an output or other intermediate), the column of the cell represents the destination (i.e. the output of intermediate that is affected by an input or other intermediate), and the value of the cell represents the constant first-order derivative in the linear relation.

making strategic decisions to benefit people, the planet and profits An interactive process with stakeholders that addresses both financial and non-financial aspects. It comprises a seven-step process that leads to a clear strategic choice. The process is empowered by a unique modelling software named the Responsible Business Simulator.

Monte Carlo simulation A sampling method that can be used to simplify a complex reality. It involves the random sampling of a probability distribution such that a specified number of trials are produced that together form the shape of the new distribution.

non-linear dependencies Non-linear relations between internal inputs, external inputs, intermediates and outputs. These dependencies require programming in the Responsible Business Simulator.

outputs The final results of the calculations based on inputs. A distinction is made between key outputs and additional outputs.

performance-based contracting A product strategy where customers do not buy specific goods or services, but rather the performance of a system.

Poisson process A random (stochastic) counting process. It is memoryless as there is a constant and continuous opportunity for an event to occur.

Responsible Business Simulator Software designed to facilitate strategic responsible business decision making. It elucidates hidden multi-dependencies and uses the power of visualization. It provides decision makers with transparency in their strategic options.

round-table format A discussion format in which a topic is chosen beforehand and all participants are given an equal right to participate.

scenario A scenario is defined by assigning a single value to all external variable inputs. It assumes that every possible future outcome of all external uncertainties with respect to the scope of the decision can be completely described by one value per external variable input. Since there typically is more than one external variable input, a scenario can be thought of as a coherent combination of future developments, where every single aspect of external uncertainty is represented by choosing a single value for the corresponding external variable input.

shared value A meaningful benefit for society that is also valuable to a business.

simulation model Part of the Responsible Business Simulator, the simulation model is a set of formulae modelling multi-dependencies. It converts the decision maker's options and scenarios into outputs.

stakeholder Anyone who is or becomes directly or indirectly involved in or affected by the activities of a company or organization.

sustainable development Development that meets the needs of the present without compromising the ability of future generations to meet their own needs.

sustainable development goals (SDGs) The goals that were unanimously adopted by the United Nations in 2015, to be achieved by 2030.

triple bottom line (TBL) Aims to measure the financial, social and environmental performance of a company over time, rather than merely the traditional measure of corporate profit, and is based on three pillars: People, Planet and Profit.

variable inputs Inputs where the user wants to explicitly investigate the effect of variations in these inputs on outputs. Two types of variable inputs are distinguished: internal variable inputs and external variable inputs.

INDEX

The index is filed in alphabetical, word-by-word order. Numbers in main headings are filed as spelt out in full, excepting Scope emissions and SDG goals, which are filed in chronological order. Acronyms are filed as presented; '@' is ignored for filing purposes. Page locators in *italics* denote information contained within a Table or Figure.

From 4 December 2025 the EU Responsible Person (GPSR) is:
eucomply oÜ, Pärnu mnt. 139b – 14, 11317 Tallinn, Estonia
www.eucompliancepartner.com

www.ingramcontent.com/pod-product-compliance
Lightning Source LLC
Chambersburg PA
CBHW041207220326
41597CB00030BA/5069

9 781398 612280